MARK TWAIN'S
SAN FRANCISCO

Sometime in May or June of 1863, Mark Twain, age 27, on his first visit to San Francisco, had this photograph taken at Edouart's Gallery, 634 Washington Street.

(Courtesy Mark Twain Papers, the Bancroft Library, University of California, Berkeley; CU-MARK)

Mark Twain's San Francisco

UNINHIBITED DISPATCHES ON "THE LIVEST HEARTIEST COMMUNITY ON OUR CONTINENT"

by America's Greatest Writer

EDITED BY

BERNARD TAPER

Heyday, Berkeley, California

Library of Congress Cataloging-in-Publication Data

Twain, Mark, 1835-1910.
Mark Twain's San Francisco / edited by Bernard Taper.
p. cm.
ISBN: 1-890771-69-4
ISBN: 978-1-890771-69-0
1. San Francisco (Calif)-Literary collections. 2. San Francisco (Calif) 1. Taper, Bernard. II. Title.
PS1303.T892003
818' .409-dc22
2003016379
ISBN for this edition: 978-1-59714-489-6

Cover Design: Ashley Ingram
Cover Photo: Earth Quakey Times, San Francisco [California], Oct[ober] 8, 1865 by Edward Jump, Courtesy of The Bancroft Library, University of California, Berkeley (BANC PIC 1963.002:0449--C)

Published by Heyday
P.O. Box 9145, Berkeley, California 94709
(510) 549-3564
heydaybooks.com

Printed in Saline, Michigan, by McNaughton and Gunn

10 9 8 7 6 5 4 3 2 1

EDITOR'S DEDICATION

To Philip, who despite the handicap of a sense of humor, proved most helpful with the proof-reading of this book—

and to Mark, Ann, and Oona

Other Books by Bernard Taper

The Arts in Boston
Balanchine: A Biography
Cellist in Exile: A Portrait of Pablo Casals
Gomillion Versus Lightfoot: The Right to Vote in Apartheid Alabama

CONTENTS

1863

1864

1865

1866

INTRODUCTION

by Bernard Taper

During the 1860s a literary movement of considerable force and originality flourished in that boisterous, gaudy, *nouveau-riche* metropolis of the frontier, San Francisco. On the scene at one time or another were Mark Twain, Bret Harte, Ambrose Bierce, Henry George, and a number of lesser lights of interest to local historians, such as the flamboyant Joaquin Miller, Ina Coolbrith, Charles Warren Stoddard, Prentice Mulford, and Charles Webb. Their activities produced perhaps the most exciting of the early provincial rebellions.

The rebellion, an unconscious one for the most part, was against the standards and taste which ruled literature in the East. Those genteel, constrictive standards could hardly cope with the raw, lusty material of life in San Francisco and its even rawer, lustier hinterlands. Imagine Henry James trying to make a story out of a jumping contest between two frogs! What a *donnée!*

Of necessity, the whole San Francisco experience was almost bound to appall a fastidious visitor. Clarence King, a member of the Henry Adams circle, visited San Francisco about this time and sniffed that it struck him as "a monument to California's march from barbarism to vulgarity."

The quality of life in the East then was imitation Victorian. That of San Francisco's West was closer to the Elizabethan in its vigor, forthrightness, and ribaldry, its acceptance of violence and excess, its excitement over the new prospects being daily unfolded, and its crude, undisguised interest in sheer wealth. I am oversimplifying, I know; no label wholly fits a culture or epoch. Yet certainly there did exist a tension between Western attitudes and Eastern standards. It's a frequent theme or device in Mark Twain's early writings. In fact, that tension, as Twain biographers have noted, was the central theme and predicament of his whole life. Hence *Mr. Clemens and Mark Twain,* the title of Justin Kaplan's prize-winning biography.

Of these Western writers of the sixties, the most important to us now, of course, is Mark Twain. San Francisco and the Far West were important to Twain, too. It was here that, in his late twenties, after trying one thing or another—typesetting, riverboat piloting, a brief spell of soldiering, mining—he entered upon his real vocation. All along he had been "scribbling," as he puts it, but it was here in the Far West that he can be said to have become a writer, and the kind of writer that he was to be. Here, in fact, Samuel Clemens became Mark Twain.

He came to the Far West in 1861, accompanying his brother Orion, who had been appointed secretary of the Nevada Territory, and after about two and a half years in that mining country, that extraordinary wasteland in which almost nothing grew except quantities of silver and gold, he moved to San Francisco. That was May 1864, when he was twenty-eight. "I fell in love with the most cordial and sociable city in the Union," he later writes in *Roughing It.* "After the sage-brush and alkali deserts of Washoe, San Francisco was Paradise to me." To Twain's mind, San Francisco was "the livest, heartiest community on our continent." Only fifteen years previously, when the Gold Rush began, it had been an obscure hamlet of a few hundred people. Now it teemed with a population of 115,000. It could boast a score of newspapers, an academy of natural sciences, six theaters, some fine hotels and numerous excellent restaurants, forty-one churches and about ten times that many saloons. It was, Twain thought, everything a man could want in a city.

By this time he was no stranger to the city. For about a year he had been contributing occasional articles to the city's pioneer literary journal, the *Golden Era,* and for a couple of years the broadly humorous and prankish pieces he had been doing as reporter and city editor of Virginia City's *Territorial Enterprise* had received wide circulation in San Francisco, winning much favor. From the very start of his writing in the West, as the literary historian Franklin Walker has pointed out, he had been addressing a San Francisco audience. In effect, Virginia City in those days was San Francisco's "mining suburb." The more than two-hundred-mile journey across the Sierra was virtually a commute for a good many people, whether business or pleasure was their bent. In the year before he settled in San Francisco, Twain made at least two long visits to the city. He wrote in a letter to his mother that when he visited San Francisco he felt as at home on Montgomery Street as he did on Main Street back in Hannibal.

It was as Samuel Clemens that he had stepped off the stagecoach in Nevada. It was as Mark Twain that he came on to San Francisco. That name—probably the most famous pen name in the history of literature and the one that feels to us now the most apt somehow—he had adopted in Virginia City just the year before, because pseudonyms were the thing among the local columnists (it first appeared in print February 3, 1863). The pseudonym still sat new on him; he had not really broken it in yet. By the time he left San Francisco a few years later he wore the name most naturally.

Already, at the time of his arrival, there were those who saw him as destined for fame as a humorist. At the urging of the famous Artemus Ward, whom he had met in Virginia City, he had in mid-January sent a couple of sketches off to the New York *Mercury* and had them accepted. Still, at that time, becoming a great writer was not yet his goal. His simple ambition in those days was to become a millionaire in a day or two—an ambition he shared with just about every other San Franciscan. "Speculation went mad," he recalls. "Bankers, merchants, lawyers, doctors, mechanics, laborers, even the very washerwomen and servant-girls, were putting up their earnings on silver stocks, and every sun that rose in the morning went down on paupers enriched and rich men beggared. What a gambling carnival it was! Stock was rising. Gould and Curry had soared to six thousand dollars a foot."

In anticipation of the wealth that would be his as soon as he chose to cash his stocks, Twain lived at first in millionaire style at the sumptuous Lick House, whose grand dining room had been modeled on the banquet hall of the palace at Versailles. And then—well, let Twain tell it: "And then—all of a sudden, out went the bottom and everything and everybody went to ruin and destruction! The wreck was complete. The bubble scarcely left a microscopic moisture behind it. I was an early beggar and a thorough one. My hoarded stocks were not worth the paper they were printed on. I threw them all away."

This was just one bubble of many which, during this and succeeding epochs, inflated enchantingly and then burst with a damp pop in San

SNOW& ROOS
BANK OF CALIFORNIA
E. Jump
STEAMER DAY IN
Published by Snow

AGENCY
PACIFIC MAIL
STEAMSHIP CO.
L. NAGEL PRINT.
FRANCISCO.

Francisco. The most recent, of course, was the Silicon Valley mirage. Will we never learn? Not Mark Twain evidently. All his long life he would have trouble resisting the seductions of a potentially ruinous speculation.

So Twain had to go to work after all. He took a job as a reporter on the *Call,* starting in early June 1864. For a time he functioned as the entire reportorial staff. It was, he later recalled, fearful drudgery. His day started at mid-morning and did not end till the paper was put to bed at two a.m. All day he used to "rake the town from end to end," looking for news, and at night he had to visit the six theaters one after another, getting only the merest glimpse of the plays and operas he would report on. Around eleven at night he sat down to write these gleanings up, doing his best, as he recalls in later memoirs, to make them "cover as much acreage as I could."

During his months on the *Call* Twain remembers doing only one story with spontaneous enthusiasm. He saw some Irish hoodlums stoning a Chinese laundryman for fun one day, while a policeman looked on with amused interest—and Twain went back to the office and wrote this scene down in undoubtedly telling fashion. The next day Twain eagerly opened the paper to look for his story. It was not to be seen. When he went to the paper's owner, George Barnes, and asked why the story had been killed, Barnes replied to him that the *Call* was, like the New York *Sun* of that day, the paper of the poor. "It gathered its livelihood from the poor," Barnes said, " and therefore must respect their prejudices or perish. The Irish were the poor…and they hated the Chinamen."

This incident reveals much about the state of things in San Francisco, at that time and for decades afterwards, in regard to the Chinese. Twain often alluded to it indignantly in later life. Yet he himself, when he first came to San Francisco, had been capable of playing such crude jokes on the Chinese as dropping beer bottles from the window of his California Street lodgings onto the tin roofs of their shacks below, just for the fun of seeing them run out into the street in fright.

Indignant as Mark Twain had been over the mistreatment of the Chinese, he would not have hesitated to employ in his speech or writings the derogatory names by which the Chinese were commonly called—nor would he avoid doing the same in regard to blacks. He was not politically correct—not then, not ever. In his time, verbal political correctness had not yet been invented, but if it had been, Twain would not have observed it—or, more likely, would have satirized it as hypocritical fastidiousness, a masquerade of righteousness.

The best thing about the *Call* for Twain was its location. Its offices were situated in the same building as the United States Mint. Whenever Twain could find the time, he would go down to the second floor and hobnob with Bret Harte, who was secretary to the Superintendent of the Mint. The two men were about the same age, but Harte was already an established literary figure. Twain deferred to him at first, and the two young men, though very different in personality and appearance—Harte elegant and dandified, Twain with his disorderly mop of hair, drawling speech, and slouched stance—got along well in those years.

Like Twain, Harte had been a compositor, and his first connection with the *Golden Era* had been as printer. It amused Twain to hear Harte tell of how he had written his first stories for that journal directly in hand-set type, much to the puzzlement of the *Golden Era's* editor upon whose desk these stories, which he had never seen in manuscript, would suddenly appear in print galleys.

They used to discuss their writing trade as well, and Twain credits Harte's advice on style as having been helpful. In later years, as Twain's star rose and Harte's declined, the two men fell out. "I think he was incapable of emotion," Twain writes in his memoirs, "for I think he had nothing to feel with. I think his heart was merely a pump and had no other function...He said to me once with a cynical chuckle that he thought he had mastered the art of pumping up the tear of sensibility. The idea conveyed was that the tear of sensibility was oil, and that by luck he had struck it."

After four months, Twain was fired by the *Call*—a not surprising development in view of Twain's lack of interest in its style and policy, but still one that would rankle all his life, even though Barnes had done the deed as gently as could be imagined. "For two months," Twain recalls, "my sole occupation was avoiding acquaintances...I became very adept at slinking." He was broke, as well as ashamed. Soon, though, he began to write for other journals—the *Golden Era,* the *Californian,* the *Sacramento Union,* the San Francisco *Dramatic Chronicle* after it was founded, and to contribute regular letters on San Francisco to the *Territorial Enterprise.*

In these signed pieces, under less deadline pressure, he could let himself go as he had not been able to on the *Call.* In them, the San Francisco of the sixties comes alive and kicking, with all its verve and foibles and delights and pretensions. All sorts of aspects, large and small, come under

Twain's amused and searching scrutiny—fashions, politics, theater critics, rival newspapers, opera, prizefights, spiritualism. He writes up an opera performance in the solemn style of a music critic—the difference being that what Twain reviews is the performance of the furniture mover: "I was particularly impressed by the able manner in which Signor Bellindo Alphonso Cellini, the accomplished basso-relievo furniture scout and sofa shifter, performed his part." He parodies the fashion writers and the city's social set in his reports on the Lick House and Pioneers' Balls: "The fan used by Mrs. B. was of real palm-leaf and cost four thousand dollars—the handle alone cost six bits. Her head dress was composed of white chantilly lace, surmounted by a few artificial worms, and butterflies and things, and a tasteful tarantula done in jet."

And he lovingly describes the easy grace with which one of the guests at the Pioneers' Ball blew her nose: her manner of doing so "marked her as a cultivated and accomplished woman of the world; its exquisitely modulated tone excited the admiration of all who had the happiness to hear it." As for the new style of hoop skirts, that merits a whole article, from which we learn that "to critically examine these hoops—to get the best effect—one should stand on the corner of Montgomery and look up a steep street like Clay or Washington…It reminds me of how I used to peep under circus tents when I was a boy and see a lot of mysterious legs about with no visible bodies attached to them. And what handsome vari-colored garters they wear now-adays!"

The ladies of fashionable South Park were shocked and infuriated by such impertinent observations, but at places like the Bank Exchange bar, where the gentlemen of the town gathered to drink Pisco punch, exchange good talk, and admire the luscious painting of Samson and

Delilah above the bar, there were roars of laughter. (Twain, in another of his articles, carefully describes this "magnificent picture" and tells how the carping stranger who comes into the bar invariably says, after taking one look at the painting, "Them scissors is too modern—there warn't no scissors like that in them days, by a d——d sight.")

All sorts of characters swim into Twain's ken—miners, millionaires, actors, bill collectors, notables, bums. He is on easy terms with them all. In the Turkish bath in the Montgomery Block he even meets a man named Tom Sawyer, with whom he likes playing penny ante. Long afterward this man enjoyed the conviction that it was he who inspired Twain's famous book, and outside of a tavern he acquired near Third and Mission he proudly hung the sign: ALE AND SPIRITS! THE ORIGINAL TOM SAWYER: PROP.

Twain had the gift of gaiety and delight, and this quality is communicated even when he is being ostensibly misanthropic, as in, for instance, his account of a trip he let himself be persuaded to take out to the Cliff House at four o'clock in the morning, at which time, according to the friend who persuaded him, the road would not be crowded and nature would be at its most pristine and bracing. Twain prefaces this piece with an epigraph:

> "Early to bed, early to rise makes a man healthy, wealthy and wise."—BENJAMIN FRANKLIN
> "I don't see it."—GEORGE WASHINGTON

"No," Twain writes, "the road was not encumbered by carriages—we had it all to ourselves. I suppose the reason was, that most people do not like to enjoy themselves too much, and therefore they do not go out to the Cliff House in the cold and the fog and the dead silence and solitude of four o'clock in the morning." The fog was so thick, he writes, that "we could not see the horse at all, and were obliged to steer by his ears, which stood up dimly out of the dense white mist that enveloped him. But for those friendly beacons, we must have been cast away and lost."

And once they got out there and the fog did lift, he found himself in no mood to enjoy any of the sights—not even the seals, "writhing and squirming like exaggerated maggots." His moral is a simple one: "If you go to the Cliff House at any time after seven in the morning, you cannot fail to enjoy it"—but not before that hour.

Subsequent trips to the Cliff House did, in fact, prove fruitful as well as enjoyable. It was there that he one day discovered Nature's eternal law of compensation, which he formulates thus, in another of his articles: "Behold, the same gust of wind that blows a lady's dress aside and exposes her ankle, fills your eyes so full of sand that you can't see it."

It is quite remarkable how much of the characteristic San Francisco experience Twain crowded into those years in the city and how many of its abiding themes and phenomena appear in his writings—including even earthquakes. There were several in 1864, comparatively modest in size but exasperating to the *Call*'s reporter, who complains in a July 22 article, "When we contracted to report for this newspaper, the important matter of two earthquakes a month was not considered in the salary. There shall be no mistake of that kind in the next contract, though."

Describing each of them was a challenge. Some of the quakes, Twain writes, "have been distinguished by a soothing kind of undulating motion, like the roll of waves on the sea..." Other shocks seemed to come straight up from below, as if possibly "freighted with urgent messages from some of our departed friends." Of the July 22 quake he writes, "The house seemed to waltz from side to side with a quick

motion, suggestive of sifting corn meal through a sieve; afterward it rocked grandly to and fro like a prodigious cradle, and in the meantime several persons started downstairs to see if there were anybody in the street so timid as to be frightened at a mere earthquake." In these reports, we see the writer playing with the language, seeking just the right simile to convey his experience. It's like watching a budding concert pianist doing his finger exercises.

The following year a much bigger quake struck. This is the one Twain describes at length in *Roughing It.* It occurred on October 8, 1865, and caught Twain as he was strolling along Third Street near Mission, enjoying the Sabbath peacefulness of the day. "Such another destruction of mantel ornaments and toilet bottles as the earthquake created, San Francisco never saw before," Twain writes, and notes, "hardly an individual escaped nausea entirely." Naturally, he sets down the numerous curiosities the event produced. "A lady," he writes, "sitting in her rocking and quaking parlor, saw the wall part at the ceiling, open and shut twice, like a mouth, and then drop the end of a brick on the floor like a tooth. She was a woman easily disgusted with foolishness, and she arose and went out of there."

Because this earthquake took place around noon of a Sunday, it bred ecclesiastical anecdotes. Twain tells, in his *Roughing It* account, of the minister who, after the first shock, said to his congregation, "Keep your seats! There is no better place to die than this," and who added, after the third shock, "But outside is good enough!", with which he skipped out the back door. As Twain related it, the hero of this anecdote was an *Oakland* minister. Oakland had already begun to fulfill its divine destiny as the butt of San Franciscans' jokes.

For the *Dramatic Chronicle,* the earthquake article Twain promptly contributed was not a piece of reporting, but a burlesque earthquake almanac, written, he says, "at the instance of several friends who feel a boding anxiety to know beforehand what sort of phenomena we may expect the elements to exhibit during the next month or two." For October 23, his almanac predicts, "Mild, balmy earthquakes." For October 27, "Universal despondency, indicative of approaching disaster. Abstain from smiling, or indulgence in humorous conversation, or exasperating jokes." For November 2, "Spasmodic but exhilarating earthquakes, accompanied by occasional showers of rain, and churches and things." And for the next day, simply, "Make your will."

In the 138 years since Mark Twain published those fanciful words, the science of seismology has come into being, with faults scrupulously mapped, the faintest of tremors recorded by sensors, and seismographic records constantly studied and collated for possible early warning signs. Yet the most recent big earthquake to hit the San Francisco Bay Area—the one that struck at 5:04 p.m., October 17, 1989, just as, of all things, a World Series baseball game between the San Francisco Giants and the Oakland A's was about to start in Candlestick Park—caught scientists, as well as the rest of us, by surprise. In the realm of predictions for San Franciscans afflicted with "boding anxiety," sober science still offers little more help than the fanciful nonsense of Twain's earthquake almanac. "Make your will" still seems smart advice.

Burlesque, parody, fantasy, the tall tale—these forms, which Twain was to employ all his life, even in his more serious works, are prominent in his San Francisco writings; his increasing deftness in their use may be noted. In many respects, these early pieces of journalism, intended as fugitive and casual reports, stand up as well as or better than later essays he polished and worked over. They are directly engaged, in a way that many of the later writings are not: they have *real* topics, drawn from immediate observation. They are less inflated than some of the later essays and there is less striving to be oracular.

Exaggerated as many of the early pieces are for humorous effect, one cannot but be constantly aware in reading them of the remarkable eye for detail and the inimitable ear for the sound of ordinary talk that Twain possessed. It was because he saw and heard so accurately that his burlesques and fantasies are as pleasing as they are. One might almost say that the first requirement for the writer of fantasy or other forms of exaggeration is an unusual sense of reality; without that the fantasy is bound to be insipid and unbelievable. So for all the playful distortions, the San Francisco of that era comes through in Twain's writings in a myriad of details which nobody else was noting.

The social satirist in Twain makes its appearance too in these early writings. He was never just a jester. As early as his Virginia City days, colleagues had styled him "the Moral Phenomenon." In San Francisco the chief target for his moral indignation was the police, whom he loathingly portrayed as lazy, stupid, brutal, callous, and corrupt. And the Police Court, which he dubbed "The Black Hole of San Francisco," reeked.

Probably the strongest satire he wrote in San Francisco was an article called "What Have the Police Been Doing?" Written for the *Territorial Enterprise* and reprinted January 21, 1866, in the *Golden Era,* it recounted the death in prison of a man who had been arrested for stealing seventy-five cents' worth of flour sacks. The man had been dumped into a cell and left there, and none of the prison officials bothered to see if he was all right. If they looked in at him at all, Twain wrote bitingly, they probably thought there was nothing unusual about him and that the prisoner was merely "sleeping with that calm serenity which is peculiar to men whose heads have been caved in with a club."

Ah yes, police scandals—still another recurring theme in San Francisco's history! It is the spring of 2003 as I write this, and for the past year the newspapers of the region have been front-paging a particularly loony and juicy scandal the press has dubbed Fajitagate.

It started, the story goes, with three off-duty rookie cops, one of them the son of the Assistant Chief of Police, out on the town carousing. Encountering a couple of men emerging from a bar with takeout fajitas in their hands, the cops demanded that the food be handed over. The men demurred. A brawl ensued. More cops were called to quell the brawl.

In due time, felony assault charges were brought against the rookie cops. But by the time those charges were brought, a widespread suspicion had been aroused that the Department's top brass had conspired to cover up the matter. The D.A. called a special Grand Jury. The Mayor deplored the D.A. and the Grand Jury as well. Conspiracy indictments were brought against top Police officials, and then dropped. The civilian watchdog agency issued a sweeping denunciation of the Department. The Mayor then offered, as his concept of reform, his intention to appoint as new Police Chief the father of the most bellicose of the rookie cops.

And so it goes in San Francisco. By this time hundreds of thousands of words have been written about the bungled attempt to hijack a bag of fajitas and the cascade of civic tumult that ensued. And all I can think, as I read what's been written, is "Mark Twain, where are you when we need you?"

And where was the Mark Twain of late 1864? He was off in the gold country, the foothills of the Sierra Nevada. In December he got out of town, and he stayed away for three months. His early biographer Albert Bigelow Paine surmised that fear of police reprisal for his stinging articles may have prompted Twain's departure, but current scholarship doubts that explanation, since it wasn't till later that most of his more scathing critiques of the police appeared. Maybe he just felt the need for a change of air and scene, though Tuolomne and Calaveras counties in the rainy season can hardly be considered the most desirable of vacation destinations.

Nevertheless, this turned out to be one of the most fortunate choices of his life. For a couple of months he lived in a shack at Jackass Hill with two brothers of his old Virginia City buddy, Steve Gillis. Then he moved on to nearby Angel's Camp, where he did a little gold mining with no great success but, more profitably, spent much time in a local tavern listening to the miners and other old-timers spin yarns.

In his notebook for that period we find one of these yarns summarized: "Coleman with his jumping frog—bet stranger $50—stranger had no frog, & C got him one—in the meantime stranger filled C's frog full of shot & he couldn't jump—the stranger's frog won." Twain wrote this yarn up as a tavern monologue delivered by a garrulous Angel's Camp local. It appeared in the New York *Saturday Press* on November 18, 1865 under the title of "Jim Smiley and His Jumping Frog," and it immediately made his name. The nation's fancy was tickled by this drawling tale of the jumping frog of Calaveras County, captivated more perhaps by the voice in which the story was told than by its plot. H. L. Mencken once said, "Twain was the first American author of world rank to write a genuinely colloquial and native American." And the first piece of writing in which the national audience encountered this voice was, of course, the little tale about the frog—a tale which, though it might tickle the fancy, gave only the slightest hint of the range of tunes this new voice would eventually produce.

To this day Angel's Camp celebrates the Twain tale with an annual jumping frog jubilee that attracts contest competitors and passels of visitors. Last year, an animal rights society sought to have the contest banned as cruelty to frogs. Twain would have relished that twist to the story.

For a writer there are apt to be two places that have a special importance in his life. One is the place where he was brought up and formed the impressions which, in various guises, will be the basic material he will draw on. The other is the place where he first discovers his vocation. For Twain that place was San Francisco; it was here that—on the verge of thirty, a quite late age—he came to the realization that he was not really ever going to be a riverboat pilot or a printer or a miner or any of the other things he had tried. Nor was he going to be a preacher of the gospel, a saver of souls, which had once been his most fervent dream. What he was going to be was a writer.

On October 19, 1865 he faced up to this realization in an earnest, self-scrutinizing letter to his brother Orion and Orion's wife Molly. In it he recognized that in the past he had pursued ambitions for which he had no true call and that such aspirations had been "the very ecstasy of presumption." And he continues, "But I *have* had a 'call' to literature, of a low order—*i.e.* humorous. It is nothing to be proud of, but it is my strongest suit, & if I were to listen to that maxim of stern *duty* which says that to do right you must multiply the one or two or three talents which the Almighty entrusts to your keeping, I would long ago have ceased to meddle with things for which I was by nature unfitted & turned my attention to seriously scribbling to excite the laughter of God's creatures. Poor, pitiful business!" This letter is considered by Robert Hirst, the director of the Mark Twain Papers, to be the most important letter Mark Twain ever wrote.

If this is a moment of conscious decision making for Twain, certainly much unconscious preparation had already gone into it. When one thinks of Twain's Western years, as he has presented this period to us in *Roughing It,* one is apt to think of it as a crude, wild time and to picture Twain as the tenderfoot on the frontier. But *Roughing It* is a work of semifiction, for all its autobiographical form, and its central character is only one aspect of the author. It is probable that fully as important to Twain's development at that stage of his career as any experience in panning for gold or encountering frontier desperadoes was the fact that for the first time in his life he had become, in San Francisco, part of a literary circle—the Bohemians, whose headquarters were the offices of the *Golden Era* and the *Californian.* Through his association with them he began to think consciously of what was involved in the craft of writing and to consider with a new sophistication, which fortunately did not dampen the old zest, the techniques and standards that would be required for one to become a master.

Twain left San Francisco about a year after the publication of the jumping frog story. During his two and a half years in San Francisco, as Bernard DeVoto has written, Twain's work had grown surer and also broader in scope. "All the rest of Mark Twain's books are embryonic in what he had written by December 1866, when he went east," DeVoto observes. "These casual pieces outline the future: the humorist, the social satirist, the pessimist, the novelist of America, Mark Twain exhilarated, sentimental, cynical, angry, and depressed, all are here. The rest is only development."

Just before he left, Twain had also discovered what was to be his second vocation—lecturing. He gave the first lecture of his life before a paying audience. It took place at the Academy of Music on October 2, 1866. The topic was the Sandwich Islands (as Hawaii was then known), where Twain had spent a number of months on assignment for the *Sacramento Union.* Those who have read Twain's account of this debut in *Roughing It* should take with a grain of salt Twain's story of how surprised he was that anyone showed up at the hall on the evening of the lecture. As Paul Fatout established in his book *Mark Twain on the Lecture Circuit,* Twain must have been fully aware that the house had been sold out for days in advance. He was, after all, one of San Francisco's favorite characters. The city's populace went to the hall that evening expecting to have a good time—and they did.

In 1868 Twain, having made a trip to Europe and the Holy Land with a shipload of American tourists as part of the first chartered pleasure cruise ever made, returned to San Francisco once more to revise and expand the letters he had written for the *Alta California* while en route. At the same time there appeared an opportunity which tempted him mightily—the chance to become postmaster at San Francisco, at a goodly stipend. But he turned it down. "I have thrown away that offer when I had it in my grasp," he wrote, in a letter dated February 6, 1868, "because it was plain enough that I could not be postmaster and write the book too...But it was worth from ten to twelve thousand a year." With that he settled down to write at a fierce clip. In two months of concentrated effort, working nightly from midnight to past daybreak, he turned his *Alta California* letters into the book he called *The Innocents Abroad*—his first full-length work. An instant success, this book sold more copies than had any other American work except *Uncle Tom's Cabin.*

So Twain had struck at last, here in the West, the bonanza he had dreamed about. With that, he left San Francisco for good. Two years later Bret Harte, then at the very peak of his fame, also departed, lured by a writing contract for the *Atlantic Monthly*—$10,000 for twelve stories or poems in a twelve-month period, the most lucrative contract, Harte boasted, ever offered to an American writer. Harte's progress across the country on this journey excited, according to Twain, "such a prodigious blaze of national interest and excitement that one might have supposed he was the Viceroy of India on a progress, or Halley's comet come again after seventy-five years of lamented absence." He was not able to sustain his success, though, and thereafter his course was downward. His works are not read now, not like Twain's; but he has survived too, in an unexpected way: the Western—story and film—is in sentiment and stereotypes of character the direct descendant of the Bret Harte tale.

Many of the lesser literary figures left around this time as well. There remained in San Francisco Henry George, to whom the next epoch of the city's history belongs, and Ambrose Bierce, sardonically announcing that he intended to stay and refine the styles of such journalists as he could, and assassinate those he couldn't. It was not until the end of the century, when Jack London and Frank Norris appeared on the scene, that San Francisco would again experience so stimulating a literary era.

This book's time span is from 1863, the year when Twain made his first coach trip from Virginia City down to San Francisco and began contributing to San Francisco journals, to December 1866, when he left the city to embark on the voyages out of which he would make *The Innocents Abroad.* They are selected from a much larger body of material. Twain wrote assiduously during this time, for any paper which would pay him a few dollars—from the *Napa County Reporter* to the *Daily Hawaiian Herald.*

In making my selection, my criteria have been to choose those pieces which best reveal the San Francisco of Twain's day, which show aspects of his development as a writer, and which—most persuasive of all, if the truth be told—delight me particularly, for one reason or another. I have left out some pieces which Twain himself admired enough to preserve in his own later collections of his essays—such as his biography of George Washington and the piece called "The Killing of Julius Caesar, 'Localized.'" My official reason for omitting them might be that they do not do anything to evoke the San Francisco of the 1860s, but my real reason is undoubtedly that I do not enjoy them much; they seem to me not to have the spark that other pieces have. I have not included any of the San Francisco sections from *Roughing It,* partly because that book is readily available to the public, but more because *Roughing It* is retrospective—even though it is the liveliest kind of retrospection—and I wish to present here simply the voice of Twain as it was to be heard at a particular time and a particular place.

Mine is a selection intended not for the scholar but for the general reader. For those wishing a more detailed, more comprehensive, impeccably scholarly collection, I recommend the two volumes of the *Works of Mark Twain* series entitled *Early Tales and Sketches,* edited by Edgar Marquess Branch and Robert H. Hirst with the assistance of Harriet Elinor Smith.

My principal sources have been the newspapers and journals of the period to be found at the Bancroft Library of the University of California and the Yale Collection of American Literature at the Yale University Library. Of particular value and interest was a scrapbook Twain kept of clippings from those years, which is to be found at the Yale Library. The scrapbook is not complete. A number of items in it are torn or illegible. But it is an essential source for the *Territorial Enterprise* articles, since the files of the *Enterprise* were all destroyed by fire or earthquake. The scrapbook contains marginalia in Twain's own handwriting, which indicate that he was at the time considering collecting the pieces for publication in book form. And, indeed, most of the material in his 1867 book *The Celebrated Jumping Frog of Calaveras County, and Other Sketches* did come from the scrapbook.

Such revisions as he made in this scrapbook are often, it may be noted, in the direction of toning down an exuberance or colloquialism. The result is not necessarily an improvement. The best evidence as to when he made these revisions suggests a date of early 1867, so one can't in this instance automatically blame the influence of his wife, Olivia, or William Dean Howells and the genteel East, as biographers have tended to do whenever encountering evidence that Twain has toned himself down a notch. There were genteel pressures within himself, as well—and certainly there were many such influences among the San Francisco literati at the time Twain was there. Bret Harte, who turned his sentences quite elegantly even when writing on cowpoke topics, was certainly one such influence, and Twain at one point gave Harte credit for helping him train and trim his style when he was starting out. At any rate, I have not attempted to incorporate any of Twain's suggested revisions, but have preferred to present the articles in their original form, as they appeared in their time.

In the preparation of the early edition of this book I received valuable assistance from Donald Gallup and Mrs. Anne Whelpley of the Collection of American Literature at Yale Library, and the staff of the

Bancroft Library of the University of California, particularly John Barr Tompkins and J. R. K. Kantor. Also most helpful was Frederick Anderson, then director of the Mark Twain Papers at the University of California.

For this new edition I gratefully acknowledge the help of Robert Hirst, the current director of that priceless institution, the Mark Twain Papers, and I also thank the present staff of the Bancroft Library, Susan Snyder in particular.

May 2003

A NOTE ON THE ILLUSTRATIONS

The large cartoons to be found throughout the book are by Edward Jump, whose work makes, I think, an apt and pungent complement, both in spirit and content, to Twain's San Francisco writings. Jump and Twain were in San Francisco for almost exactly the same period of time. Jump's earliest San Francisco drawing is dated 1863, and his last is 1867. During that period he was San Francisco's favorite caricaturist, as Twain was its favorite writer. Twain admired Jump's work. In his lecture on the Sandwich Islands, Twain announced that he planned to make a book out of the articles he had written there, and that Jump would provide the illustrations. But that project never found a publisher.

Born in Paris in 1831 or maybe 1832—the reference books disagree on the exact date—Jump came to the United States as a young man, lured by the Gold Rush. Jump learned his craft, it is said, by designing the labels for whisky bottles. If so, that would have been in San Francisco—saloon city. His earliest known work, though, preceded his arrival in San Francisco; this was a group of sketches of the Fall River waterfall published in *Hutching's California Magazine* in 1857.

After leaving San Francisco in 1867, he lived for a while in Washington, D.C., where he was a successful portrait artist, commanding high fees. Around that time he married a singer from a traveling French opera company. Their marriage was, from all accounts, stormy. No matter what Jump earned, there was never enough money and there was always too much alcohol.

For a time he was a leading artist for *Leslie's* magazine in New York. He left that to start an illustrated paper in Montreal. When that failed, he moved on from one city to another—New Orleans, St. Louis, Cincinnati, Chicago—making an uncertain living by whatever means his pen could enable—portraits, cartoons, bawdy illustrations to adorn the walls of saloons. In Chicago, where he and his wife and daughter settled in 1880, his main source of income was drawing circus and theater posters. On April 21, 1883, leaving a note for his wife that read, "Poor darling, I have done it at last. I know it is bad, but I can't bear poverty, and I have had too much of it lately," he put a revolver to his head and pulled the trigger.

Jump's work—in particular the genre of crowd scenes—was really quite remarkable. Though his sense of overall composition is sometimes weak, he had a gift for accurate, vivid detail even when his aim was burlesque. He was like Mark Twain in that respect. One of the pleasures Jump's audience got from his drawings was that in his crowd scenes it was always possible to recognize the faces of scores of notable San Franciscans of one sort or another—respectable citizens, low types, town characters, politicians, even well-known dogs.

His cartoons, mainly lithographs signed on the stone, were usually issued in the form of broadside sheets. A few of his drawings appeared in *Puck,* a short-lived California pictorial journal. As far as I have been able to determine, only twenty-one of Jump's San Francisco cartoons are extant. I have included fourteen of them in this book, which is, I believe, substantially more than have been printed in any volume hitherto—in fact, this book comes out several jumps ahead in that regard.

Most of the smaller illustrations sprinkled throughout the text are by True W. Williams, who illustrated *The Innocents Abroad, Roughing It, Sketches New and Old, The Gilded Age,* and other Twain books. Of him, Twain's biographer Albert Bigelow Paine wrote: "Williams was a man of great talent, of fine imagination and sweetness of spirit, but it was necessary to lock him in a room when industry was required, with nothing more exciting than cold water as a beverage."

TABLE OF ILLUSTRATIONS BY JUMP

1863

[This account of what the stagecoach trip over the Sierra from Virginia City to San Francisco was like was written some months before Twain moved to San Francisco. He made the trip at least twice to see the sights and report on them. When Twain speaks of "Virginia" in these writings, it is, of course, Virginia City he means; and Nevada, throughout these pieces, is almost always called Washoe by Twain, as it was by the general public.]

OVER THE MOUNTAINS

The trip from Virginia to Carson by Messrs. Carpenter & Hoog's stage is a pleasant one, and from thence over the mountains by the Pioneer would be another, if there were less of it. But you naturally want an outside seat in the daytime, and you feel a good deal like riding inside when the cold night winds begin to blow; yet if you commence your journey on the outside, you will find that you will be allowed to enjoy the desire I speak of unmolested from twilight to sunrise. An outside seat is preferable, though, day or night. All you want to do is to prepare for it thoroughly. You should sleep forty-eight hours in succession before starting so that you may not have to do anything of that kind on the box. You should also take a heavy overcoat with you. I did neither. I left Carson feeling very miserable for want of sleep, and the voyage from there to Sacramento did not refresh me perceptibly. I took no overcoat and I almost shivered the shirt off myself during that long night ride from Strawberry Valley to Folsom. Our driver was a very companionable man, though, and this was a happy circumstance for me, because, being drowsy and worn out, I would have gone to sleep and fallen overboard if he had not enlivened the dreary hours with his conversation. Whenever I stopped coughing, and went to nodding, he always watched me out of the corner of his eye until I got to pitching in his direction, and then he would stir me up and inquire if I were asleep. If I said "No" (and I was apt to do that), he always said "it was a bully good thing for me that I warn't, you know," and then went on to relate cheerful anecdotes of people who had got to nodding by his side when he wasn't noticing, and had fallen off and broken their necks. He said he could see those fellows before him now, all jammed and bloody and quivering in death's agony—"G'lang! d——n that horse, he knows there's a parson and an old maid inside, and that's what makes him cut up so; I've saw him act jes' so more'n a thousand times!" The driver always lent an additional charm to his conversation by mixing his horrors and his general information together in this way. "Now," said he, after urging his team at a furious speed down the grade for a while, plunging into deep bends in the road brimming with a thick darkness almost palpable to the touch, and darting out again and again on the verge of

what instinct told me was a precipice, "Now, I seen a poor cuss—but you're asleep again, you know, and you've rammed your head agin' my side-pocket and busted a bottle of nasty rotten medicine that I'm taking to the folks at the Thirty-five Mile House; do you notice that flavor? ain't it a ghastly old stench? The man that takes it down there don't live on anything else—it's vittles and drink to him; anybody that ain't used to him can't go a-near him; he'd stun 'em—he'd suffocate 'em; his breath smells like a graveyard after an earthquake—you Bob! I allow to skelp that ornery horse, yet, if he keeps on this way; you see he's been on the overland till about two weeks ago, and every stump he sees he cal'lates it's an Injun." I was awake by this time, holding on with both hands and bouncing up and down just as I do when I ride a horseback. The driver took up the thread of his discourse and proceeded to soothe me again: "As I was a saying, I see a poor cuss tumble off along here one night—he was monstrous drowsy, and went to sleep when I'd took my eye off of him for a moment—and he fetched up agin a boulder, and in a second there wasn't anything left of him but a promiscus pile of hash! It was moonlight, and when I got down and looked at him he was quivering like jelly, and sorter moaning to himself, like, and the bones of his legs was sticking out through his pantaloons every which way, like that." (Here the driver mixed his fingers up after the manner of a stack of muskets, and illuminated them with the ghostly light of his cigar.) "He warn't in misery long though. In a minute and a half he was deader'n a smelt—Bob! I say I'll cut that horse's throat if he stays on this route another week." In this way the genial driver caused the long hours to pass sleeplessly away, and if he drew upon his imagination for his fearful histories, I shall be the last to blame him for it, because if they had taken a milder form I might have yielded to the dullness that oppressed me, and got my own bones smashed out of my hide in such a way as to render me useless forever after—unless, perhaps, some one chose to turn me to account as an uncommon sort of hat-rack.

Sept. 13, 1863—*Territorial Enterprise.*

[The most obvious sight to be seen on this occasion in San Francisco was Adah Isaacs Menken, who, dressed in tights and a Greek chiton, was playing the male lead in *Mazeppa.* The play had a sensational scene in which she was strapped to the back of a horse for a "death ride" up the mountains. Some thirty thousand people saw the play in less than three weeks in San Francisco, and she was paid $500 a night for her performance. Charles Warren Stoddard wrote that she was "a living and breathing poem that set the heart to music and throbbed rhythmically to a passion that was as splendid as it was pure." The inveterate punster Charles Henry Webb, who wrote for the *Golden Era* under the pseudonym of Inigo, said, "One touch of nature makes all Men Kin." She had once been married to John Heenan, the pugilist—"The Benicia Boy," as he was known—but she also wrote poetry and inspired Swinburne to write his "Our Lady of Sorrows" for her. In San Francisco she immediately became part of the literary and Bohemian circle.]

THE MENKEN—WRITTEN ESPECIALLY FOR GENTLEMEN

When I arrived in San Francisco, I found there was no one in town—at least there was no body in town but "the Menken"—or rather, that no one was being talked about except that manly young female. I went to see her play "Mazeppa," of course. They said she was dressed from head to foot in flesh-colored "tights," but I had no opera-glass, and I couldn't see it, to use the language of the inelegant rabble. She appeared to me to have but one garment on—a thin tight white linen one, of unimportant dimensions; I forget the name of the article, but it is indispensable to infants of tender age—I suppose any young mother can tell you what it is, if you have the moral courage to ask the question. With the exception of this superfluous rag, the Menken dresses like the Greek Slave; but some of her postures are not so modest as the suggestive attitude of the latter. She is a finely formed woman down to her knees; if she could be herself that far, and Mrs. H. A. Perry the rest of the way, she would pass for an unexceptionable Venus. Here every tongue sings the praises of her matchless grace, her supple gestures, her charming attitudes. Well, possibly, these tongues are right. In the first act, she rushes on the stage, and goes cavorting around after "Olinska"; she bends herself back like a bow; she pitches headforemost at the atmosphere like a battering-ram; she works her arms, and her legs, and her whole body like a dancing-jack: her every movement is as quick as thought; in a word, without any apparent reason for it, she carries on like a lunatic from the beginning of the act to the end of it. At other times she "whallops" herself down on the stage, and rolls over as does the sportive pack-mule after his burden is removed. If this be grace then the Menken is eminently graceful. After a while they proceed to strip her, and the high chief Pole calls for the "fiery untamed steed"; a subordinate Pole brings in the fierce brute, stirring him up occasionally to make him run away, and then hanging to him like death to keep him from doing it; the monster looks around pensively upon the brilliant audience in the theatre, and seems very willing to stand still—but a lot of those Poles grab him and hold on to him, so as to be prepared for him in case he changes his mind. They are posted as to his fiery untamed nature, you know, and they give him no chance to get loose and eat up the orchestra. They strap Mazeppa on his back, fore and aft, and face uppermost, and the horse goes cantering up-stairs over the painted mountains, through tinted clouds of theatrical mist, in a brisk exciting way, with the wretched victim he bears unconsciously digging her heels into his hams, in the agony of her sufferings, to make him go faster. Then a tempest of applause bursts forth, and the curtain falls. The fierce old circus horse carries his prisoner around through the back part of the theatre, behind the scenery, and although assailed at every step by the savage wolves of the desert, he makes his way at last to his dear old home in Tartary down by the footlights, and beholds once more, O, gods! the familiar faces of the fiddlers in the orchestra. The noble old steed is happy, then, but poor Mazeppa is insensible—"ginned out" by his trip, as it were. Before the act closes, however, he is restored to consciousness and his doting old father, the king of Tartary; and the next day, without taking time to dress—without even borrowing a shirt, or stealing a fresh horse—he starts off on the fiery untamed, at the head of the Tartar nation, to exterminate the Poles, and carry off his own sweet Olinska from the Polish court. He succeeds, and the curtain falls upon a bloody combat, in which the Tartars are victorious. "Mazeppa" proved a great card for Maguire here; he put it on the boards in first-class style, and crowded houses went crazy over it every night it was played. But Virginians will soon have an opportunity of seeing it themselves, as "the Menken" will go direct from our town there without stopping on the way. The "French Spy" was played last night and the night before, and as this spy is a frisky Frenchman, and as dumb as an oyster, Miss Menken's extravagant gesticulations do not seem so overdone in it as they do in "Mazeppa." She don't talk well, and as she goes on her shape and her acting, the character of a fidgety "dummy" is peculiarly suited to her line of business. She plays the Spy, without words, with more feeling than she does Mazeppa with them.

I am tired writing, now, so you will get no news in this letter. I have got a note-book full of interesting hieroglyphics, but I am afraid that by the time I am ready to write them out, I shall have forgotten what they mean. The lady who asked me to furnish her with the Lick House fashions, shall have them shortly—or if I ever get time, I will dish up those displayed at the great Pioneer ball, at Union Hall, last Wednesday night.

Sept. 13, 1863—*Territorial Enterprise.*

[This article was Twain's first contribution to San Francisco's *Golden Era,* a weekly that Franklin Walker, author of *San Francisco's Literary Frontier,* has called "the livest literary sheet west of New York." Twain was pleased enough with the piece to include it in his collection, *Sketches New and Old.* The "Lake Bigler" he refers to is Lake Tahoe, a name which, for some reason, Twain could not abide and refused to accept—he said it sounded "as weak as soup for a sick infant."]

HOW TO CURE A COLD

It is a good thing, perhaps, to write for the amusement of the public, but it is a far higher and nobler thing to write for their instruction—their profit—their actual and tangible benefit.

The latter is the sole object of this article.

If it prove the means of restoring to health one solitary sufferer among my race—of lighting up once more the fire of hope and joy in his faded eyes—of bringing back to his dead heart again the quick, generous impulses of other days—I shall be amply rewarded for my labor; my soul will be permeated with the sacred delight a Christian feels when he has done a good, unselfish deed.

Having led a pure and blameless life, I am justified in believing that no man who knows me will reject the suggestions I am about to make, out of fear that I am trying to deceive him.

Let the public do itself the honor to read my experience in doctoring a cold, as herein set forth, and then follow in my footsteps.

When the White House was burned in Virginia, I lost my home, my happiness, my constitution and my trunk.

The loss of the two first named articles was a matter of no great consequence, since a home without a mother or a sister, or a distant young female relative in it, to remind you by putting your soiled linen out of sight and taking your boots down off the mantel-piece, that there are those who think about you and care for you, is easily obtained.

And I cared nothing for the loss of my happiness, because, not being a poet, it could not be possible that melancholy would abide with me long.

But to lose a good constitution and a better trunk were serious misfortunes.

I had my Gould and Curry in the latter, you recollect; I may get it back again, though—I came down here this time partly to bully-rag the Company into restoring my stock to me.

On the day of the fire, my constitution succumbed to a severe cold caused by undue exertion in getting ready to do something.

I suffered to no purpose, too, because the plan I was figuring at for the extinguishing of the fire was so elaborate that I never got it completed until the middle of the following week.

The first time I began to sneeze, a friend told me to go and bathe my feet in hot water and go to bed.

I did so.

Shortly afterward, another friend advised me to get up and take a cold shower-bath.

I did that also.

Within the hour, another friend assured me that it was policy to "feed a cold and starve a fever."

I had both.

I thought it best to fill myself up for the cold, and then keep dark and let the fever starve a while.

In a case of this kind, I seldom do things by halves; I ate pretty heartily; I conferred my custom upon a stranger who had just opened his restaurant that morning; he waited near me in respectful silence until I had finished feeding my cold, when he inquired if the people about Virginia were much afflicted with colds?

I told him I thought they were.

He then went out and took in his sign.

I started down toward the office, and on the way encountered another bosom friend, who told me that a quart of salt water, taken warm, would come as near curing a cold as anything in the world.

I hardly thought I had room for it, but I tried it anyhow.

The result was surprising; I must have vomited three-quarters of an hour; I believe I threw up my immortal soul.

Now, as I am giving my experience only for the benefit of those who are troubled with the distemper I am writing about, I feel that they will see the propriety of my cautioning them against following such portions of it as proved inefficient with me—and acting upon this conviction, I warn them against warm salt water.

It may be a good enough remedy, but I think it is too severe. If I had another cold in the head, and there was no course left me but to take either an earthquake or a quart of warm salt water, I would cheerfully take my chances on the earthquake.

After the storm which had been raging in my stomach had subsided, and no more good Samaritans happening along, I went on borrowing handkerchiefs again and blowing them to atoms, as had been my custom in the early stages of my cold, until I came across a lady who had just arrived from over the plains, and who said she had lived in a part of the country where doctors were scarce and had from necessity acquired considerable skill in the treatment of simple "family complaints."

I knew she must have had much experience, for she appeared to be a hundred and fifty years old.

She mixed a decoction composed of molasses, aqua fortis, turpentine, and various other drugs, and instructed me to take a wine-glass full of it every fifteen minutes.

I never took but one dose; that was enough; it robbed me of all moral principle, and awoke every unworthy impulse of my nature.

Under its malign influence, my brain conceived miracles of meanness but my hands were too feeble to execute them; at that time had it not been that my strength had surrendered to a succession of assaults from infallible remedies for my cold, I am satisfied that I would have tried to rob the graveyard.

Like most other people, I often feel mean, and act accordingly, but until I took that medicine I had never reveled in such supernatural depravity and felt proud of it.

At the end of two days, I was ready to go to doctoring again. I took a few more unfailing remedies, and finally drove my cold from my head to my lungs.

I got to coughing incessantly, and my voice fell below Zero; I conversed in a thundering bass two octaves below my natural tone; I could only compass my regular nightly repose by coughing myself down to a state of utter exhaustion, and then the moment I began to talk in my sleep, my discordant voice woke me up again.

My case grew more and more serious every day.

Plain gin was recommended; I took it.

Then gin and molasses; I took that also.

Then gin and onions; I added the onions and took all three.

I detected no particular result, however, except that I had acquired a breath like a buzzard's.

I found I had to travel for my health.

I went to Lake Bigler with my reportorial comrade, Adair Wilson. It is gratifying to me to reflect that we traveled in considerable style; we went in the Pioneer coach, and my friend took all his baggage with him, consisting of two excellent silk handkerchiefs and a daguerreotype of his grandmother.

I had my regular gin and onions along.

Virginia, San Francisco and Sacramento were well represented at the Lake House, and we had a very healthy time of it for a while. We sailed and hunted and fished and danced all day, and I doctored my cough all night.

By managing in this way, I made out to improve every hour in the twenty-four.

But my disease continued to grow worse.

A sheet-bath was recommended. I had never refused a remedy yet, and it seemed poor policy to commence then; therefore I determined to take a sheet-bath, notwithstanding I had no idea what sort of arrangement it was.

It was administered at midnight, and the weather was very frosty. My breast and back were bared, and a sheet (there appeared to be a thousand yards of it) soaked in ice-water, was wound around me until I resembled a swab for a Columbiad.

It is a cruel expedient. When the chilly rag touches one's warm flesh, it makes him start with sudden violence and gasp for breath just as men do in the death agony. It froze the marrow in my bones and stopped the beating of my heart.

I thought my time had come.

Young Wilson said the circumstance reminded him of an anecdote about a negro who was being baptised, and who slipped from the Parson's grasp and came near being drowned; he floundered around, though, finally rose up out of the water considerably strangled and furiously angry, and started ashore at once, spouting water like a whale, and remarking with great asperity that "One o' dese days, some gen'man's nigger gwyne to git killed wid jes' sich dam foolishness as dis!"

Then young Wilson laughed at his silly, pointless anecdote, as if he had thought he had done something very smart. I suppose I am not to be affronted every day, though, without resenting it—I coughed my bed-fellow clear out of the house before morning.

Never take a sheet-bath—never. Next to meeting a lady acquaintance, who, for reasons best known to herself, don't see you when she looks at you and don't know you when she does see you, it is the most uncomfortable thing in the world.

It is singular that such a simile as that happened to occur to me; I haven't thought of that circumstance a dozen times to-day. I used to think she was so pretty, and gentle, and graceful, and considerate, and all that sort of thing.

But I suspect it was all a mistake.

In reality, she is as ugly as a crab; and there is no expression in her countenance, either; she reminds me of one of those dummies in the milliner shops. I know she has got false teeth, and I think one of her eyes is glass. She can never fool me with that French she talks, either; that's Cherokee—I have been among that tribe myself. She has already driven two or three Frenchmen to the verge of suicide with that unchristian gibberish. And that complexion of hers is the dingiest that ever a white woman bore—it is pretty nearly Cherokee itself. It shows out strongest when it is contrasted with her monstrous white sugar-shoveled bonnet; when she gets that on, she looks like a sorrel calf under a new shed. I despise that woman, and I'll never speak to her again. Not unless she speaks to me, anyhow.

But as I was saying, when the sheet-bath failed to cure my cough, a lady friend recommended the application of a mustard plaster to my breast.

I believe that would have cured me effectually, if it had not been for young Wilson.

When I went to bed I put my mustard plaster—which was a very gorgeous one, eighteen inches square—where I could reach it when I was ready for it.

But young Wilson got hungry in the night, and ate it up.

I never saw anybody have such an appetite; I am confident that lunatic would have eaten me if I had been healthy.

After sojourning a week at Lake Bigler, I went to Steamboat Springs, and besides the steam baths, I took a lot of the vilest medicines that were ever concocted. They would have cured me, but I had to go back to Virginia, where, notwithstanding the variety of new remedies I absorbed every day, I managed to aggravate my disease by carelessness and undue exposure.

I finally concluded to visit San Francisco, and the first day I got here a lady at the Lick House told me to drink a quart of whisky every twenty-four hours, and a friend at the Occidental recommended precisely the same course.

Each advised me to take a quart—that makes half a gallon.

I calculate to do it or perish in the attempt.

Now, with the kindest motives in the world, I offer for the consideration of consumptive patients the variegated course of treatment I have lately gone through. Let them try it—if it don't cure them, it can't more than kill them.

Sept. 20, 1863—*Golden Era.*

[In this piece Twain manages to parody contemporary sportswriters' style while at the same time satirizing bloodthirsty California politics. San Francisco was always an ardent fight town, and the California *Police Gazette* gave vivid reports on the pugilistic encounters of the period in language almost, but not quite, as sanguinary as that employed here by Twain.]

THE GREAT PRIZE FIGHT

THE ONLY TRUE AND RELIABLE ACCOUNT OF THE GREAT PRIZE FIGHT FOR $100,000 AT SEAL ROCK POINT, ON SUNDAY LAST, BETWEEN HIS EXCELLENCY GOV. STANFORD AND HON. F. F. LOW, GOVERNOR-ELECT OF CALIFORNIA.

For the past month the sporting world has been in a state of feverish excitement on account of the grand prize fight set for last Sunday between the two most distinguished citizens of California, for a purse of a hundred thousand dollars. The high social standing of the competitors, their exalted position in the arena of politics, together with the princely sum of money staked upon the issue of the combat, all conspired to render the proposed prize fight a subject of extraordinary importance, and to give it an eclat never before vouchsafed to such a circumstance since the world began. Additional lustre was shed upon the coming contest by the lofty character of the seconds or bottle-holders chosen by the two champions, these being no other than Judge Field (on the part of Gov. Low), Associate Justice of the Supreme Court of the United States, and Hon. Wm. M. Stewart (commonly called "Bill Stewart," or "Bullyragging Bill Stewart"), of the city of Virginia, the most popular as well as the most distinguished lawyer in Nevada Territory, member of the Constitutional Convention, and future U.S. Senator for the State of Washoe, as I hope and believe—on the part of Gov. Stanford. Principals and seconds together, it is fair to presume that such an array of talent was never entered for a combat of this description upon any previous occasion.

Stewart and Field had their men in constant training at the Mission during the six weeks preceding the contest, and such was the interest taken in the matter that thousands visited that sacred locality daily to pick up such morsels of information as they might, concerning the physical and scientific improvement being made by the gubernatorial acrobats. The anxiety manifested by the populace was intense. When it was learned that Stanford had smashed a barrel of flour to atoms with a single blow of his fist, the voice of the people was on his side. But when the news came that Low had caved in the head of a tubular boiler with one stroke of his powerful "mawley" (which term is in strict accordance with the language of the ring), the tide of opinion changed again. These changes were frequent, and they kept the minds of the public in such a state of continual vibration that I fear the habit thus acquired is confirmed, and that they will never more cease to oscillate.

The fight was to take place on last Sunday morning at ten o'clock. By nine every wheeled vehicle and every species of animal capable of bearing burthens, were in active service, and the avenues leading to the Seal Rock swarmed with them in mighty processions whose numbers no man might hope to estimate.

I determined to be upon the ground at an early hour. Now I dislike to be exploded, as it were, out of my balmy slumbers, by a sudden, stormy assault upon my door, and an imperative order to "Get up!"—wherefore I requested one of the intelligent porters of the Lick House to call at my palatial apartments, and murmur gently through the keyhole the magic monosyllable "Hash!" That "fetched me."

The urbane livery-stable keeper furnished me with a solemn, short-bodied, long-legged animal—a sort of animated counting-house stool, as it were—which he called a "Morgan" horse. He told me who the brute was "sired" by, and was proceeding to tell me who he was "dammed" by, but I gave him to understand that I was competent to damn the horse myself, and should probably do it very effectually before I got to the battle-ground. I mentioned to him, however, that as I was not proposing to attend a funeral, it was hardly necessary to furnish me an animal gifted with such oppressive solemnity of bearing as distinguished his "Morgan." He said in reply, the Morgan was only pensive when in the stable, but that on the road I would find him one of the liveliest horses in the world.

He enunciated the truth.

The brute "bucked" with me from the foot of Montgomery street to the Occidental Hotel. The laughter which he provoked from the crowds of citizens along the side-walks, he took for applause, and honestly made every effort in his power to deserve it, regardless of consequences.

He was very playful, but so suddenly were the creations of his fancy conceived and executed, and so much ground did he take up with them, that it was safest to behold them from a distance. In the selfsame moment of time, he shot his heels through the side of a street-car, and then backed himself into Barry and Patten's and sat down on the free-lunch table.

Such was the length of this Morgan's legs.

Between the Occidental and the Lick House, having become thoroughly interested in his work, he planned and carried out a series of the most extraordinary maneuvers ever suggested by the brain of any horse. He arched his neck and went tripping daintily across the street sideways, "rairing up" on his hind legs occasionally, in a very disagreeable way, and looking into the second-story win-

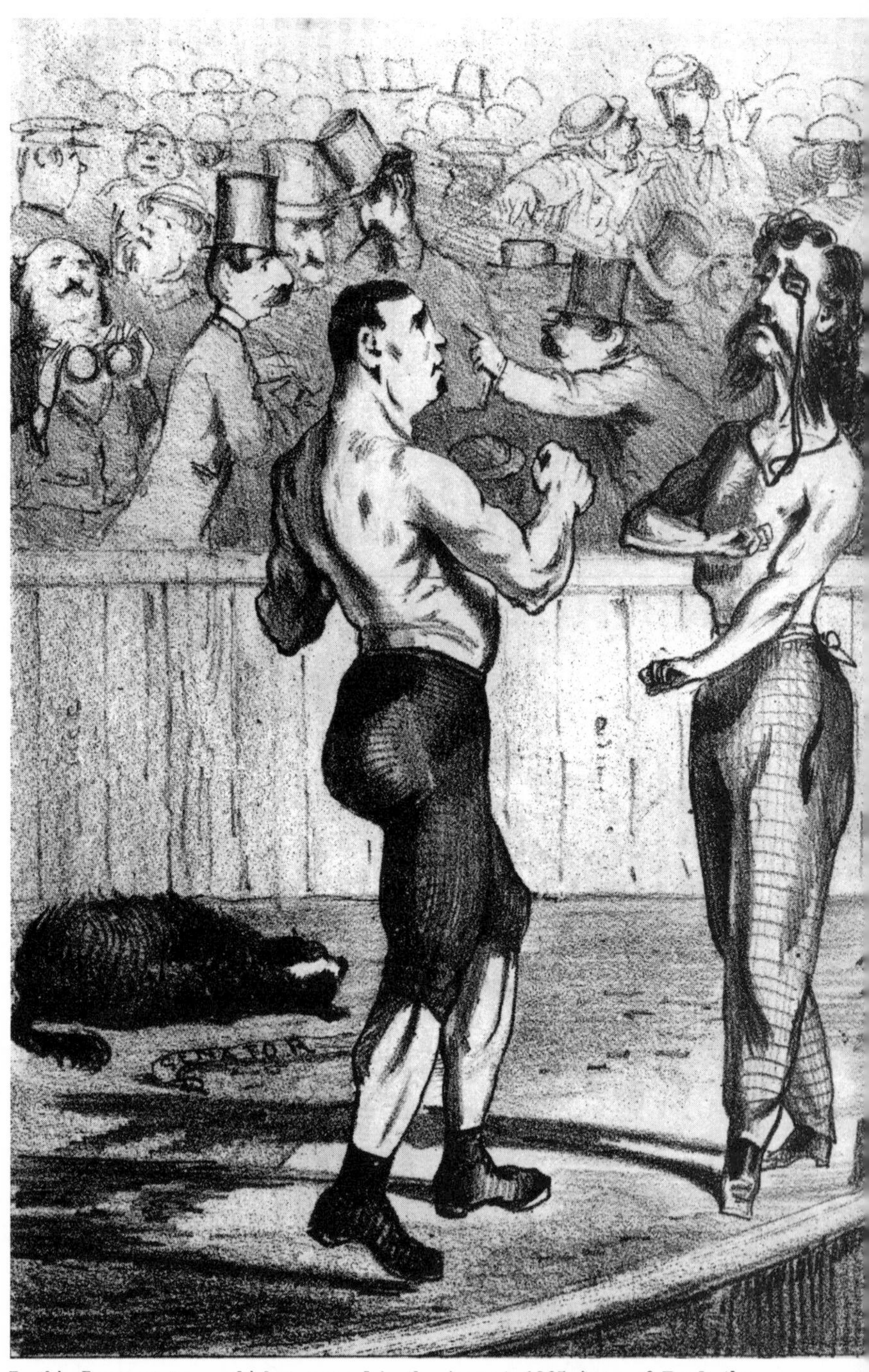

In this Jump cartoon, which appeared in the August, 1865, issue of *Puck,* the California pictorial, the antagonists are the candidates for United States Senator. The two party factions were familiarly known as the Short Hairs and

the Long Hairs. Jump probably drew his inspiration from Twain's "Great Prize Fight" article—as well as from the fact that the party convention ended in a disgraceful brawl.

dows. He finally waltzed into the large ice cream saloon opposite the Lick House, and—

But the memory of that perilous voyage hath caused me to digress from the proper subject of this paper, which is the great prize fight between Governors Low and Stanford. I will resume.

After an infinitude of fearful adventures, the history of which would fill many columns of this newspaper, I finally arrived at the Seal Rock Point at a quarter to ten—two hours and a half out from San Francisco, and not less gratified than surprised that I ever got there at all—and anchored my noble Morgan to a boulder on the hill-side. I had to swathe his head in blankets also, because, while my back was turned for a single moment, he developed another atrocious trait of his most remarkable character. He tried to eat little Augustus Maltravers Jackson, the "humbly" but interesting off-spring of Hon. J. Belvidere Jackson, a wealthy barber from San Jose. It would have been a comfort to me to leave the infant to his fate, but I did not feel able to pay for him.

When I reached the battle-ground, the great champions were already stripped and prepared for the "mill." Both were in splendid condition and displayed a redundancy of muscle about the breast and arms which was delightful to the eye of the sportive connoisseur. They were well matched. Adepts said that Stanford's "heft" and tall stature were fairly offset by Low's superior litheness and activity. From their heads to the Union colors around their waists, their costumes were similar to that of the Greek Slave; from thence down they were clad in flesh-colored tights and grenadier boots.

The ring was formed upon the beautiful level sandy beach above the Cliff House, and within twenty paces of the snowy surf of the broad Pacific ocean, which was spotted here and there with monstrous sea-lions attracted shoreward by curiosity concerning the vast multitudes of people collected in the vicinity.

At five minutes past ten, Brigadier General Wright, the Referee, notified the seconds to bring their men "up to the scratch." They did so, amid the shouts of the populace, the noise whereof rose high above the roar of the sea.

First Round.—The pugilists advanced to the centre of the ring, shook hands, retired to their respective corners, and at the call of the time-keeper, came forward and went at it. Low dashed out handsomely with his left and gave Stanford a paster in the eye, and at the same moment his adversary mashed him in the ear. [These singular phrases are entirely proper, Mr. Editor—I find them in the copy of "Bell's Life in London" now lying before me.] After some beautiful sparring, both parties went down—that is to say, they went down to the bottle-holders, Stewart and Field, and took a drink.

Second Round.—Stanford launched out a well intended plunger, but Low parried it admirably and instantly busted him in the snoot. [Cries of "Bully for the Marysville Infant!"] After some lively fibbing (both of them are used to it in political life), the combatants went to the grass. [See "Bell's Life."]

Third Round.—Both came up panting considerably. Low let go a terrific side-winder, but Stanford stopped it handsomely and replied with an earthquake on Low's bread-basket. [Enthusiastic shouts of "Sock it to him, my Sacramento Pet!"] More fibbing—both down.

Fourth Round.—The men advanced and sparred warily for a few moments, when Stanford exposed his cocoanut an instant, and Low struck out from the shoulder and split him in the mug. [Cries of "Bully for the Fat Boy!"]

Fifth Round.—Stanford came looking wicked, and let drive a heavy blow with his larboard flipper which caved in the side of his adversary's head. [Exclamations of "Hi! at him again Old Rusty!"]

From this time until the end of the conflict, there was nothing regular in the proceedings. The two champions got furiously angry, and used up each other thus:

No sooner did Low realize that the side of his head was crushed in like a dent in a plug hat, than he "went after" Stanford in the most desperate manner. With one blow of his fist he mashed his nose so far into his face that a cavity was left in its place the size and shape of an ordinary soup-bowl. It is scarcely necessary to mention that in making room for so much nose, Gov. Stanford's eyes were crowded to such a degree as to cause them to "bug out'' like a grasshopper's. His face was so altered that he scarcely looked like himself at all.

I never saw such a murderous expression as Stanford's countenance now assumed; you see it was so concentrated—it had such a small number of features to spread around over. He let fly one of his battering rams and caved in the other side of Low's head. Ah me, the latter was a ghastly sight to contemplate after that—one of the boys said it looked ''like a beet which somebody had trod on it.''

Low was ''grit'' though. He dashed out with his right and stove Stanford's chin clear back even with his ears. Oh, what a horrible sight he was, gasping and reaching after his tobacco, which was away back among his under-jaw teeth.

Stanford was unsettled for a while, but he soon rallied, and watching his chance, aimed a tremendous blow at his favorite mark, which crushed in the rear of Gov. Low's head in such a way that the crown thereof projected over his spinal column like a shed.

He came up to the scratch like a man, though, and sent one of his ponderous fists crashing through his opponent's ribs and in among his vitals, and instantly afterward he hauled out poor Stanford's left lung and smacked him in the face with it.

If ever I saw an angry man in my life it was Leland Stanford. He fairly raved. He jumped at his old speciality, Gov. Low's head; he tore it loose from his body and knocked him down with it. [Sensation in the crowd.]

Staggered by his extraordinary exertion, Gov. Stanford reeled, and before he could recover himself the headless but indomitable Low sprang forward, pulled one of his legs out by the roots, and dealt him a smashing paster over the eye with the end of it. The ever watchful Bill Stewart sallied out to the assistance of his crippled principal with a pair of crutches, and the battle went on again as fiercely as ever.

At this stage of the game the battle ground was strewn with a sufficiency of human remains to furnish material for the construction of three or four men of ordinary size, and good sound brains enough to stock a whole county like the one I came from in the noble old state of Missouri. And so dyed were the combatants in their own gore that they looked like shapeless, mutilated, red-shirted firemen.

The moment a chance offered, Low grabbed Stanford by the hair of the head, swung him thrice round and round in the air like a lasso, and then slammed him on the ground with such mighty force that he quivered all over, and squirmed painfully, like a worm; and behold, his body and such of his limbs as he had left, shortly assumed a swollen aspect like unto those of a rag doll-baby stuffed with saw-dust.

He rallied again, however, and the two desperadoes clinched and never let up until they had minced each other into such insignificant odds and ends that neither was able to distinguish his own remnants from those of his antagonist. It was awful.

Bill Stewart and Judge Field issued from their corners and gazed upon the sanguinary reminiscences in silence during several minutes. At the end of that time, having failed to discover that either champion had got the best of the fight, they threw up their sponges simultaneously, and Gen. Wright proclaimed in a loud voice that the battle was "drawn." May my ears never again be rent asunder with a burst of sound similar to that which greeted this announcement, from the multitude. Amen.

By order of Gen. Wright, baskets were procured, and Bill Stewart and Judge Field proceeded to gather up the fragments of their late principals, while I gathered up my notes and went after my infernal horse, who had slipped his blankets and was foraging among the neighboring children. I—* * * * * * *

P. S.—Messrs. Editors, I have been the victim of an infamous hoax. I have been imposed upon by that ponderous miscreant, Mr. Frank Lawler, of the Lick House. I left my room a moment ago, and the first man I met on the stairs was Gov. Stanford, alive and well, and as free from mutilation as you or I. I was speechless. Before I reached the street, I actually met Gov. Low also, with his own head on his own shoulders, his limbs intact, his inner mechanism in its proper place, and his cheeks blooming with gorgeous robustitude. I was amazed. But a word of explanation from him convinced me that I had been swindled by Mr. Lawler with a detailed account of a fight which had never occurred, and was never likely to occur; that I had believed him so implicitly as to sit down and write it out (as other reporters have done before me) in language calculated to deceive the public into the conviction that I was present at it myself, and to embellish it with a string of falsehoods intended to render that deception as plausible as possible. I ruminated upon my singular position for many minutes, arrived at no conclusion—that is to say, no satisfactory conclusion, except that Lawler was an accomplished knave and I was a consummate ass. I had suspected the first before, though, and been acquainted with the latter fact for nearly a quarter of a century.

In conclusion, permit me to apologize in the most abject manner to the present Governor of California, to Hon. Mr. Low, the Governor-elect, to Judge Field and to Hon. Wm. M. Stewart, for the great wrong which my natural imbecility has impelled me to do them in penning and publishing the foregoing sanguinary absurdity. If it were to do over again, I don't really know that I would do it. It is not possible for me to say how I ever managed to believe that refined and educated gentlemen like these could stoop to engage in the loathsome and degrading pastime of prize fighting. It was just Lawler's work, you understand—the lubberly, swelled-up effigy of a nine-days drowned man! But I shall get even with him for this. The only excuse he offers is that he got the story from John B. Winters, and thought of course it must be just so—as if a future Congressman for the State of Washoe could by any possibility tell the truth! Do you know that if either of these miserable scoundrels were to cross my path while I am in this mood I would scalp him in a minute? That's me—that's my style.

Oct. 11, 1863—*Golden Era.*

1864

[Thinking this essay a "pearl which ought for the eternal welfare of my race to have a more extensive circulation than is afforded by a local daily paper," Twain sent it off to the New York *Sunday Mercury,* from which the *Golden Era* later reprinted it. It was the first signed piece by Twain to appear in an Eastern periodical. Twain dates the piece 1864 in the heading, but his stay at the Lick House was on one of his visits in 1863, at a time when his Gould and Curry stock was still soaring and he was living in the style "of a man worth a hundred thousand dollars (prospectively) and likely to reach absolute affluence when that silver-mine sale should be ultimately achieved in the East." The Lick House, with its flagged marble floors and fine woodwork, was San Francisco's first palatial hotel; its banquet hall was perhaps the handsomest in America.]

THOSE BLASTED CHILDREN

Lick House, San Francisco,
Wednesday, 1864

No. 165 is a pleasant room. It is situated at the head of a long hall, down which, on either side, are similar rooms occupied by sociable bachelors, and here and there one tenanted by an unsociable nurse or so. Charley Creed sleeps in No. 157. He is my timepiece—or, at least, his boots are. If I look down the hall and see Charley's boots still before his door, I know it is early yet, and I may hie me sweetly to bed again. But if those unerring boots are gone, I know it is after eleven o'clock, and time for me to be rising with the lark.

This reminds me of the lark of yesterday and last night which was altogether a different sort of bird from the one I am talking about now. Ah me! Summer girls and summer dresses, and summer scenes at the "Willows," Seal Rock Point, and the grim sea-lions wallowing in the angry surf; glimpses through the haze of stately ships far away at sea, a dash along the smooth beach, and the exhilaration of watching the white startled horse's feet; reveries beside the old wreck, half buried in sand, and compassion for the good ship's fate; home again in a soft twilight, oppressed with the odor of flowers—home again to San Francisco, drunk, perhaps, but not disorderly. Dinner at six, with ladies and gentlemen, very quiet and well-bred—unaccountably so, under the circumstances, it seemed to my cloudy brain. Many things happened after that, I remember,—such as visiting some of their haunts with those dissipated *Golden Era* fellows, and—Here come those young savages again—those noisy and inevitable children. God be with them!—or they with him, rather, if it be not asking too much. They are another timepiece of mine. It is two o'clock now; they are invested with their regular lunch, and have come up here to settle it. I will soothe my troubled spirit with a short season of blasphemy, after which I will expose their infamous feelings with a relentless pen. They have driven me from labor many and many a time; but behold! the hour of retribution is at hand.

That is young Washington Billings, now—a little dog in long flaxen curls and Highland costume.

"Hi, Johnny! look through the keyhole! here's that feller with a long nose, writing again—less stir him up!" [A double kick against the door—a grand infant war-whoop in full chorus—and then a clatter of scampering feet down the echoing corridors.] Ah—one of them has fallen, and hurt himself. I hear the intelligent foreign nurse boxing his ears for it (the parents, Mr. and Mrs. Kerosene, having gone up to Sacramento on the evening boat, and left their offspring properly cared for).

Here they come again, as soldiers—infantry. I know there are not more than thirty or forty of them, yet they are under no sort of discipline, and they make noise enough for a thousand. Young Oliver Higgins is in command. They assault my works—they try to carry my position by storm—they finally draw off with boisterous cheers, to harass a handful of skirmishers thrown out by the enemy—a bevy of chambermaids.

Once more they come trooping down the hall. This time as cavalry. They must have captured and disarmed the skirmishers, for half my young ruffians are mounted on broomsticks. They make a reconnoissance in force. They attack my premises in a body, but they achieve nothing approaching a success. I am too strongly intrenched for them.

They invest my stronghold, and lay siege to it—that is to say, they sit down before my camp, and betake themselves to the pastimes of youth. All talking at once, as they do, their conversation is amusing, but not instructive to me:

"Ginn me some o' that you're eat'n." "I won't—you wouldn't lemme play with that dead rat, the peanut-boy give you yesterday." "Well! I don't care; I reckon I know summun't you don't; Oho, Mr. Smarty, 'n' I ain't a goin' to tell you, neither; now, see what you got by it; it's summun't my ma said about your ma, too. I'll tell you, if you'll gimme ever so little o' that, will you? Well." (I imagine from the break in this conversation, while the other besiegers go on talking noisily, that a compromise is being effected.) "There, don't take so much. Now, what'd she say?" "Why, ma told my pa't if your ma is so mighty rich now she wasn't nobody till she come to Sanf'cisco. That's what she said." "Your ma's a big story-teller, 'n' I'm going jus' as straight as I can walk, 'n' tell my ma. You'll see what she'll do." (I foresee a diversion in one or two family circles.) "Flora Low, you quit pulling that doll's legs out, it's mine." "Well, take your old doll, then. I'd thank you to know, Miss Florence Hillyer, 't my pa's Governor, 'n' I can have a thousan' dolls if I want to, 'n' gold ones, too, or silver, or anything." (More trouble brewing.) "What do I care for that. I guess my pa could be Governor, too, if he wanted to; but he don't. He owns two hundred feet in the Chollar, 'n' he's got lots more silver mines in Washoe besides. He could fill this house full of silver, clear up to that chandelier, so he could, now, Miss." "You, Bob Miller, you leg go that string—I'll smack you in the eye." "You will, will you? I'd like to see you try it. You jes' hit me if you dare!" "You lay your hands on me, 'n' I will hit you." "Now I've laid my hand on you, why don't you hit?" "Well, I mean, if you lay em' on me so's to hurt." "Ah-h! you're afraid, that's the reason!" "No I ain't, neither, you big fool." (Ah, now they're at it. Discord shall invade the ranks of my foes, and they shall fall by their own hands. It appears from the sound without that two nurses have made a descent upon the combatants, and are bearing them from the field. The nurses are abusing each other. One boy proclaims that the other struck him when he wasn't doin' nothin'; and the other boy says he was called a big fool. Both are going right straight, and tell their pa's. Verily, things are going along as comfortably as I could wish, now.) "Sandy Baker, I know what makes your pa's hair kink so; it's cause he's a mulatter; I heard my ma say so." "It's a lie!" (Another row, and more skirmishing with the nurses. Truly, happiness flows in upon me most bountifully this day.)

Hi, boys! here comes a Chinaman. (God pity any Chinaman who chances to come in the way of the boys hereabouts, for the eye of the law regardeth him not, and the youth of California in their generation are down upon him.) Now, boys! grab his clothes basket —take him by the tail! (There they go, now, like a pack of young demons; they have confiscated the basket, and the dismayed Chinaman is towing half the tribe down the hall by his cue. Rejoice, O my soul, for behold, all things are lovely, etc.—to speak after the manner of the vulgar.) "Oho, Miss Susy Badger, my uncle Tom's goin' across the bay to Oakland, 'n' down to Santa Clara, 'n' Alamedy, 'n' San Leandro, 'n' everywheres—all over the world, 'n' he's goin' to take me with him—he said so." "Humph! that ain't noth'n—I been there. My aunt Mary'd take me to any place I wanted to go, if I wanted her to, but I don't; she's got horses 'n' things—O, ever so many—millions of 'em; but my ma says it don't look well for little girls to be always gadd'n about. That's why you don't ever see me goin' to places like some girls do. I despise to—" (The end is at hand; the nurses have massed themselves on the left; they move in serried phalanx on my besiegers; they surround them, and capture the last miscreant—horse, foot, and dragoons, munitions of war, and camp equipage. The victory is complete. They are gone—my castle is no longer menaced, and the rover is free. I am here, staunch and true!)

It is a living wonder to me that I haven't scalped some of those children before now. I expect I would have done it, but then I hardly felt well enough acquainted with them. I scarcely ever show them any attention anyhow, unless it is to throw a bootjack at them or some little nonsense of that kind when I happen to feel playful. I am confident I would have destroyed several of them though, only it might appear as if I were making most too free.

I observe that that young officer of the Pacific squadron—the one with his nostrils turned up like port-holes—has become a great favorite with half the mothers in the house, by imparting to them much useful information concerning the manner of doctoring children among the South American savages. His brother is a brigadier in the Navy. The drab-complexioned youth with the Solferino mustache has corralled the other half with the Japanese treatment.—The more I think of it, the more I admire it. Now, I am no peanut. I have an idea that I could invent some little remedies that would stir up a commotion among these women, if I chose to try. I always had a good general notion of physic, I believe. It is one of my natural gifts, too, for I have never studied a single day under a regular physician. I will jot down a few items here, just to see how likely I am to succeed.

In the matter of measles, the idea is, to bring it out—bring it to the surface. Take the child and fill it up with saffron tea. Add something to make the patient sleep—say a table-spoonful of arsenic. Don't rock it, it will sleep anyhow.

As far as brain fever is concerned: This is a very dangerous disease, and must be treated with decision and dispatch. In every case where it has proved fatal, the sufferer invariably perished. You must strike at the root of the distemper. Remove the brains; and then—. Well, that will be sufficient—that will answer—just remove the brains. This remedy has never been known to fail. It was invented by the lamented J. W. Macbeth, Thane of Cawdor, Scotland, who refers to it thus: "Time was, that when the brains were out, the man would die; but, under different circumstances, I think not; and, all things being equal, I believe you, my boy." Those were his last words.

Concerning worms: Administer a catfish three times a week. Keep the room very quiet; the fish won't bite if there is the least noise.

When you come to fits, take no chances on fits. If the child has them bad, soak it in a barrel of rain water over night, or a good article of vinegar. If this does not put an end to its troubles, soak it a week. You can't soak a child too much when it has fits.

In cases wherein an infant stammers, remove the under-jaw. In proof of the efficacy of this treatment, I append the following certificate, voluntarily forwarded to me by Mr. Zeb. Leavenworth, of St. Louis, Mo.:

St. Louis, May 26, 1863.

"Mr. Mark Twain—Dear Sir:—Under Providence, I am beholden to you for the salvation of my Johnny. For a matter of three years, that suffering child stuttered to that degree that it was a pain and a sorrow to me to hear him stagger over the sacred name of 'p-p-p-pap.' It troubled me so that I neglected my business; I refused food; I took no pride in my dress, and my hair began to actually fall off. I could not rest; I could not sleep. Morning, noon, and night, I did nothing but moan pitifully, and murmur to myself: 'Hell's fire, what am I going to do about my Johnny?' But in a blessed hour you appeared unto me like an angel from the skies; and without hope of reward, revealed your sovereign remedy—and that very day, I sawed off my Johnny's under-jaw. May Heaven bless you, noble Sir. It afforded instant relief; and my Johnny has never stammered since. I honestly believe he never will again. As to disfigurement, he does seem to look sorter ornery and hog-mouthed, but I am too grateful in having got him effectually saved from that dreadful stuttering, to make much account of small matters. Heaven speed you in your holy work of healing the afflictions of humanity. And if my poor testimony can be of any service to you, do with it as you think will result in the greatest good to our fellow creatures. Once more, Heaven bless you.

Zeb. Leavenworth."

Now, that has such a plausible ring about it, that I can hardly keep from believing it myself. I consider it a very fair success.

Regarding cramps. Take your offspring—let the same be warm and dry at the time—and immerse it in a commodious soup-tureen filled with the best quality of camphene. Place it over a slow fire, and add reasonable quantities of pepper, mustard, horse-radish, saltpetre, strychnine, blue vitriol, aqua fortis, a quart of flour, and eight or ten fresh eggs, stirring it from time to time, to keep up a healthy reaction. Let it simmer fifteen minutes. When your child is done, set the tureen off, and allow the infallible remedy to cool. If this does not confer an entire insensibility to cramps you must lose no time, for the case is desperate. Take your offspring, and parboil it. The most vindictive cramps cannot survive this treatment; neither can the subject, unless it is endowed with an iron constitution. It is an extreme measure, and I always dislike to resort to it. I never parboil a child until everything else has failed to bring about the desired end.

Well, I think those will do to commence with. I can branch out, you know, when I get more confidence in myself.

O infancy! thou art beautiful, thou art charming, thou art lovely to contemplate! But thoughts like these recall sad memories of the past, of the halycon days of my childhood, when I was a sweet, prattling innocent, the pet of a dear home-circle and the pride of the village.

Enough, enough! I must weep, or this bursting heart will break.

March 27, 1864—*Golden Era*
(as reprinted from the New York *Sunday Mercury*).

UNION TICKET.
Dr. I. ROWELL,
I. BLUXOME, Jr.
H. HASBACH,
JNO. MULLENEY,
C.S. HIGGINS,
D.W. THOMPSON.
H.M. HASTINGS
JOHN C. PELTON.
A.W. VON SCHMIDT.
MARCUS HARLOE
JAMES LAIDLEY.
Dr. JAS. MURPHY.
THE PRIZE
Doctor you must bring down that old COON
CLEAR THE TRACK

The race for Mayor between Rowell of the Union party and Coon of the People's party—with San Francisco's favorite stray dog, Bummer, bounding ahead to proclaim, "Clear the track." The People's party won.

WASHOE—INFORMATION WANTED

(A citizen of Virginia, Washoe's world-famed metropolis, lately received a letter from a friend in Missouri who "Wanted Information" concerning Silver-Land. This letter was handed over to Mark Twain. In the Territorial Enterprise *we find the whole correspondence:)*

Springfield, Mo. April 12.

Dear Sir:—My object in writing to you is to have you give me a full history of Nevada: What is the character of its climate? What are the productions of the earth? Is it healthy? What diseases do they die of mostly? Do you think it would be advisable for a man who can make a living in Missouri to emigrate to that part of the country? There are several of us who would emigrate there in the spring if we could ascertain to a certainty that it is a much better country than this. I suppose you know Joel H. Smith? He used to live here; he lives in Nevada now; they say he owns considerable in a mine there. Hoping to hear from you soon, etc., I remain yours, truly,

William ———

Dearest William:—Pardon my familiarity—but that name touchingly reminds me of the loved and lost, whose name was similar. I have taken the contract to answer your letter, and although we are now strangers, I feel we shall cease to be so if we ever become acquainted with each other. The thought is worthy of attention, William. I will now respond to your several propositions in the order in which you have fulminated them.

Your object in writing is to have me give you a full history of Nevada. The flattering confidence you repose in me, William, is only equalled by the modesty of your request. I could detail the history of Nevada in five hundred pages octavo, but as you have never done me any harm, I will spare you, though it will be apparent to everybody that I would be justified in taking advantage of you if I were a mind to do it.

However, I will condense. Nevada was discovered many years

ago by the Mormons, and was called Carson county. It only became Nevada in 1861, by act of Congress. There is a popular tradition that God Almighty created it; but when you come to see it, William, you will think differently. Do not let that discourage you, though. The country looks something like a singed cat, owing to the scarcity of shrubbery, and also resembles that animal in the respect that it has more merits than its personal appearance would seem to indicate. The Grosch brothers found the first silver lead here in 1857. They also founded Silver City, I believe. (Observe the subtle joke, William.) But the "history" of Nevada which you demand, properly begins with the discovery of the Comstock lead, which event happened nearly five years ago. The opinion now prevailing in the East that the Comstock is on the Gould & Curry is erroneous; on the contrary, the Gould & Curry is on the Comstock. Please make the correction, William. Signify to your friends, also, that all the mines here do not pay dividends as yet; you may make this statement with the utmost unyielding inflexibility—it will not be contradicted from this quarter. The population of this Territory is about 35,000, one-half of which number reside in the united cities of Virginia and Gold Hill. However, I will discontinue this history for the present, lest I get you too deeply interested in this distant land and cause you to neglect your family or your religion. But I will address you again upon the subject next year. In the meantime, allow me to answer your inquiry as to the character of our climate.

It has no character to speak of, William, and alas! in this respect it resembles many, ah, too many chambermaids in this wretched, wretched world. Sometimes we have the seasons in their regular order, and then again we have winter all the summer and summer all winter. Consequently, we have never yet come across an almanac that would just exactly fit this latitude. It is mighty regular about not raining, though, William. It will start in here in November and rain about four, and sometimes as much as seven days on a stretch; after that, you may loan out your umbrella for twelve months, with the serene confidence which a Christian feels in four aces. Sometimes the winter begins in November and winds up in June; and sometimes there is a bare suspicion of winter in March and April, and summer all the balance of the year. But as a general thing, William, the climate is good, what there is of it.

What are the productions of the earth? You mean in Nevada, of course. On our ranches here, anything can be raised that can be produced on the fertile fields of Missouri. But ranches are very scattering—as scattering, perhaps, as lawyers in heaven. Nevada, for the most part, is a barren waste of sand, embellished with melancholy sage-brush, and fenced in with snowclad mountains. But these ghastly features were the salvation of the land, William, for no rightly constituted American would have ever come here if the place had been easy of access, and none of our pioneers would have staid after they got here if they had not felt satisfied that they could not find a smaller chance for making a living anywhere else. Such is man, William, as he crops out in America.

"Is it healthy?" Yes, I think it is as healthy here as it is in any part of the West. But never permit a question of that kind to vegetate in your brain, William, because as long as providence has an eye on you, you will not be likely to die until your time comes.

"What diseases do they die of mostly?" Well, they used to die of conical balls and cold steel, mostly, but here lately erysipelas and the intoxicating bowl have got the bulge on those things, as was very justly remarked by Mr. Rising last Sunday. I will observe, for your information, William, that Mr. Rising is our Episcopal minister, and has done as much as any man among us to redeem this community from its pristine state of semi-barbarism. We are

afflicted with all the diseases incident to the same latitude in the States, I believe, with one or two added and half a dozen subtracted on account of our superior altitude. However, the doctors are about as successful here, both in killing and curing, as they are anywhere.

Now, as to whether it would be advisable for a man who can make a living in Missouri to emigrate to Nevada, I confess I am somewhat mixed. If you are not content in your present condition, it naturally follows that you would be entirely satisfied if you could make either more or less than a living. You would exult in the cheerful exhilaration always produced by a change. Well, you can find your opportunity here, where, if you retain your health, and are sober and industrious, you will inevitably make more than a living, and if you don't you won't. You can rely upon this statement, William. It contemplates any line of business except the selling of tracts. You cannot sell tracts here, William; the people take no interest in tracts; the very best efforts in the tract line—even with pictures on them—have met with no encouragement here. Besides, the newspapers have been interfering; a man gets his regular text or so from the Scriptures in his paper, along with the stock sales and the war news, every day, now. If you are in the tract business, William, take no chances on Washoe; but you can succeed at anything else here.

"I suppose you know Joel H. Smith?" Well—the fact is—I believe I don't. Now isn't that singular? Isn't it very singular? And he owns "considerable" in a mine here, too. Happy man. Actually owns in a mine here in Nevada Territory, and I never even heard of him. Strange—strange—do you know, William, it is the strangest thing that ever happened to me? And then he not only owns in a mine, but owns "considerable"; that is the strangest part about it—how a man could own "considerable" in a mine in Washoe and I not know anything about it. He is a lucky dog, though. But I strongly suspect that you have made a mistake in the name; I am confident you have; you mean John Smith—I know you do; I know it from the fact that he owns considerable in a mine here, because I sold him the property at a ruinous sacrifice on the very day he arrived here from over the plains. That man will be rich one of these days. I am just as well satisfied of it as I am of any precisely similar instance of the kind that has come under my notice. I said as much to him yesterday, and he said he was satisfied of it, also. But he did not say it with that air of triumphant exultation which a heart like mine so delights to behold in one to whom I have endeavored to be a benefactor in a small way. He looked pensive a while, but, finally, says he, "Do you know, I think I'd a been a rich man long ago if they'd ever found the d——d ledge?" That was my idea about it. I always thought, and I still think, that if they ever do find that ledge, his chances will be better than they are now. I guess Smith will be all right one of these centuries, if he keeps up his assessments—he is a young man yet. Now, William, I have taken a liking to you, and I would like to sell you "considerable" in a mine in Washoe. I think I could get you a commanding interest in the "Union," Gold Hill, on easy terms. It is just the same as the "Yellow Jacket," which is one of the richest mines in the Territory. The title was in dispute between the two companies some two years ago, but that is all settled now. Let me hear from you on the subject. Greenbacks at par is as good a thing as I want. But seriously, William, don't you ever invest in a mining stock which you don't know anything about; beware of John Smith's experience.

You hope to hear from me soon? Very good. I shall also hope to hear from you soon, about that little matter above referred to. Now, William, ponder this epistle well; never mind the sarcasm, here and there, and the nonsense, but reflect upon the plain facts set forth, because they *are* facts and are meant to be so understood and believed.

Remember me affectionately to your friends and relations, and especially to your venerable grandmother, with whom I have not the pleasure to be acquainted—but that is of no consequence, you know. I have been in your town many a time, and all the towns of the neighboring counties—the hotel keepers will recollect me vividly. Remember me to them—I bear them no animosity.

Yours affectionately,
Mark Twain

May 22, 1864—*Golden Era* (as reprinted from *Territorial Enterprise*).

[The "Dan" whom Twain suggests that the editors of the *Enterprise* send down into the Gould and Curry mine to get some facts with which to counteract the panic rumors in the air was Dan De Quille (William Wright), the *Enterprise*'s feature writer, with whom Twain roomed when he lived in Virginia City. The Bank Exchange, in the Montgomery Block, was San Francisco's most hallowed saloon. Its "Samson and Delilah" painting was later purchased by Milton S. Latham for $10,500 and presented by him to one of the San Francisco museums.]

IN THE METROPOLIS

To a Christian who has toiled months and months in Washoe; whose hair bristles from a bed of sand, and whose soul is caked with a cement of alkali dust; whose nostrils know no perfume but the rank odor of sage-brush—and whose eyes know no landscape but barren mountains and desolate plains; where the winds blow, and the sun blisters, and the broken spirit of the contrite heart finds joy and peace only in Limberger cheese and lager beer—unto such a Christian, verily the Occidental Hotel is Heaven on the half shell. He may even secretly consider it to be Heaven on the entire shell, but his religion teaches a sound Washoe Christian that it would be sacrilege to say it.

Here you are expected to breakfast on salmon, fried oysters and other substantials from 6 till half-past 12; you are required to lunch on cold fowl and so forth, from half-past 12 until 3; you are obliged to skirmish through a dinner comprising such edibles as the world produces, and keep it up, from 3 until half-past 7; you are then compelled to lay siege to the tea-table from half-past 7 until 9 o'clock, at which hour, if you refuse to move upon the supper works and destroy oysters gotten up in all kinds of seductive styles until 12 o'clock, the landlord will certainly be offended, and you might as well move your trunk to some other establishment. (It is a pleasure to me to observe, incidentally, that I am on good terms with the landlord yet.)

Why don't you send Dan down into the Gould & Curry mine, to

see whether it has petered out or not, and if so, when it will be likely to peter in again. The extraordinary decline of that stock has given rise to the wildest surmises in the way of accounting for it, but among the lot there is harm in but one, which is the expressed belief on the part of a few that the bottom has fallen out of the mine. Gould & Curry is climbing again, however.

It has been many a day since San Francisco has seen livelier times in her theatrical department than at present. Large audiences are to be found nightly at the Opera House, the Metropolitan, the Academy of Music, the American, the New Idea, and even the Museum, which is not as good a one as Barnum's. The Circus company, also, played a lucrative engagement, but they are gone on their travels now. The graceful, charming, clipper-built Ella Zoyara was very popular.

Miss Caroline Richings has played during the past fortnight at Maguire's Opera House to large and fashionable audiences, and has delighted them beyond measure with her sweet singing. It sounds improbable, perhaps, but the statement is true, nevertheless.

You will hear of the Metropolitan, now, from every visitor to Washoe. It opened under the management of the new lessees, Miss Annette Ince and Julia Dean Hayne, with a company who are as nearly all stars as it was possible to make it. For instance—Annette Ince, Emily Jordan, Mrs. Judah, Julia Dean Hayne, James H.

Taylor, Frank Lawlor, Harry Courtaine and Fred Franks (my favorite Washoe tragedian, whose name they have put in small letters in the programme, when it deserves to be in capitals—because, whatever part they give him to play don't he always play it well? and does he not possess the first virtue of a comedian, which is to do humorous things with grave decorum and without seeming to know that they are funny).

The birds, and the flowers, and the Chinamen, and the winds, and the sunshine, and all things that go to make life happy, are present in San Francisco to-day, just as they are all days in the year. Therefore, one would expect to hear these things spoken of, and gratefully, and disagreeable matters of little consequence allowed to pass without comment. I say, one would suppose that. But don't you deceive yourself—any one who supposes anything of the kind, supposes an absurdity. The multitude of pleasant things by which the people of San Francisco are surrounded are not talked of at all. No—they damn the wind, and they damn the dust, and they give all their attention to damning them well, and to all eternity. The blasted winds and the infernal dust—these alone form the eternal topics of conversation, and a mighty absurd topic it seems to one just out of Washoe. There isn't enough wind here to keep breath in my body, or dust enough to keep sand in my craw. But it is human nature to find fault—to overlook that which is pleasant to the eye, and seek after that which is distasteful to it. You take a stranger into the Bank Exchange and show him the magnificent picture of Samson and Delilah, and what is the first object he notices?—Samson's fine face and flaming eye? or the noble beauty of his form? or the lovely, half-nude Delilah? or the muscular Philistine behind Samson, who is furtively admiring her charms? or the perfectly counterfeited folds of the rich drapery below her knees? or the symmetry and truth to nature of Samson's left foot? No, sir, the first thing that catches his eye is the scissors on the floor at Delilah's feet, and the first thing he says, "Them scissors is too modern—there warn't no scissors like that in them days, by a d——d sight!"

June 26, 1864—*Golden Era*
(as reprinted from *Territorial Enterprise*).

["The moon, riding high, touched the rough rocks as tenderly as though they were the crags of Latmos . . ." That is Bret Harte, rhapsodizing on the view from the Cliff House, when the poetic soul is all alone out there at the verge of the mighty ocean. Now here's Mark Twain. "The Unreliable" was Twain's nickname for one of his friendly rivals, Clement T. Rice, of the Virginia City *Union*.]

EARLY RISING AS REGARDS EXCURSIONS TO THE CLIFF HOUSE

Early to bed, and early to rise,
Makes a man healthy, wealthy and wise.
—BENJAMIN FRANKLIN.

I don't see it. —GEORGE WASHINGTON.

Now both of these are high authorities—very high and respectable authorities—but I am with General Washington first, last, and all the time on this proposition.

Because I don't see it, either.

I have tried getting up early, and I have tried getting up late—and the latter agrees with me best. As for a man's growing any wiser, or any richer, or any healthier, by getting up early, I know it is not so; because I have got up early in the station-house many and many a time, and got poorer and poorer for the next half a day, in consequence, instead of richer and richer. And sometimes, on the same terms, I have seen the sun rise four times a week up there at Virginia, and so far from my growing healthier on account of it, I got to looking blue, and pulpy and swelled, like a drowned man, and my relations grew alarmed and thought they were going to lose me. They entirely despaired of my recovery, at one time, and began to grieve for me as one whose days were numbered—whose fate was sealed—who was soon to pass away from them forever, and from the glad sunshine, and the birds, and the odorous flowers, and murmuring brooks, and whispering winds, and all the cheerful scenes of life, and go down into the dark and silent tomb—and they went forth sorrowing, and jumped a lot in the graveyard, and made up their minds to grin and bear it with that fortitude which is the true Christian's brightest ornament.

You observe that I have put a stronger test on the matter than even Benjamin Franklin contemplated, and yet it would not work. Therefore, how is a man to grow healthier, and wealthier, and wiser by going to bed early and getting up early, when he fails to accomplish these things even when he does not go to bed at all? And as far as becoming wiser is concerned, you might put all the wisdom I acquired in these experiments in your eye, without obstructing your vision any to speak of.

As I said before, my voice is with George Washington's on this question.

Another philosopher encourages the world to get up at sunrise because "it is the early bird that catches the worm."

It is a seductive proposition, and well calculated to trap the unsuspecting. But its attractions are all wasted on me, because I have no use for the worm. If I had, I would adopt the Unreliable's plan. He was much interested in this quaint proverb, and directed the powers of his great mind to its consideration for three or four consecutive hours. He was supposing a case. He was supposing, for instance, that he really wanted the worm—that the possession of the worm was actually necessary to his happiness—that he yearned for it and hankered after it, therefore, as much as a man *could* yearn for and hanker after a worm under such circumstances—and he was supposing, further, that he was opposed to getting up early in order to catch it (which was much the more plausible of the two suppositions). Well, at the end of three or four hours' profound meditation upon the subject, the Unreliable rose up and said: "If he were so anxious about the worm, and he couldn't get along without him, and he didn't want to get up early in the morning to catch him—why then, by George, he would just lay for him the night before." I never would have thought of that. I looked at the youth, and said to myself, he is malicious, and dishonest, and unhandsome, and does not smell good—yet how quickly do these trivial demerits disappear in the shadow, when the glare from this great intellect shines out above them!

I have always heard that the only time in the day that a trip to the Cliff House could be thoroughly enjoyed was early in the morning (and I suppose it might be as well to withhold an adverse impression while the flow-tide of public opinion continues to set in that direction).

I tried it the other morning with Harry, the stock-broker, rising at 4 A.M., to delight in the following described things, to wit:

A road unencumbered by carriages, and free from wind and dust; a bracing atmosphere; the gorgeous spectacle of the sun in the dawn of his glory; the fresh perfume of flowers still damp with dew; a solitary drive on the beach while its smoothness was yet unmarred by wheel or hoof, and a vision of white sails glinting in the morning light far out at sea.

These were the considerations, and they seemed worthy a sacrifice of seven or eight hours' sleep.

We sat in the stable, and yawned, and gaped, and stretched, until the horse was hitched up, and then drove out into the bracing atmosphere. (When another early voyage is proposed to me, I want it understood that there is to be no bracing atmosphere in the programme. I can worry along without it.) In half an hour we were so thoroughly braced up with it that it was just a scratch that we were not frozen to death. Then the harness came unshipped, or got broken, or something, and I waxed colder and drowsier while Harry fixed it. I am not fastidious about clothes, but I am not used to wearing fragrant, sweaty horse-blankets, and not partial to them, either; I am not proud, though, when I am freezing, and I added the horse-blanket to my overcoats, and tried to wake up and feel warm and cheerful. It was useless, however—all my senses slumbered and continued to slumber, save the sense of smell.

When my friend drove past suburban gardens and said the flowers never exhaled so sweet an odor before, in his experience, I dreamily but honestly endeavored to think so too, but in my secret soul I was conscious that they only smelled like horse-blankets. (When another early voyage is proposed to me, I want it understood that there is to be no "fresh perfume of flowers" in the programme, either. I do not enjoy it. My senses are not attuned to the flavor—there is too much horse about it and not enough eau de cologne.)

The wind was cold and benumbing, and blew with such force that we could hardly make headway against it. It came straight from the ocean, and I think there are icebergs out there somewhere. True, there was not much dust, because the gale blew it all to Oregon in two minutes; and by good fortune, it blew no gravel-stones, to speak of—only one of any consequence, I believe—a three-cornered one—it struck me in the eye. I have it there yet. However, it does not matter—for the future I suppose I can manage to see tolerably well out of the other. (Still, when another early voyage is proposed to me, I want it understood that the dust is to be put in, and the gravel left out of the programme. I might want my other eye if I continue to hang on until my time comes; and besides, I shall not mind the dust much hereafter, because I have only got to shut one eye, now, when it is around.)

No, the road was not encumbered by carriages—we had it all to ourselves. I suppose the reason was, that most people do not like to enjoy themselves too much, and therefore they do not go out to the Cliff House in the cold and the fog, and the dread silence and solitude of four o'clock in the morning. They are right. The impressive solemnity of such a pleasure trip is only equalled by an excursion to Lone Mountain in a hearse. Whatever of advantage there may be in having that Cliff House road all to yourself we had—but to my mind a greater advantage would be in dividing it up in small sections among the entire community; because, in consequence of the repairs in progress on it just now, it's as rough as a corduroy bridge—(in a good many places) and consequently the less you have of it, the happier you are likely to be and the less shaken up and disarranged on the inside. (Wherefore, when another early voyage is proposed to me, I want it understood that the road is not to be unencumbered with carriages, but just the reverse—so that the balance of the people shall be made to stand their share of the jolting and the desperate lonesomeness of the thing.)

From the moment we left the stable, almost, the fog was so

thick that we could scarcely see fifty yards behind or before, or overhead; and for a while, as we approached the Cliff House, we could not see the horse at all, and were obliged to steer by his ears, which stood up dimly out of the dense white mist that enveloped him. But for those friendly beacons, we must have been cast away and lost.

I have no opinion of a six-mile ride in the clouds; but if I ever have to take another, I want to leave the horse in the stable and go in a balloon. I shall prefer to go in the afternoon, also, when it is warm, so that I may gape, and yawn, and stretch, if I am drowsy, without disarranging my horse-blanket and letting in a blast of cold wind.

We could scarcely see the sportive seals out on the rocks, writhing and squirming like exaggerated maggots, and there was nothing soothing in their discordant barking, to a spirit so depressed as mine was.

Harry took a cocktail at the Cliff House, but I scorned such ineffectual stimulus; I yearned for fire, and there was none there; they were about to make one, but the bar-keeper looked altogether too cheerful for me—I could not bear his unnatural happiness in the midst of such a ghastly picture of fog, and damp, and frosty surf, and dreary solitude. I could not bear the sacrilegious presence of a pleasant face at such a time; it was too much like sprightliness at a funeral, and we fled from it down the smooth and vacant beach.

We had that all to ourselves, too, like the road—and I want it divided up, also, hereafter. We could not drive in the roaring surf and seem to float abroad on the foamy sea, as one is wont to do in the sunny afternoon, because the very thought of any of that icy-looking water splashing on you was enough to congeal your blood, almost. We saw no white-winged ships sailing away on the billowy ocean, with the pearly light of morning descending upon them like a benediction—"because the fog had the bulge on the pearly light," as the Unreliable observed when I mentioned it to him afterwards; and we saw not the sun in the dawn of his glory, for the same reason. Hill and beach, and sea and sun were all wrapped in a ghostly mantle of mist, and hidden from our mortal vision. (When another early voyage is proposed to me, I want it understood that the sun in his glory, and the morning light, and the ships at sea, and all that sort of thing are to be left out of the programme, so that when we fail to see them, we shall not be so infernally disappointed.)

We were human icicles when we got to the Ocean House, and there was no fire there, either. I banished all hope, then, and succumbed to despair; I went back on my religion, and sought surcease of sorrow in soothing blasphemy. I am sorry I did it, now, but it was a great comfort to me, then. We could have had breakfast at the Ocean House, but we did not want it; can statues of ice feel hunger? But we adjourned to a private room and ordered red-hot coffee, and it was a sort of balm to my troubled mind to observe that the man who brought it was as cold, and as silent, and as solemn as the grave itself. His gravity was so impressive, and so appropriate and becoming to the melancholy surroundings, that it won upon me and thawed out some of the better instincts of my nature, and I told him he might ask a blessing if he thought it would lighten him up any—because he looked as if he wanted to, very bad—but he only shook his head resignedly and sighed.

That coffee did the business for us. It was made by a master artist, and it had not a fault; and the cream that came with it was so rich and thick that you could hardly have strained it through a wire fence. As the generous beverage flowed down our frigid throats, our blood grew warm again, our muscles relaxed, our torpid bodies awoke to life and feeling, anger and uncharitableness departed from us and we were cheerful once more. We got good cigars, also, at the Ocean House, and drove into town over a smooth road, lighted by the sun and unclouded by fog.

Near the Jewish cemeteries we turned a corner too suddenly, and got upset, but sustained no damage, although the horse did what he honestly could to kick the buggy out of the State while we were grovelling in the sand. We went on down to the steamer, and while we were on board, the buggy was upset again by some outlaw, and an axle broken.

However, these little accidents, and all the deviltry and misfortune that preceded them, were only just and natural consequences of the absurd experiment of getting up at an hour in the morning when all God-fearing Christians ought to be in bed. I consider that the man who leaves his pillow, deliberately, at sun-rise, is taking his life in his own hands, and he ought to feel proud if he don't have to put it down again at the coroner's office before dark.

Now, for that early trip, I am not any healthier or any wealthier than I was before, and only wiser in that I know a good deal better than to go and do it again. And as for all those notable advantages, such as the sun in the dawn of his glory, and the ships, and the perfume of the flowers, etc., etc., etc., I don't see them, any more than myself and Washington see the soundness of Benjamin Franklin's attractive little poem.

If you go to the Cliff House at any time after seven in the morning, you cannot fail to enjoy it—but never start out there before daylight, under the impression that you are going to have a pleasant time and come back insufferably healthier and wealthier and wiser than your betters on account of it. Because if you do you will miss your calculation, and it will keep you swearing about it right straight along for a week to get even again.

Put no trust in the benefits to accrue from early rising, as set forth by the infatuated Franklin—but stake the last cent of your substance on the judgment of old George Washington, the Father of his Country, who said "he couldn't see it."

And you hear me endorsing that sentiment.

July 3, 1864—*Golden Era.*

[Twain's reporting for the *Call* was unsigned. For long this was one of only two items established as by him. In *Clemens of the Call,* however, Edgar M. Branch has now creditably attributed to Twain a total of 471 items, many of them routine but some clearly bearing Twain's mark.]

A SMALL PIECE OF SPITE

Some witless practical joker made a false entry, a few days ago, on a slate kept at the dead-house for the information of the public, concerning dead bodies found, deaths by accident, etc. The *Alta, Bulletin,* and *Flag,* administered a deserved rebuke to the Coroner's understrappers, for permitting the entry to remain there, and pass into the newspapers and mislead the public, and for this reason the slate has been removed from the office. Now it is too late in the day for such men as these to presume to deny to the public, information which belongs to them, and which they have a right to demand, merely to gratify a ridiculous spite against two or three reporters. It is a matter of no consequence to reporters whether the slate is kept there or not; but it *is* a matter of consequence to the public at large, who are the real injured parties when the newspapers are denied the opportunity of conveying it to them. If the Coroner permits his servants to close the door against reporters, many a man may lose a friend in the Bay, or by assassination, or suicide, and never hear of it, or know anything about it; in that case, the public and their servant, the Coroner, are the victims, not the reporter. Coroner Sheldon needs not to be told that he is a public officer; that his doings, and those of his underlings at the coffin shop, belong to the people; that the public do not recognize his right or theirs to suppress the transactions of his department of the public service; and, finally, that the people will not see the propriety of the affairs of his office being hidden from them, in order that the small-potato malice of his reporters may be gratified. Those employees have *always* shown a strong disinclination to tell a reporter anything about their ghastly share in the Coroner's business, and it was easy to see that they longed for some excuse to abolish that slate. Their motive for such conduct did not concern reporters, but it might interest the public and the Coroner if they would explain it. Those official corpse-planters always put on as many airs as if the public and their master, the Coroner, belonged to them, and they had a right to do as they pleased with both. They told us yesterday that their Coronial affairs should henceforth be a sealed book, and they would give us *no* information.

As if *they*—a lot of forty-dollar understrappers—had authority to proclaim that the affairs of a public office like the Coroner's should be kept secret from the people, whose minions they are! If the credit of that office suffers from their impertinence, who is the victim, Mr. Sheldon or the reporters? We cannot suffer greatly, for we never succeeded in getting any information out of one of those fellows yet. You see the dead-cart leaving the place, and ask one of them where it is bound, and without looking up from his newspaper, he grunts, lazily, and says, *"Stiff,"* meaning that it is going in quest of the corpse of some poor creature whose earthly troubles are over. You ask one of them a dozen questions calculated to throw more light upon a meagre entry in the slate, and he invariably answers, *"Don't know"*—as if the grand end and aim of his poor existence was not to know anything, and to come as near accomplishing his mission as his opportunities would permit. They would vote for General Jackson at the "Body-snatchers' Retreat," but for the misfortune that they "don't know" such a person ever existed. What do you suppose the people would ever know about how their interests were being attended to if the employees in all public offices were such unmitigated ignoramuses as these? One of these fellows said to us yesterday, "We have taken away the slate; we are not going to give you any more information; the reporters have got too sharp—by George, they know more'n *we* do!" God help the reporter that don't! It is as fervent a prayer as ever welled up from the bottom of our heart. Now, a reporter can start any day and travel through the whole of the long list of employees in the public offices in this city, and not in a solitary instance will he find any difficulty in getting any information which the public have a right to know, until he arrives at the inquest office of the Coroner. There all knowledge concerning the dead who die in mysterious ways and mysterious places, and who may have friends and relatives near at hand who would give the world and all its wealth for even the poor consolation of knowing their fate, is denied us. Who are the sufferers by this contemptible contumacy—we or the hundred thousand citizens of San Francisco? The responsibility of this state of things rests with the Coroner, and it is only right and just that he should amend it.

Sept. 6, 1864—*Call.*

[The annual Mechanics Fair was one of San Francisco's most popular events. Its most interesting exhibits were its various heavy mining machines. By this time San Francisco was becoming industrialized and could boast of 13 iron foundries and 30 machine shops. The Fair also featured art exhibits of rather less distinction than the machines. As Harte commented in regard to one Fair, "If the woolen fabrics and quartz crushers were better than the pictures, it was because gold medals were provided for the former and silver for the latter, and the comparative *status* settled before competition." The Fair was also, as Twain makes clear, one of the best places in town for a rendezvous. The Weller whose broken bust gives Twain the opportunity for the pun he is so becomingly modest about was a former governor of California. The sanitary scarecrow was a fund-raising device of the Sanitary Commission, which was the equivalent of the Red Cross. This slight passing mention is one of the few reminders to be found in Twain's writings from this period that there was a war going on elsewhere in the country.

With this piece Twain makes his debut in the *Californian,* whose editorship Harte had assumed about a month before. It sought to be a high-toned and sophisticated journal, and it generally allowed Twain more length for his pieces than did other papers, which was not always an advantage.]

A NOTABLE CONUNDRUM

The fair continues, just the same. It is a nice place to hunt for people in. I have hunted for a friend there for as much as two hours of an evening, and at the end of that time found the hunting just as good as it was when I commenced.

If the projectors of this noble Fair never receive a dollar or even a kindly word of thanks for the labor of their hands, the sweat of their brows and the wear and tear of brain it has cost them to plan their work and perfect it, a consciousness of the incalculable good they have conferred upon the community must still give them a placid satisfaction more precious than money or sounding compliments. They have been the means of bringing many a pair of loving hearts together that could not get together anywhere else on account of parents and other obstructions. When you see a young lady standing by the sanitary scarecrow which mutely appeals to the public for quarters and swallows them, you may know by the expectant look upon her face that a young man is going to happen along there presently; and, if you have my luck, you will notice by that look still remaining upon her face that you are not the young man she is expecting. They court a good deal at the Fair, and the young fellows are always exchanging notes with the girls. For this purpose the business cards scattered about the place are found very convenient. I picked up one last night which was printed on both sides, but has been interlined in pencil, by somebody's Arabella, until one could not read it without feeling dizzy. It ran about in this wise—though the interlineations were not in parentheses in the original:

"John Smith, (My Dearest and Sweetest:) Soap Boiler and Candle Factor; (If you love me, if you love) Bar Soap, Castile Soap and Soft Soap, peculiarly suitable for (your Arabella, fly to the) Pacific coast, because of its non-liability to be affected by the climate. Those who may have kitchen refuse to sell, can leave orders, and our soap-fat carts will visit the (Art Gallery. I will be in front of the big mirror in an hour from now, and will go with you to the) corner designated. For the very best Soap and Candles the market affords, apply at the (Academy of Music. And from there, O joy! how my heart thrills with rapture at the prospect! with souls surcharged with bliss, we will wander forth to the) Soap Factory, or to the office, which is located on the (moonlit beach,) corner of Jackson street, near the milk ranch. (From Arabella, who sends kisses to her darling) JOHN SMITH, Pioneer Soap Boiler and Candle Factor."

Sweethearts usually treasure up these little affectionate billets,

The Squarza's Punch exhibit at the San Francisco Mechanics Fair in 1864.

and that this one was lost in the Pavilion, seemed proof to me that its contents were rather distracting to the mind of the young man who received it. He never would have lost it if he had not felt unsettled about something. I think it is likely he got mixed, so to speak, as to whether he was the lucky party, or whether it was the soap-boiler. However, I have possession of her extraordinary document now, and this is to inform Arabella that, in the hope that I may answer for the other young man, and do to fill a void or so in her aching heart, I am drifting about, in an unsettled way, on the look-out for her—sometimes on the Pacific Coast, sometimes at the Art Gallery, sometimes at the soap factory, and occasionally at the moonlit beach and the milk ranch. If she happen to visit either of those places shortly, and will have the goodness to wait a little while, she can calculate on my drifting around in the course of an hour or so.

I cannot say that all visitors to the Fair go there to make love, though I have my suspicions that a good many of them do. Numbers go there to look at the machinery and misunderstand it, and still greater numbers, perhaps, go to criticise the pictures. There is a handsome portrait in the Art Gallery of a pensive young girl. Last night it fell under the critical eye of a connoisseur from Arkansas. She examined it in silence for many minutes, and then she blew her nose calmly, and, says she, "I like it—it is so sad and thinkful."

Somebody knocked Weller's bust down from its shelf at the Fair, the other night, and destroyed it. It was wrong to do it, but it gave rise to a very able pun by a young person who has had much experience in such things, and was only indifferently proud of it. He said it was Weller enough when it was a bust, but just the reverse when it was busted. Explanation: He meant that it looked like Weller in the first place, but it did not after it was smashed to pieces. He also meant that it was well enough to leave it alone and not destroy it. The Author of this fine joke is among us yet, and I can bring him around if you would like to look at him. One would expect him to be haughty and ostentatious, but you would be surprised to see how simple and unpretending he is and how willing to take a drink.

But I have been playing the noble game of "Muggins." In that game, if you make a mistake of any kind, however trivial it may be, you are pronounced a muggins by the whole company, with great unanimity and enthusiasm. If you play the right card in the wrong place, you are a muggins; no matter how you play, in nine cases out of ten you are a muggins. They inform you of it with a shout which has no expression in it of regret. I have played this fine game all the evening, and although I knew little about it at first, I got to be quite a muggins at last. I played it very successfully on a policeman as I went home. I had forgotten my night-key and was climbing in at the window. When he clapped his hand on my shoulder, I smiled upon him and, says I, "Muggins!" with much vivacity. Says he, "How so?" and I said, "Because I live here, and you play the wrong card when you arrest me for entering my own house." I thought it was rather neat. But then there was nobody at home to identify me, and I had to go all the way to the station-house with him and give bail to appear and answer to a charge of burglary. As I turned to depart says he "Muggins!" I thought that was rather neat also.

But the conundrum I have alluded to in the heading of this article, was the best thing of the kind that has ever fallen under my notice. It was projected by a young man who has hardly any education at all, and whose opportunities have been very meagre, even from his childhood up. It was this: "Why was Napoleon when he crossed the Alps, like the Sanitary cheese at the Mechanics' Fair?"

It was very good for a young man just starting in life; don't you think so? He has gone away now to Sacramento. Probably we shall never see him more. He did not state what the answer was.

Oct. 1, 1864—*Californian.*

[San Francisco had shown itself, from the early days of the Gold Rush, receptive to opera as well as to theatre—and its writers were constantly pointing out what a cultured city it was, not the crude frontier town that Easterners might think. Twain had his doubts about the sincerity of both audience and critics in their admiration for this opera stuff. He himself was allergic to it all his life. He once petulantly exclaimed, some years later on, "I hate Art. I hate Opera. I hate Travel."]

STILL FURTHER CONCERNING THAT CONUNDRUM

In accordance with your desire, I went to the Academy of Music on Monday evening, to take notes and prepare myself to write a careful critique upon the opera of the *Crown Diamonds*. That you considered me able to acquit myself creditably in this exalted sphere of literary labor, was gratifying to me, and I should even have felt flattered by it had I not known that I was so competent to perform the task well, that to set it for me could not be regarded as a flattering concession. But, on the contrary, only a just and deserved recognition of merit.

Now, to throw disguise aside and speak openly, I have long yearned for an opportunity to write an operatic diagnostical and analytical dissertation for you. I feel the importance of carefully-digested newspaper criticism in matters of this kind—for I am aware that by it the dramatic and musical tastes of a community are moulded, cultivated and irrevocably fixed—that by it these tastes are vitiated and debased, or elevated and ennobled, according to the refinement or vulgarity, and the competency or incompetency of the writers to whom this department of the public training is entrusted. If you would see around you a people who are filled with the keenest appreciation of perfection in musical execution and dramatic delineation, and painfully sensitive to the slightest departures from the true standard of art in these things, you must employ upon your newspapers critics capable of discriminating between merit and demerit, and alike fearless in praising the one and condemning the other. Such a person—although it may be in some degree immodest in me to say so—I claim to be. You will not be surprised, then, to know that I read your boshy criticisms on the opera with the most exquisite anguish—and not only yours, but those which I find in every paper in San Francisco.

You do nothing but sing one everlasting song of praise; when an artist, by diligence and talent, makes an effort of transcendent excellence, behold, instead of receiving marked and cordial attention, both artist and effort sink from sight, and are lost in the general slough of slimy praise in which it is your pleasure to cause the whole company, good, bad and indifferent, to wallow once a week. With this brief but very liberal and hearty expression of sentiment, I will drop the subject and leave you alone for the present, for it behooves me now to set you a model in criticism.

The opera of the *Crown Diamonds* was put upon the stage in creditable shape on Monday evening, although I noticed that the curtains of the "Queen of Portugal's" drawing-room were not as gorgeous as they might have been, and that the furniture had a second-hand air about it, of having seen service in the preceding reign. The acting and the vocalization, however, were, in the main, good. I was particularly charmed by the able manner in which Signor Bellindo Alphonso Cellini, the accomplished basso-relievo furniture-scout and sofa-shifter, performed his part. I have before observed that this rising young artist gave evidence of the rarest genius in his peculiar department of operatic business, and have been annoyed at noticing with what studied care a venomous and profligate press have suppressed his name and suffered his sublimest efforts to pass unnoticed and unglorified. Shame upon such grovelling envy and malice! But, with all your neglect, you have failed to crush the spirit of the gifted furniture-scout, or seduce from him the affectionate encouragement and appreciation of the people. The moment he stepped upon the stage on Monday evening, to carry out the bandit chieftain's valise, the upper circles, with one accord, shouted, "Supe! supe!" and greeted him with warm and generous applause. It was a princely triumph for Bellindo; he told me afterwards it was the proudest moment of his life.

I watched Alphonso during the entire performance and was never so well pleased with him before, although I have admired him from the first. In the second act, when the eyes of the whole audience were upon him—when his every movement was the subject of anxiety and suspense—when everything depended upon his nerve and self-possession, and the slightest symptom of hesitation or lack of confidence would have been fatal—he stood erect in front of the cave, looking calmly and unflinchingly down upon the camp-stool for several moments, as one who has made up his mind to do his great work or perish in the attempt, and then seized it and bore it in triumph to the foot-lights! It was a sublime spectacle. There was not a dry eye in the house. In that moment, not even the most envious and uncharitable among the noble youth's detractors would have had the hardihood to say he was not endowed with a lofty genius.

Again, in the scene where the Prime Minister's nephew is imploring the female bandit to fly to the carriage and escape impending wrath, and when dismay and confusion ruled the hour, how quiet, how unmoved, how grandly indifferent was Bellindo in the midst of it all!—what stolidity of expression lay upon his countenance! While all save himself were unnerved by despair, he serenely put forth his finger and mashed to a shapeless pulp a mosquito that loitered upon the wall, yet betrayed no sign of agitation the while. Was there nothing in this lofty contempt for the dangers which surrounded him that marked the actor destined hereafter to imperishable renown?

Possibly upon that occasion when it was necessary for Alphonso to remove two chairs and a table during the shifting of the scenes, he performed his part with undue precipitation; with the table upside down upon his head, and grasping the corners with hands burdened with the chairs, he appeared to some extent undignified when he galloped across the stage. Generally his conception of his part is excellent, but in this case I am satisfied he threw into it an enthusiasm not required and also not warranted by the circumstances. I think that careful study and reflection will convince him that I am right, and that the author of the opera intended that in this particular instance the furniture should be carried out with impressive solemnity. That he had this in view is evidenced by the slow and stately measure of the music played by the orchestra at that juncture.

But the crowning glory of Cellini's performance that evening was the placing of a chair for the Queen of Portugal to sit down in after she had become fatigued by earnestly and elaborately abusing the Prime Minister for losing the Crown Diamonds. He did not grab the chair by the hind leg and shove it awkwardly at her Majesty; he did not seize it by the seat and thrust it ungracefully toward her; he did not handle it as though he was undecided about the strict line of his duty or ignorant of the proper manner of performing it. He did none of these things. With a coolness and confidence that evinced the most perfect conception and the most consummate knowledge of his part, he came gently forward and laid hold of that chair from behind, set it in its proper place with a movement replete with grace, and then leaned upon the back of it, resting his chin upon his hand, and in this position smiled a smile of transfigured sweetness upon the audience over the Queen of Portugal's head. There shone the inspired actor! and the people saw and acknowledged him; they waited respectfully for Miss Richings to finish her song, and then with one impulse they poured forth upon him a sweeping tempest of applause.

At the end of the piece the idolized furniture-scout and sofa-skirmisher was called before the curtain by an enthusiastic shouting and clapping of hands, but he was thrust aside, as usual, and other artists, (who chose to consider the compliment as intended for themselves), swept bowing and smirking along the footlights and received it. I swelled with indignation, but I summoned my fortitude and resisted the pressure successfully. I am still intact.

Take it altogether, the *Crown Diamonds* was really a creditable performance. I feel that I would not be doing my whole duty if I closed this critique without speaking of Miss Caroline Richings, Miss Jenny Kempton, Mr. Hill, Mr. Seguin and Mr. Peakes, all of whom did fair justice to their several parts, and deserve a passing notice. With study, perseverance and attention I have no doubt these vocalists will in time achieve a gratifying success in their profession.

I believe I have nothing further to say. I will call around, to-morrow, after you have had time to read, digest and pass your judgment upon my criticism, and, if agreeable, I will hire out to you for some years in that line. Mark Twain.

P. S.—No answer to that conundrum this week. On account of over-exertion on it the old woman has got to having fits here lately. However, it will be forthcoming yet, when she runs out of them, if she don't die in the meantime, and I trust she will not. We may as well prepare ourselves for the worst, though it is not to be disguised that they are shaking her up mighty lively.

Oct. 15, 1864—*Californian.*

[As it originally appeared in the *Californian,* this piece was prefaced by a long and rather spun-out fantasy, which was set off in Twain's mind by seeing a sign over a store at the corner of Third and Minna streets reading LOVE'S BAKERY. He indulges in a reverie about the kind of hearts that are baked there, et cetera. This preface may have amused the proprietor of the bakery—one William Love—but it was in a strained vein, and Twain later cut it out when he included the sad tale of Aurelia's accident-prone lover in his *Sketches New and Old.* I follow his later judgment here.]

AURELIA'S UNFORTUNATE YOUNG MAN

The facts in the following case came to me by letter from a young lady who lives in the beautiful city of San José; she is perfectly unknown to me, and simply signs herself "Aurelia Maria," which may possibly be a fictitious name. But no matter, the poor girl is almost heartbroken by the misfortunes she has undergone, and so confused by the conflicting counsels of misguided friends and insidious enemies that she does not know what course to pursue in order to extricate herself from the web of difficulties in which she seems almost hopelessly involved. In this dilemma she turns to me for help, and supplicates for my guidance and instruction with a moving eloquence that would touch the heart of a statue. Hear her sad story:

She says that when she was sixteen years old she met and loved, with all the devotion of a passionate nature, a young man from New Jersey, named Williamson Breckinridge Caruthers, who was some six years her senior. They were engaged, with the free consent of their friends and relatives, and for a time it seemed as if their career was destined to be characterized by an immunity from sorrow beyond the usual lot of humanity. But at last the tide of fortune turned; young Caruthers became infected with smallpox of the most virulent type, and when he recovered from his illness his face was pitted like a waffle-mold, and his comeliness gone forever. Aurelia thought to break off the engagement at first, but pity for her unfortunate lover caused her to postpone the marriage-day for a season, and give him another trial.

The very day before the wedding was to have taken place, Breckinridge, while absorbed in watching the flight of a balloon, walked into a well and fractured one of his legs, and it had to be taken off above the knee. Again Aurelia was moved to break the engagement, but again love triumphed, and she set the day forward and gave him another chance to reform.

And again misfortune overtook the unhappy youth. He lost one arm by the premature discharge of a Fourth of July cannon, and within three months he got the other pulled out by a carding-machine. Aurelia's heart was almost crushed by these latter calamities. She could not but be deeply grieved to see her lover passing from her by piecemeal, feeling, as she did, that he could not last forever under this disastrous process of reduction, yet knowing of no way to stop its dreadful career, and in her tearful despair she almost regretted, like brokers who hold on and lose, that she had not taken him at first, before he had suffered such an alarming

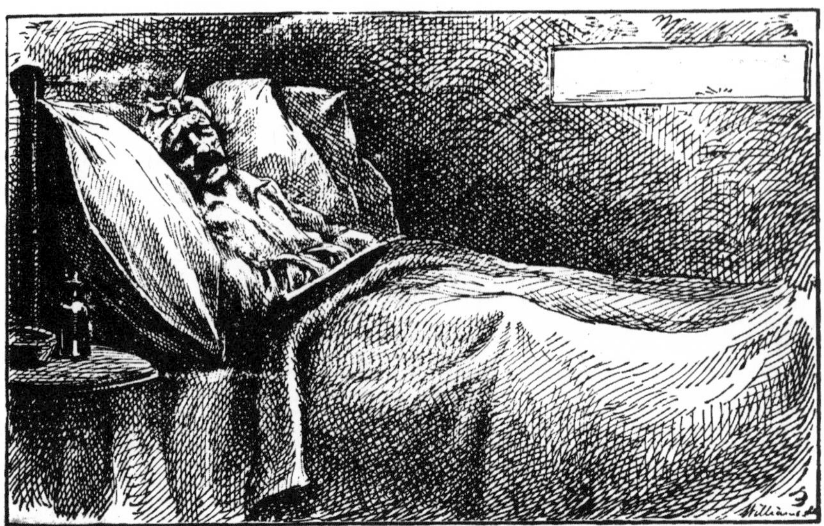

depreciation. Still, her brave soul bore her up, and she resolved to bear with her friend's unnatural disposition yet a little longer.

Again the wedding-day approached, and again disappointment over-shadowed it; Caruthers fell ill with the erysipelas, and lost the use of one of his eyes entirely. The friends and relatives of the bride, considering that she had already put up with more than could reasonably be expected of her, now came forward and insisted that the match should be broken off; but after wavering awhile, Aurelia, with a generous spirit which did her credit, said she had reflected calmly upon the matter, and could not discover that Breckinridge was to blame.

So she extended the time once more, and he broke his other leg.

It was a sad day for the poor girl when she saw the surgeons reverently bearing away the sack whose uses she had learned by previous experience, and her heart told her the bitter truth that some more of her lover was gone. She felt that the field of her affections was growing more and more circumscribed every day, but once more she frowned down her relatives and renewed her betrothal.

Shortly before the time set for the nuptials another disaster occurred. There was but one man scalped by the Owens River Indians last year. That man was Williamson Breckinridge Caruthers of New Jersey. He was hurrying home with happiness in his heart, when he lost his hair forever, and in that hour of bitterness he almost cursed the mistaken mercy that had spared his head.

At last Aurelia is in serious perplexity as to what she ought to do. She still loves her Breckinridge, she writes, with truly womanly feeling—she still loves what is left of him—but her parents are bitterly opposed to the match, because he has no property and is disabled from working, and she has not sufficient means to support both comfortably. "Now, what should she do?" she asked with painful and anxious solicitude.

It is a delicate question; it is one which involves the lifelong happiness of a woman, and that of nearly two-thirds of a man, and I feel that it would be assuming too great a responsibility to do more than make a mere suggestion in the case. How would it do to build to him? If Aurelia can afford the expense, let her furnish her mutilated lover with wooden arms and wooden legs, and a glass eye and a wig, and give him another show; give him ninety days, without grace, and if he does not break his neck in the mean time, marry him and take the chances. It does not seem to me that there is much risk, anyway, Aurelia, because if he sticks to his singular propensity for damaging himself every time he sees a good opportunity, his next experiment is bound to finish him, and then you are safe, married or single. If married, the wooden legs and such other valuables as he may possess revert to the widow, and you see you sustain no actual loss save the cherished fragment of a noble but most unfortunate husband, who honestly strove to do right, but whose extraordinary instincts were against him. Try it, Maria. I have thought the matter over carefully and well, and it is the only chance I see for you. It would have been a happy conceit on the part of Caruthers if he had started with his neck and broken that first, but since he has seen fit to choose a different policy and string himself out as long as possible, I do not think we ought to upbraid him for it if he has enjoyed it. We must do the best we can under the circumstances, and try not to feel exasperated at him.

Oct. 22, 1864—*Californian.*

[Nearly everybody in San Francisco was speculating in mining stocks in those days, but the profession of stockbroker was regarded as a disreputable one. Blatant rigging of stock values went on, but that did not seem to deter the public from eagerly rushing to be duped. There were some 160 brokers in town, in three boards, or organizations. The brokers' offices were along Montgomery Street, and their window displays usually consisted of saucers full of gold nuggets.]

DANIEL IN THE LION'S DEN— AND OUT AGAIN ALL RIGHT

Some people are not particular about what sort of company they keep. I am one of that kind. Now for several days I have been visiting the Board of Brokers, and associating with brokers, and drinking with them, and swapping lies with them, and being as familiar and sociable with them as I would with the most respectable people in the world. I do this because I consider that a broker goes according to the instincts that are in him, and means no harm, and fulfils his mission according to his lights, and has a right to live, and be happy in a general way, and be protected by the law to some extent, just the same as a better man. I consider that brokers come into the world with souls—I am satisfied they do; and if they wear them out in the course of a long career of stock-jobbing, have they not a right to come in at the eleventh hour and get themselves half-soled, like old boots, and be saved at last? Certainly—the father of the tribe did that, and do we say anything against Barabbas for it to-day? No! we concede his right to do it; we admire his mature judgment in selling out of a worked-out mine of iniquity and investing in righteousness, and no man denies, or even doubts, the validity of the transaction. Other people may think as they please, and I suppose I am entitled to the same privilege; therefore, notwithstanding what others may believe, I am of the opinion that a broker can be saved. Mind, I do not say that a broker *will* be saved, or even that it is uncommon likely that such a thing will happen—I only say that Lazarus was raised from the dead, the five thousand were fed with twelve loaves of bread, the water was turned into wine, the Israelites crossed the Red Sea dry-shod, and a broker *can* be saved. True, the angel that accomplishes the task may require all eternity to rest himself in, but has that got anything to do with the establishment of the proposition? Does it invalidate it? does it detract from it? I think not. I am aware that this enthusiastic and may-be highly-colored vindication of the brokers may lay me open to suspicion of bribery, but I care not; I am a native of Washoe, and I will stand by anybody that stands by Washoe.

The place where stocks are daily bought and sold is called by interested parties the Hall of the San Francisco Board of Brokers, but by the impartial and disinterested the Den of the Forty Thieves; the latter name is regarded as the most poetic, but the former is considered the most polite. The large room is well stocked with small desks, arranged in semi-circular ranks like the seats of an amphitheatre, and behind these sit the th—the brokers. The portly President, with his gavel of office in his hand, an abundance of whiskers and moustaches on his face, spectacles on nose, an expression of energy and decision on his countenance and an open plaza on his head, sits, with his three clerks, in a pulpit at the head of the hall, flanked on either hand by two large cases, with glass doors, containing mineralogical specimens from Washoe and California mines—the emblems of the traffic. Facing the President, at the opposite end of the hall, is a blackboard, whereon is written in accusing capitals, "John Smith delinquent to John Jones, $1,550; William Brown delinquent to Jonas White, $475!" You might think brokers wouldn't mind that, maybe, but they do; a delinquent loses caste, and that touches his fine moral sensibilities —and he is suspended from active membership for the time being, and even expelled if his delinquency savors of blundering and ungraceful rascality—a thing which the Board cannot abide—and this inflicts exquisite pain upon the delicate nerves and tissues of his pocket, now when a seat in the Den is worth twelve or fifteen hundred dollars, and in brisker times even three thousand.

The session of the Board being duly opened, the roll is rapidly called, the members present responding, and the absentees being noted by the clerks for fines:

"Ackerman, (Here!) Adams, Atchison, (Here!) Babcock, Bocock, (Here!) Badger, Blitzen, Bulger, Buncombe, (Here!) Caxton, (Here!) Cobbler, Crowder, Clutterback, (Here!) Dashaway, Dilson, Dodson, Dummy (Here!)"—and so on, the place becoming lively and animated, and the members sharpening their pencils, disposing their printed stock-lists before them, and getting ready for a sowing of unrighteousness and a harvest of sin.

In a few moments the roll-call was finished, the pencils all sharpened, and the brokers prepared for business—some with a leg thrown negligently over the arms of their chairs, some tilted back comfortably with their knees against their desks, some sitting half upright and glaring at the President, hungry for the contention to begin—but not a rascal of them tapping his teeth with his pencil—only dreamy, absent-minded people do that.

Then the President called "Ophir!" and after some bidding and counter-bidding, "Gould and Curry!" and a Babel arose—an infernal din and clatter of all kinds and tones of voices, inextricably jumbled together like original chaos, and above it all the following observation by the President pealed out clearly and distinctly, and with a rapidity of enunciation that was amazing:

"Fift'naitassfrwahn fift'nseftfive bifferwahn fift'naitfive botherty!"

I said I believed I would go home. My broker friend who had procured my admission to the Board asked why I wanted to go so soon, and I was obliged to acknowledge to him that I was very unfamiliar with the Kanaka language, and could not understand it at all unless a man spoke it exceedingly slow and deliberately.

"Oh," said he, "sit still; that isn't Kanaka; it's English, but he talks fast and runs one word into another; it is easy SOLD! to understand when you GIVE FIFTEEN-NINETY BUYER TEN NO DEPOSIT! come to get used to it. He always talks so, and sometimes he says THAT'S MINE! JIGGERS SOLD ON SLADDERY'S BID! his words so fast that even some of the members cannot comprehend them readily. Now what he said then was NO SIR! I DIDN'T SAY BUYER THIRTY, I

SAID REGULAR WAY! 'Fifteen-eighty, (meaning fifteen hundred and eighty dollars,) asked for one, (one foot), fifteen-seventy-five bid for one, fifteen-eighty-five buyer thirty,' (thirty days' time on the payment,) 'TWASN'T MY BID, IT WAS SWIGGINS TO BABCOCK! and he was repeating the bids and offers of the members after them as fast as they were made. I'LL TAKE IT, CASH!"

I felt relieved, but not enlightened. My broker's explanation had got so many strange and incomprehensible interpolations sandwiched into it that I began to look around for a suitable person to translate that for me also, when it occurred to me that these interpolations were bids, offers, etc., which he had been throwing out to the assembled brokers while he was talking to me. It was all clear, then, so I have put his side-remarks in small capitals so that they may be clear to the reader likewise, and show that they have no connection with the subject matter of my friend's discourse.

And all this time, the clatter of voices had been going on. And while the storm of ejaculations hurtled about their heads, these brokers sat calmly in their several easy attitudes, but when a sale was made—when, in answer to some particularly liberal bid, somebody sung out "Sold!" down came legs from the arms of chairs, down came knees propped against desks, forward shot the heads of the whole tribe with one accord, and away went the long ranks of pencils dancing over the paper! The sale duly recorded by all, the heads, the legs and the knees came up again, and the negligent attitudes were resumed once more.

The din moderated now, somewhat, and for awhile only a random and desultory fire was kept up as the President drifted down the stock-list, calling at intervals, "Savage!" "Uncle Sam!" "Chollar!" "Potosi!" "Hale and Norcross" "Imperial" "Sierra Nevada!" "Daney!" the monotony being broken and the uncomfortable attitudes demolished, now and then, by a lucky-shot that went to the mark and made a sale. But when the old gentleman called "Burning Moscow" you should have seen the fiends wake up! you should have heard the racket! you should have been there to behold the metaphorical bull in the China shop! The President's voice and his mallet went into active service, then, and mingled their noise with the clamors of the mob. The members thus:

On Montgomery Street, outside of the stockbrokers' offices, Jump has placed, along with a few rapacious-looking stockbrokers, some of the town's favorite characters—among them Emperor Norton; The Great Unknown, who was

never heard to say a word; the phrenologist, Professor Coombs, better known as George Washington the Second; the Little Drummer Boy; and the dogs, Bummer and Lazarus.

"Sell ten forty-five cash!" "Give forty-three for ten, regular way!" "Give forty-one cash for any part fifty!" "Twenty thirty-eight seller sixty!" "Give forty-four for ten buyer thirty!" "Sold" (Down with your legs again, forward with your heads, and out with your pencils!) "Sell ten forty-three cash!" "Sold!" Then from every part of the house a din like this: "Ten more!" "Sold!" "Ten more!" "Sold!" "Ten More!" "Sold!" "Ten more!" "Sold!" "Ten—"

President (rap with his gavel)—Silence! Orfuplease, (order if you please,) gentlemen! Higgins ten to Smithers—Dodson ten to Snodgrass—"

Billson—"No, sir! Billson to Snodgrass! It was me that sold 'em, sir!"

Dodson—"I didn't sell, sir, I bought—Jiggers ten to Dodson!"

President—"Billson ten to Snodgrass—Jiggers ten to Dodson—Slushbuster ten to Bladders—Simpson ten to Blivens—Guttersnipe ten to Hogwash—aw-right! go on!"

And they did go on, hotter and heavier than ever. And as they yelled their terms, the President repeated after them—the words flowing in a continuous stream from his mouth with inconceivable rapidity, and melting and mingling together like bottle-glass and cinders after a conflagration:

"Fortwahnasscash fortray bidbortenn fortsix botherty fortsevnoffsetherty fortfourbiffertenn—(smash! with the gavel) whasthat?—aw right! fortfive offranparfortbotherty nodeposit fortfivenaf botherty bid fortsix biglerway!"

Which, translated, means: "Forty-one asked cash; forty-three bid, buyer ten; forty-six, buyer thirty; forty-seven offered, seller thirty; forty-four bid for ten—(pause)—What's that? All right—forty-five offered for any part of forty, buyer thirty, no deposit; forty-five and a half, buyer thirty, bid; forty-six bid, regular way!"

And I found out that a "Bull" is a broker who raises the market-price of a stock by every means in his power, and a "Bear" is one who depresses it; that "cash" means that the stock must be delivered and paid for immediately—that is, before the banks close; that "regular way" means that delivery of the stock and payment must be made within two days, that it is the seller who "offers" stock, and the buyer who "bids" for it; that "buyer ten, thirty," or whatever the specified number may be, signifies the number of days the purchaser is allowed in which to call for the stock, receive it and pay for it, and it implies also that he must deposit in somebody's hands a fifth part of the price of the stock purchased, to be forfeited to the seller in case the full payment is not made within the time set—full payment must be made, though, nothwithstanding the forfeit, or the broker loses his seat if the seller makes complaint to the Board within forty-eight hours after the occurrence of the delinquency; that when the words "no deposit" are added to "buyer thirty," they imply that the twenty per cent. deposit is not to be made, of course; that "seller thirty" means that any time the seller chooses, during the thirty days, he can present the stock to the buyer and demand payment—the seller generally selling at a figure below the market rate, in the hope that before his time is up a depression may occur that will enable him to pick up the stock at half price and deliver it—and the buyer taking chances on a great advance, within the month, that will accrue to his profit. Think of one of these adventurous "seller thirty's" "selling short," at thirty dollars a foot, several feet of a stock that was all corralled and withdrawn from the market within a fortnight and went to about fifteen hundred! It is not worth while to mention names—I suppose you remember the circumstance.

But I digress. Sometimes on the "second call" of stocks—that is, after the list has been gone through with in regular order, and the members are privileged to call up any stock they please—strategy is driven to the utmost limit by the friends of some pet wildcat or other, to effect sales of it to disinterested parties. The seller "offers" at a high figure, and the "bidder" responds with a low one; then the former comes warily down a dollar at a time, and the latter approaches him from below at about the same rate; they come nearer and nearer, skirmish a little in close proximity, get to a point where another bid or another offer would commit the parties to a sale, and then in the imminence of the impending event, the seller hesitates a second and is silent. But behold! as has been said of Woman, "The Broker that hesitates is lost!" The nervous and impatient President can brook no silence, no delay, and calls out: "Awstock?" (Any other stock?) Somebody yells "Burning Moscow!" and the tender wildcat, almost born, miscarries. Or perhaps the skirmishers fight shyly up to each other, counter and cross-counter, feint and parry, back and fill, and finally clinch a sale in the centre—the bidder is bitten, a smile flits from face to face, down come the legs, forward the ranks of heads, the pencils charge on the stock-lists, and the neat transaction is recorded with a rare gusto.

But twelve pages of foolscap are warning me to cut this thrilling sketch short, notwithstanding it is only half finished. However, I cannot leave the subject without saying I was agreeably disappointed in those brokers; I expected to see a set of villains with the signs of total depravity hung out all over them, but now I am satisfied there is some good in them; that they are not entirely and irredeemably bad; and I have been told by a friend, whose judgment I respect, that they are not any more unprincipled than they look. This was said by a man who would scorn to stoop to flattery. At the same time, though, as I scanned the faces assembled in that hall, I could not help imagining I could see old St. Peter admitting that band of Bulls and Bears into Paradise—see him standing by the half-open gate with his ponderous key pressed thoughtfully against his nose, and his head canted critically to one side, as he looks after them tramping down the gold-paved avenue, and mutters to himself: "Well, *you're* a nice lot, any way! Humph! I think you'll find it sort of lonesome in heaven, for if my judgment is sound, you'll not find a good many of *your* stripe in there!"

Nov. 5, 1864—*Californian.*

1865

IMPORTANT CORRESPONDENCE

BETWEEN MR. MARK TWAIN OF SAN FRANCISCO, AND REV. BISHOP HAWKS, D.D., OF NEW YORK, REV. PHILLIPS BROOKS OF PHILADELPHIA, AND REV. DR. CUMMINGS OF CHICAGO, CONCERNING THE OCCUPANCY OF GRACE CATHEDRAL.

For a long time I have taken a deep interest in the efforts being made to induce the above-named distinguished clergymen—or, rather, some of them—to come out here and occupy the pulpit of the noble edifice known as Grace Cathedral. And when I saw that the vestry were uniformly unsuccessful, although doing all that they possibly could to attain their object, I felt it my duty to come forward and throw the weight of my influence—such as it might be—in favor of the laudable undertaking. That by so doing I was not seeking to curry favor with the vestry—and that my actions were prompted by no selfish motive of any kind whatever—is sufficiently evidenced by the fact that I am not a member of Grace Church, and never had any conversation with the vestry upon the subject in hand, and never even hinted to them that I was going to write to the clergymen. What I have done in the matter I did of my own free will and accord, without any solicitation from anybody, and my actions were dictated solely by a spirit of enlarged charity and good feeling toward the congregation of Grace Cathedral. I seek no reward for my services; I desire none but the approval of my own conscience and the satisfaction of knowing I have done that which I conceived to be my duty, to the best of my ability.

M.T.

The correspondence which passed between myself and the Rev. Dr. Hawks was as follows:

Letter from Myself to Bishop Hawks.

San Francisco, March, 1865.

Rev. Dr. Hawks—Dear Doctor.—Since I heard that you have telegraphed the vestry of Grace Cathedral here, that you cannot come out to San Francisco and carry on a church at the terms offered you, viz: $7,000 a year, I have concluded to write you on the subject myself. A word in your ear: say nothing to anybody—keep dark—but just pack up your traps and come along out here—I will see that it is all right. That $7,000 dodge was only a *bid*—nothing more. They never expected you to clinch a bargain like that. I will go to work and get up a little competition among the cloth, and the result of it will be that you will make more money in six months here than you would in New York in a year. I can do it. I have a great deal of influence with the clergy here, and especially with the Rev. Dr. Wadsworth and the Rev. Mr. Stebbins—I write their sermons for them. (This latter fact is not generally known, however, and maybe you had as well not mention it.) I can get them to strike for higher wages any time.

You would like this berth. It has a greater number of attractive features than any I know of. It is such a magnificent field, for one thing,—why, sinners are so thick that you can't throw out your line without hooking several of them; you'd be surprised—the flattest old sermon a man can grind out is bound to corral half a dozen. You see, you can do such a land-office business on such a small capital. Why, I wrote the most rambling, incomprehensible harangue of a sermon you ever heard in your life for one of the Episcopalian ministers here and he landed seventeen with it at the first dash; then I trimmed it up to suit Methodist doctrine, and the Rev. Mr. Thomas got eleven more; I tinkered the doctrinal points again, and Stebbins made a lot of Unitarian converts with it; I worked it over once more, and Dr. Wadsworth did almost as well with it as he usually does with my ablest compositions. It was passed around, after that, from church to church, undergoing changes of dress as before, to suit the vicissitudes of doctrinal climate, until it went the entire rounds. During its career we took in, altogether, a hundred and eighteen of the most abject reprobates that ever traveled on the broad road to destruction.

You would find this a remarkably easy berth—one man to give out the hymns, another to do the praying, another to read the chapter from the Testament—you would have nothing in the world to do but read the litany and preach—no, not *read* the litany, but sing it. They sing the litany here, in the Pontifical Grand Mass style, which is pleasanter and more attractive than to read it. You need not mind that, though; the tune is not difficult, and requires no more musical taste or education than is required to sell "Twenty-four—self-sealing—envelopes—for f-o-u-r cents," in your city. I like to hear the litany sung. Perhaps there is hardly enough variety in the music, but still the effect is very fine. Bishop Kip never could sing worth a cent, though. However, he has gone to Europe now to learn. Yes, as I said before, you would have nothing in the world to do but preach and sing that litany; and, between you and me, Doc, as regards the music, if you could manage to ring in a few of the popular and familiar old tunes that the people love so well you would be almost certain to create a sensation. I think I can safely promise you that. I am satisfied that you could do many a

thing that would attract less attention than would result from adding a spirited variety to the music of the litany.

Your preaching will be easy. Bring along a barrel of your old obsolete sermons; the people here will never know the difference.

Drop me a line, Hawks; I don't know you, except by reputation, but I like you all the same. And don't you fret about the salary. I'll make *that* all right, you know. You need not mention to the vestry of Grace Cathedral, though, that I have been communicating with you on this subject. You see, I do not belong to their church, and they might think I was taking too much trouble on their account—though I assure you, upon my honor, it is no trouble in the world to me; I don't mind it; I am not busy now, and I would rather do it than not. All I want is to have a sure thing that you get your rights. You can depend upon me. I'll see you through this business as straight as a shingle; I haven't been drifting around all my life for nothing. I know a good deal more than a boiled carrot, though I may not appear to. And although I am not of the elect, so to speak, I take a strong interest in these things, nevertheless, and I am not going to stand by and see them come any seven-thousand-dollar arrangement over you. I have sent them word in your name that you won't take less than $18,000, and that you can get $25,000 in greenbacks at home. I also intimated that I was going to write your sermons—I thought it might have a good effect and every little helps, you know. So you can just pack up and come along—it will be all right—I am satisfied of that. You needn't bring any shirts, I have got enough for us both. You will find there is nothing mean about *me*—I'll wear your clothes, and you can wear mine, just the same as so many twin brothers. When I like a man, I *like* him, and I go my death for him. My friends will all be fond of you, and will take to you as naturally as if they had known you a century. I will introduce you, and you will be all right. You can always depend on them. If you were to point out a man and say you did not like him, they would carve him in a minute.

Hurry along, Bishop. I shall be on the lookout for you, and will take you right to my house and you can stay there as long as you like, and it shan't cost you a cent.

Very truly, yours,
Mark Twain.

Reply of Bishop Hawks.

New York, April, 1865.

My Dear Mark.—I had never heard of you before I received your kind letter, but I feel as well acquainted with you now as if I had known you for years. I see that you understand how it is with us poor laborers in the vineyard, and feel for us in our struggles to gain a livelihood. You will be blessed for this—you will have your reward for the deeds done in the flesh—you will get your deserts hereafter. I am really sorry I cannot visit San Francisco, for I can see now that it must be a pleasant field for the earnest worker to toil in; but it was ordered otherwise, and I submit with becoming humility. My refusal of the position at $7,000 a year was not precisely meant to be final, but was intended for what the ungodly term a "flyer"—the object being, of course, to bring about an increase of the amount. That object was legitimate and proper, since it so nearly affects the interests not only of myself but of those who depend upon me for sustenance and support. Perhaps you remember a remark I made once to a vestry who had been solicited to increase my salary, my family being a pretty large one: they declined, and said it was promised that Providence would take care of the young ravens. I immediately retorted, in my happiest vein, that there was no similar promise concerning the young Hawks, though! I thought it was very good, at the time. The recollection of it has solaced many a weary hour since then, when all the world around me seemed dark and cheerless, and it is a source of tranquil satisfaction to me to think of it even at this day.

No; I hardly meant my decision to be final, as I said before, but subsequent events have compelled that result in spite of me. I threw up my parish in Baltimore, although it was paying me very handsomely, and came to New York to see how things were going in our line. I have prospered beyond my highest expectations. I selected a lot of my best sermons—old ones that had been forgotten by everybody—and once a week I let one of them off in the Church of the Annunciation here. The spirit of the ancient sermons bubbled forth with a bead on it and permeated the hearts of the congregation with a new life, such as the worn body feels when it is refreshed with rare old wine. It was a great hit. The timely arrival of the "call" from San Francisco insured success to me. The people appreciated my merits at once. A number of gentlemen immediately clubbed together and offered me $10,000 a year, and agreed to purchase for me the Church of St. George the Martyr, up town, or to build a new house of worship for me if I preferred it. I closed with them on these terms, my dear Mark, for I feel that so long as not even the little sparrows are suffered to fall to the ground unnoted, I shall be mercifully cared for; and besides, I know that come what may, I can always eke out an existence so long as the cotton trade holds out as good as it is now. I am in cotton to some extent, you understand, and that is one reason why I cannot venture to leave here just at present to accept the position offered me in San Francisco. You see I have some small investments in that line which are as yet in an undecided state, and must be looked after.

But time flies, Mark, time flies; and I must bring this screed to a close and say farewell—and if forever, then forever fare thee well. But I shall never forget you, Mark—never!

Your generous solicitude in my behalf—your splendid inventive ability in conceiving of messages to the vestry calculated to make them offer me a higher salary—your sublime intrepidity in tendering those messages as having come from me—your profound sagacity in chaining and riveting the infatuation of the vestry with the intimation that you were going to write my sermons for me—your gorgeous liberality in offering to divide your shirts with me and to make common property of all other wearing apparel belonging to both parties—your cordial tender of your friends' affections and their very extraordinary services—your noble hospitality in providing a home for me in your palatial mansion—all these things call for my highest admiration and gratitude, and call not in vain, my dearest Mark. I shall never cease to pray for you and hold you in kindly and tearful remembrance. Once more, my gifted friend, accept the fervent thanks and the best wishes of

Your obliged servant,
Rev. Dr. Hawks

Writes a beautiful letter, don't he?

But when the Bishop uses a tabooed expression, and talks glibly about doing a certain thing "just for a flyer," don't he shoulder the responsibility of it on to "the ungodly," with a rare grace?

And what a solid comfort that execrable joke has been to his declining years, hasn't it? If he goes on thinking about it and swelling himself up on account of it, he will be wanting a salary after a while that will break any church that hires him. However, if he enjoys it, and really thinks it *was* a good joke, I am very sure I don't want to dilute his pleasure in the least by dispelling the illusion. It reminds me, though, of a neat remark which the editor of *Harper's Magazine* made three years ago, in an article wherein he was pleading for charity for the harmless vanity of poor devil scribblers who imagine they are gifted with genius. He said *they* didn't know but what their writing was fine—and then he says: "Don't poor Martin Farquhar Tupper fondle his platitudes and think they are poems?" That's it. Let the Bishop fondle his little joke—no doubt it is just as good to him as if it were the very soul of humor.

But I wonder who in the mischief is "St.-George-the-Martyr-Up-Town?" However, no matter—the Bishop is not going to take his chances altogether with St.-George-the-Martyr-Up-Town, or with the little sparrows that are subject to accidents, either—he has a judicious eye on cotton. And he is right, too. Nobody deserves to be helped who don't try to help himself, and "faith without works" is a risky doctrine.

Now, what is your idea about his last paragraph? Don't you think he is spreading it on rather thick?—as "the ungodly" would term it. Do you really think there is any rain behind all that thunder and lightning? Do you suppose he really means it? They are mighty powerful adjectives—uncommonly powerful adjectives—and sometimes I seem to smell a faint odor of irony about them. But that could hardly be. He evidently loves me. Why, if I could be brought to believe that that reverend old humorist was discharging any sarcasm at me, I would never write to him again as long as I live. Thinks I will "get my deserts hereafter"—I don't hardly like the ring of that, altogether.

He says he will pray for me, though. Well, he couldn't do anything that would fit my case better, and he couldn't find a subject who would thank him more kindly for it than I would. I suppose

I shall come in under the head of "sinners at large"—but I don't mind that; I am no better than any other sinner and I am not entitled to especial consideration. They pray for the congregation first, you know—and with considerable vim; then they pray mildly for other denominations; then for the near relations of the congregation; then for their distant relatives; then for the surrounding community; then for the State; then for the Government officers; then for the United States; then for North America; then for the whole Continent; then for England, Ireland and Scotland; France, Germany and Italy; Russia, Prussia and Austria; then for the inhabitants of Norway, Sweden and Timbuctoo; and those of Saturn, Jupiter and New Jersey; and then they give the niggers a lift, and the Hindoos a lift, and the Turks a lift, and the Chinese a lift; and then, after they have got the fountain of mercy baled out as dry as an ash-hopper, they bespeak the sediment left in the bottom of it for us poor "sinners at large."

It ain't just exactly fair, is it? Sometimes, (being a sort of a Presbyterian in a general way, and a brevet member of one of the principal churches of that denomination), I stand up in the devout attitude, with downcast eyes, and hands clasped upon the back of the pew before me, and listen attentively and expectantly for a while; and then rest upon one foot for a season; and then upon the other; and then insert my hands under my coat-tails and stand erect and look solemn; and then fold my arms and droop forward and look dejected; and then cast my eyes furtively at the minister; and then at the congregation; and then grow absent-minded, and catch myself counting the lace bonnets; and marking the drowsy members; and noting the wide-awake ones; and averaging the bald heads; and afterwards descend to indolent conjectures as to whether the buzzing fly that keeps stumbling up the windowpane and sliding down backwards again will ever accomplish his object to his satisfaction; and, finally, I give up and relapse into a dreary reverie—and about this time the minister reaches my department, and brings me back to hope and consciousness with a kind word for the poor "sinners at large."

Sometimes we are even forgotten altogether and left out in the cold—and then I call to mind the vulgar little boy who was fond of hot biscuits, and whose mother promised him that he should have all that were left if he would stay away and keep quiet and be a good little boy while the strange guest ate his breakfast; and who watched that voracious guest till the growing apprehension in his young bosom gave place to demonstrated ruin and then sung out: "There! I know'd how it was goin' to be—I know'd how it was goin' to be, from the start! Blamed if he hain't gobbled the last biscuit!"

I do not complain, though, because it is very seldom that the Hindoos and the Turks and the Chinese get all the atoning biscuits and leave us sinners at large to go hungry. They *do* remain at the board a long time, though, and we often get a little tired waiting for our turn. How would it do to be less diffuse? How would it do to ask a blessing upon the specialities—I mean the congregation and the immediate community—and then include the whole broad universe in one glowing fervent appeal? How would it answer to adopt the simplicity and the beauty and the brevity and the comprehensiveness of the Lord's Prayer as a model? But perhaps I am wandering out of my jurisdiction.

The letters I wrote to the Rev. Phillips Brooks of Philadelphia, and the Rev. Dr. Cummings of Chicago, urging them to come here and take charge of Grace Cathedral, and offering them my countenance and support, will be published next week, together with their replies to the same.

May 6, 1865—*Californian.*

THE LAW AND
E Jump

THE "PROFITS".
65&6
BULLETIN
UNION

FURTHER OF MR. MARK TWAIN'S IMPORTANT CORRESPONDENCE

I promised, last week, that I would publish in the present number of the *Californian* the correspondence held between myself and Rev. Phillips Brooks of Philadelphia, and Rev. Dr. Cummings of Chicago, but I must now beg you to release me from that promise. I have just received telegrams from the distinguished clergymen suggesting the impolicy of printing their letters; the suggestion is accompanied by arguments so able, so pointed and so conclusive that, although I saw no impropriety in it before, I am forced now to concede that it *would* be very impolitic to publish their letters. It could do but little good, perhaps, and might really do harm, in awakening a diseased curiosity in the public mind concerning the private matters of ministers of the gospel. The telegrams and accompanying arguments are as follows:

From Rev. Phillips Brooks.

Philadelphia, Friday, May 12.

Mr. Mick Twine: * Am told you have published Bishop Hawks' letter. You'll ruin the clergy! Don't—*don't* publish mine. Listen to reason—come, now, don't make an ass of yourself. Draw on me for five hundred dollars. Rev. Phillips Brooks.

[Although I feel it my duty to suppress his letter, it is proper to state for the information of the public, that Phil. gets a higher salary where he is, and consequently he cannot come out here and take charge of Grace Cathedral. *Mem.*—He is in petroleum to some extent, also.—M.T.]

From Rev. Dr. Cummings.

Chicago, Thursday, May 11.

Mr. MacSwain: * Have you really been stupid enough to publish Bishop Hawks' letter? Ge-whilikins! don't publish mine. Don't be a fool, Mike.* Draw on me for five or six hundred.

Rev. Dr. Cummings.

* Excuse the unhappy telegraph—it never spells names right.—M.T.

[I am conscious that it would be improper to print the Doctor's letter, but it may be as well to observe that *he* also gets a higher salary where he is, and consequently he cannot come out here and take charge of Grace Cathedral. *Mem.*—He is speculating a little in grain.—M.T.]

I am afraid I was rather hasty in publishing Bishop Hawks' letter. I am sorry I did it. I suppose there is no chance now to get an Argument out of him, this late in the day.

Foreign Correspondence.

I am a suffering victim of my infernal disposition to be always trying to oblige somebody without being asked to do it. Nobody asked me to help the vestry of Grace Cathedral to hire a minister: I dashed into it on my own hook, in a spirit of absurd enthusiasm, and a nice mess I have made of it. I have not succeeded in securing either of the three clergymen I wanted, but that is not the worst of it—I have brought such a swarm of low-priced back-country preachers about my ears that I begin to be a little appalled at the work of my own hands. I am afraid I have evoked a spirit that I cannot lay. A single specimen of the forty-eight letters addressed to me from the interior will suffice to show the interest my late publication has excited:

From Rev. Mr. Brown.

Grasshopper Chateau, 1865.

Bro. Twain: I feel that the opportunity has arrived at last for me to make a return somewhat in kind for the countless blessings which have been poured—poured, as it were—upon my unworthy head. If you get the vacancy in Grace Cathedral for me, I will accept of it at once, and at any price, notwithstanding I should sacrifice so much here in a worldly point of view, and entail so much unhappiness upon my loving flock by so doing—for I feel that I am "called," and it is not for me, an humble instrument, to disobey. [The splotch you observe here is a tear.] It stirs the deepest emotions in my breast to think that I shall soon leave my beloved flock: bear with this seeming childishness, my friend, for I have reared this dear flock, and tended it for years, and I fed it with spiritual food, and sheared it—ah, me, and sheared it—I cannot go on—the subject is too harrowing. But I'll take that berth for less than any man on the continent, if you'll get it for me. I send you specimen sermons—some original and some selected and worked over.

Your humble and obedient servant,
T. St. Matthew Brown.

They all want the berth at Grace Cathedral. They would all be perfectly satisfied with $7,000 a year. They are all willing to sacrifice their dearest worldly interests and break the tenderest ties that bind them to their rural homes, to come and fight the good fight in our stately church. They all feel that they could do more good and serve their master better in a wider sphere of action. They all feel stirring within them souls too vast for confinement in narrow flats and gulches. And they all want to come here and spread. And worse than all, they all devil *me* with their bosh, and send *me* their sermons to read, and come and dump their baggage in *my* hall, and take possession of *my* bed-rooms by assault, and carry *my* dinner-table by storm, instead of inflicting these miseries upon the vestry of Grace Cathedral, who are the proper victims, by virtue of their office. Why in thunder do they come harassing *me?* What have *I* got to do with the matter? Why, I do not even belong to the church, and have got no more to do with hiring pastors for it than the Dey of Algiers has. I wish they would ease up a little on me; I mixed into this business a little too brashly—so to speak—and without due reflection; but if I get out of it once all right, I'll not mix in any more—never any more; now that's honest—I never will.

I have numerous servants, but they are all worked down. My housekeeper is on the verge of open rebellion. Yesterday she said: "I lay I'll take and hyste some of them preachers out of this mighty soon, now." And she'll do it. I shall regret it. I could entertain no sentiment but that of regret to see a clergyman "hysted" out of my establishment, but what am I to do? I cannot help it. If I were to interfere I should get "hysted" myself.

My clerical guests are healthy. Their appetites are good. They are not particular as to food. They worry along very well on spring chickens. I don't feel safe with them, though, because if it is considered that a steamboat on the Mississippi is inviting disaster when she ventures to carry more than two ministers at a time, isn't it likely that the dozen I have got in my house will eventually produce an earthquake? The tradition goes that three clergymen on a steamboat will ground her, four will sink her, and five and a gray mare added will blow her up. If I had a gray mare in my stable, I would leave this city before night.

May 13, 1865—*Californian.*

[The sporting event of the year was the test of speed and stamina between two Kentucky race horses. It took place May 23 at the new Ocean House track, about ten miles from downtown, which one reached by way of a toll road south from the Cliff House. Twain assumes that all his readers know who won. Since I'm not sure I can make the same assumption, I'll mention that Norfolk carried the day easily. The course times were: 3:43; 3:42; 3:50; 3:51; 4:5.]

HOW I WENT TO THE GREAT RACE BETWEEN LODI AND NORFOLK

There can be no use in my writing any account whatever of the great race, because that matter has already been attended to in the daily papers. Therefore, I will simply describe to you *how* I went to the race. But before I begin, I would like to tell you about Homestead—Benj. W. Homestead, of the Incidental Hotel. (I do not wish to be too severe, though, and so I use fictitious names, to prevent your finding out who it is I refer to, and where his place of business is.)

It will ease my mind to tell you about him. You know Homestead, clerk at the Incidental Hotel, and you know he has the reputation of being chatty, and sociable, and accommodating—a man, in fact, eminently fitted to make a guest feel more at home in the hotel than in his own house with his own wife, and his own mother, and his wife's mother, and her various friends and relatives, and all the other little comforts that go to make married life a blessing, and create what is known as "Sweet Home," and which is so deservedly popular—I mean among people who have not tried it. You know Homestead as that kind of a man. Therefore, you would not suppose that attractive exterior of his, and that smiling visage, and that seductive tongue capable of dark and mysterious crimes.

Very well, I will ask you to listen to a plain, unprejudiced statement of facts:

On or about the 21st of the present month, it became apparent to me that the forthcoming race between *Norfolk* and *Lodi* was awakening extraordinary attention all over the Pacific coast, and even far away in the Atlantic States. I saw that if I failed to see this race I might live a century, perhaps, without ever having an opportunity to see its equal. I went at once to a livery stable—the man

said his teams had all been engaged a week before I called. I got the same answer at all the other livery stables, except one. They told me there that they had a nice dray, almost new, and a part of a horse—they said part of a horse because a good deal of him was gone, in the way of a tail, and one ear and a portion of the other, and his upper lip, and one eye; and, inasmuch as his teeth were exposed, and he had a villainous cast in his remaining eye, these defects, added to his damaged ears and departed tail, gave him an extremely "gallus" and unprepossessing aspect—but they only asked two hundred and forty dollars for the turn-out for the day.

I resisted the yearning I felt to hire this unique establishment.

Then they said they had a capacious riding-horse left, but all the seats on him except one had been engaged; they said he was an unusually long horse, and he could seat seven very comfortably; and that he was very gentle, and would not kick up behind; and that one of the choicest places on him for observation was still vacant, and I could have it for nineteen dollars—and so on and so on; and while the passenger agent was talking, he was busy measuring off a space of nine inches for me pretty high up on the commodious animal's neck.

It seemed to me that the prospect of going to the races was beginning to assume a very "neck-or-nothing" condition, but nevertheless I steadfastly refused the supercargo's offer, and he sold the vacancy to a politician who was used to being on the fence and would naturally consider a seat astride a horse's neck in the light of a pleasant variety.

I then walked thoughtfully down to the Incidental, turning over in my mind various impossible expedients for getting out to the Ocean Race-Course. I thought of the horse-cars and the steam-cars, but without relief, for neither of these conveyances could carry me within four miles of the place. At the hotel I met the abandoned Homestead, and as nearly as I can recollect, the following conversation ensued:

"Ah, Mark, you're the very man I was looking for. Take a drink?"

I cannot be positive, but it is my impression that I either stated that I would, or else signified assent by a scarcely perceptible eagerness of manner common to me under circumstances of this nature.

While we were drinking, Homestead remarked, with considerable vivacity:

"Yes, I was just looking for you. I am going out to the great race on Tuesday, and I've a vacancy and want company. I'd like to have you go along with me if you will."

I set my glass down with a suddenness and decision unusual with me on such occasions, and seizing his hand, I wrung it with heartfelt warmth and cordiality. It is humiliating to me to reflect, now, that at that moment I even shed some tears of gratitude, and felt them coursing down the backbone of my nose and dripping from the end of it.

Never mind the remainder of the conversation—suffice it that I was charged to be at the Incidental punctually at ten o'clock on Tuesday morning, and that I promised to do so.

Well, at the appointed time, I *was* there. That is, I was as near as I could get—I was on the outskirts of a crowd that occupied all the pavement outside and filled the office inside. Young Smith, of Buncombe and Brimstone, approached me with an air of superiority, and remarked languidly that he guessed he would go to the races. He dropped his airs, though, very suddenly, and came down to my level when I told him *I* was going to the races also. He said he thought all the conveyances in town had been secured a week ago. I assumed a crushing demeanor of wealthy indifference, and remarked, rather patronizingly, that I had seen greater races—in Europe and other places—and did not care about seeing this one, but then Homestead had insisted so on my going with him that—

"The very devil!" says young Smith, "give us your hand! we're *compangyongs dew vo-yaj!"* (he affects the French, does young Smith,)—*"I'm* going with Homestead, too, my boy!"

We grew cordial in a moment, and went around, arm-in-arm, patronizing the balance of the crowd. But somehow, every man we accosted silenced our batteries as I had silenced young Smith's in the first place—they were all going with Homestead. I tell you candidly, and in all seriousness, that when I came to find out that there were a hundred and fifty men there, all going to the races, and all going with Homestead, I began to think it was—was—singular, at the very least, not to say exceedingly strange.

But I am tired of this infamous subject—I am tired of this disgraceful narrative, and I shall not finish it.

However, as I have gone this far, I *will* quote from a conversation that occurred in front of the hotel at ten o'clock. The degraded Homestead stepped out at the door, and bowed, and smiled his hated smile, and said, blandly:

"Ah, you are all here, I see. I am glad you are so punctual, for there is nothing that worries me so much when I am going on a little trip like this for recreation, as to be delayed. Well, boys, time presses—let's make a start."

"I guess we're all ready, Mr. Homestead," said one gentleman, "but—but how are you going?"

The depraved Homestead smiled, as if he were going to say something very smart, and then, "Oh," says he, "I'M GOING TO WALK!"

I have made a plain, simple statement of the facts connected with this outrage, and they can be substantiated by every man who was present upon that occasion. I will now drop this subject forever.

May 27, 1865—*Californian.*

[For six weeks in a row, beginning June 3, Twain ran a free-wheeling "Answers to Correspondents" column for the *Californian*. Twain made a selection of them for his *Sketches New and Old,* and I have done the same. Some of the country papers of the region thought Twain was being serious in printing as a submission from a Dutch Flat correspondent the lines of poetry about the Assyrian coming down like a wolf on the fold. Twain's critique of these lines as sounding "like buttermilk gurgling from a jug" and his estimate that they were good enough, maybe, for Dutch Flat but certainly not for the metropolis provoked the country editors exceedingly. They denounced Twain's ignorance in not knowing that the lines were by Byron.]

ANSWERS TO CORRESPONDENTS

"Moral Statistician."—I don't want any of your statistics; I took your whole batch and lit my pipe with it. I hate your kind of people. You are always ciphering out how much a man's health is injured, and how much his intellect is impaired, and how many pitiful dollars and cents he wastes in the course of ninety-two years' indulgence in the fatal practice of smoking; and in the equally fatal practice of drinking coffee; and in playing billiards occasionally; and in taking a glass of wine at dinner, etc., etc., etc. And you are always figuring out how many women have been burned to death because of the dangerous fashion of wearing expansive hoops, etc., etc., etc. You never see more than one side of the question. You are blind to the fact that most old men in America smoke and drink coffee, although, according to your theory, they ought to have died young; and that hearty old Englishmen drink wine and survive it, and portly old Dutchmen both drink and smoke freely, and yet grow older and fatter all the time. And you never try to find out how much solid comfort, relaxation and enjoyment a man derives from smoking in the course of a lifetime (which is worth ten times the money he would save by letting it alone), nor the appalling aggregate of happiness lost in a lifetime by your kind of people from *not* smoking. Of course you can save money by denying yourself all those little vicious enjoyments for fifty years; but then what can you do with it? What use can you put it to? Money can't save your infinitesimal soul. All the use that money can be put to is to purchase comfort and enjoyment in this life; therefore, as you are an enemy to comfort and enjoyment, where is the use of accumulating cash? It won't do for you to say that you can use it to better purpose in furnishing a good table, and in charities, and in supporting tract societies, because you know yourself that you people who have no petty vices are never known to give away a cent, and that you stint yourselves so in the matter of food that you are always feeble and hungry. And you never dare to laugh in the daytime for fear some poor wretch, seeing you in a good humor, will try to borrow a dollar of you; and in church you are always down on your knees, with your eyes buried in the cushion, when the contribution-box comes around; and you never give the revenue officers a full statement of your income. Now you know all these things yourself, don't you? Very well, then, what is the use of your stringing out your miserable lives to a lean and withered old age? What is the use of your saving money that is so utterly

worthless to you? In a word, why don't you go off somewhere and die, and not be always trying to seduce people into becoming as "ornery" and unlovable as you are yourselves, by your villainous "moral statistics"? Now I don't approve of dissipation, and I don't indulge in it, either; but I haven't a particle of confidence in a man who has no redeeming petty vices, and so I don't want to hear from you any more. I think you are the very same man who read me a long lecture last week about the degrading vice of smoking cigars, and then came back, in my absence, with your reprehensible fire-proof gloves on, and carried off my beautiful parlor stove.

"Young Author."—Yes, Agassiz *does* recommend authors to eat fish, because the phosphorus in it makes brain. So far you are correct. But I cannot help you to a decision about the amount you need to eat—at least, not with certainty. If the specimen composition you send is about your fair usual average, I should judge that perhaps a couple of whales would be all you would want for the present. Not the largest kind, but simply good, middling-sized whales.

"Simon Wheeler," *Sonora.*—The following simple and touching remarks and accompanying poem have just come to hand from the rich gold-mining region of Sonora:

"To Mr. Mark Twain: *The within parson, which I have set to poetry under the name and style of "He Done His Level Best," was one among the whitest men I ever see, and it ain't every man that knowed him that can find it in his heart to say he's glad the poor cuss is busted and gone home to the States. He was here in an early day, and he was the handyest man about takin' holt of anything that come along you most ever see, I judge. He was a cheerful, stirrin' cretur, always doin' somethin', and no man can say he ever see him do anything by halvers. Preachin' was his nateral gait, but he warn't a man to lay back and twidle his thumbs because there didn't happen to be nothin' doin' in his own especial line—no, sir, he was a man who would meander forth and stir up something for hisself. His last acts was to go his pile on* "*Kings-*and" (*calklatin' to fill, but which he didn't fill*), *when there was a* "*flush*" *out agin him, and naterally, you see, he went under. And so he was cleaned out, as you may say, and he struck the home-trail, cheerful but flat broke. I knowed this talonted man in Arkansaw, and if you would print this humbly tribute to his gorgis abilities, you would greatly obleege his onhappy friend.*"

HE DONE HIS LEVEL BEST

Was he a mining on the flat—
He done it with a zest;
Was he a leading of the choir—
He done his level best.

If he'd a reg'lar task to do,
He never took no rest;
Or if 'twas off-and-on—the same—
He done his level best.

If he was preachin' on his beat,
He'd tramp from east to west,
And north to south—in cold and heat
He done his level best.

He'd yank a sinner outen (Hades),[1]
And land him with the blest;
Then snatch a prayer'n waltz in again,
And do his level best.

He'd cuss and sing and howl and pray,
And dance and drink and jest,
And lie and steal—all one to him—
He done his level best.

Whate'er this man was sot to do,
He done it with a zest;
No matter what *his contract was,*
HE'D DO HIS LEVEL BEST.

Verily, this man *was* gifted with "gorgis abilities," and it is a happiness to me to embalm the memory of their luster in these columns. If it were not that the poet crop is unusually large and rank in California this year, I would encourage you to continue writing, Simon Wheeler; but, as it is, perhaps it might be too risky in you to enter against so much opposition.

"Professional Beggar."—No; you are not obliged to take greenback at par.

"Melton Mowbray." *Dutch Flat.*—This correspondent sends a lot of doggerel, and says it has been regarded as very good in Dutch Flat. I give a specimen verse:

The Assyrian came down like a wolf on the fold,
And his cohorts were gleaming with purple and gold;
And the sheen of his spears was like stars on the sea,
When the blue wave rolls nightly on deep Galilee.

There, that will do. That may be very good Dutch Flat poetry, but it won't do in the metropolis. It is too smooth and blubbery; it reads like buttermilk gurgling from a jug. What the people ought

1 Here I have taken a slight liberty with the original MS. "Hades" does not make such good meter as the other word of one syllable, but it sounds better.

to have is something spirited—something like "Johnny Comes Marching Home." However, keep on practising, and you may succeed yet. There is genius in you, but too much blubber.

"*St. Clair Higgins.*" Los Angeles.—"*My life is a failure; I have adored, wildly, madly, and she whom I love has turned coldly from me and shed her affections upon another. What would you advise me to do?*"

You should set your affections on another also—or on several, if there are enough to go round. Also, do everything you can to make your former flame unhappy. There is an absurd idea disseminated in novels, that the happier a girl is with another man, the happier it makes the old lover she has blighted. Don't allow yourself to believe any such nonsense as that. The more cause that girl finds to regret that she did not marry you, the more comfortable you will feel over it. It isn't poetical, but it is mighty sound doctrine.

"*Arithmeticus.*" Virginia, Nevada.—"*If it would take a cannon-ball $3\frac{1}{3}$ seconds to travel four miles, and $3\frac{3}{8}$ seconds to travel the next four, and $3\frac{5}{8}$ to travel the next four, and if its rate of progress continued to diminish in the same ratio, how long would it take it to go fifteen hundred million miles?*"

I don't know.

"Ambitious Learner." *Oakland.*—Yes; you are right—America was not discovered by Alexander Selkirk.

"*Discarded Lover.*"—"*I loved, and still love, the beautiful Edwitha Howard, and intended to marry her. Yet, during my temporary absence at Benicia, last week, alas! she married Jones. Is my happiness to be thus blasted for life? Have I no redress?*"

Of course you have. All the law, written and unwritten, is on your side. The *intention* and not the *act* constitutes crime—in other words, constitutes the *deed.* If you call your bosom friend a fool, and *intend* it for an insult, it *is* an insult; but if you do it playfully, and meaning no insult, it is *not* an insult. If you discharge a pistol *accidentally,* and kill a man, you can go free, for you have done no murder; but if you try to kill a man, and manifestly *intend* to kill him, but fail utterly to do it, the law still holds that the *intention* constituted the crime, and you are guilty of murder. Ergo, if you had married Edwitha *accidentally,* and without really *intending* to do it you would not actually be married to her at all, because the *act* of marriage could not be complete without the *intention.* And ergo, in the strict spirit of the law, since you deliberately *intended* to marry Edwitha, and didn't do it, you are married to her all the same—because, as I said before, the *intention* constitutes the crime. It is as clear as day that Edwitha is your wife, and your redress lies in taking a club and mutilating Jones with it as much as you can. Any man has a right to protect his own wife from the advances of other men. But you have another alternative—you were married to Edwitha *first,* because of your deliberate intention, and now you can prosecute her for bigamy, in subsequently marrying Jones. But there is another phase in this complicated case: You *intended* to marry Edwitha, and consequently, according to law, she is your wife—there is no getting around that; but she didn't marry you, and if she *never intended* to marry you, *you are not her husband, of course.* Ergo, in marrying Jones, she was guilty of bigamy, because she was the wife of another man at the time; which is all very well as far as it goes—but then, don't you see, she had no other *husband* when she married Jones, and consequently she was *not* guilty of bigamy. Now, according to this view of the case, Jones married a *spinster,* who was a *widow* at the same time and another man's *wife* at the same time, and yet who had no *husband* and *never had one,* and never had any *intention* of getting married, and therefore, of course, *never had* been married; and by the same reasoning you are a *bachelor,* because you have never been any one's *husband;* and a *married man,* because you have a wife living; and to all intents and purposes a *widower,* because you have been deprived of that wife; and a consummate *ass* for going off to Benicia in the first place, while things were so mixed. And by this time I have got myself so tangled up in the intricacies of this extraordinary case that I shall have to give up any further attempt to advise you—I might get confused and fail to make myself understood. I think I could take up the argument where I left off, and by following it closely awhile, perhaps I could prove to your satisfaction, either that you never existed at all, or that you are dead now, and consequently don't need the faithless Edwitha—I think I could do that, if it would afford you any comfort.

"Arthur Augustus."—No; you are wrong; that is the proper way to throw a brickbat or a tomahawk; but it doesn't answer so well for a bouquet; you will hurt somebody if you keep it up. Turn your nosegay upside down, take it by the stems, and toss it with an upward sweep. Did you ever pitch quoits? that is the idea. The practice of recklessly heaving immense solid bouquets, of the general size and weight of prize cabbages, from the dizzy altitude of the galleries, is dangerous and very reprehensible. Now, night before last, at the Academy of Music, just after Signorina ——— had finished that exquisite melody, "The Last Rose of Summer," one of these floral pile-drivers came cleaving down through the atmosphere of applause, and if she hadn't deployed suddenly to the right, it would have driven her into the floor like a shingle-nail. Of course that bouquet was well meant; but how would you like to have been the target? A sincere compliment is always grateful to a lady, so long as you don't try to knock her down with it.

"Young Mother."—And so you think a baby is a thing of beauty and a joy forever? Well, the idea is pleasing, but not original; every cow thinks the same of its own calf. Perhaps the cow may not think it so elegantly, but still she thinks it nevertheless. I honor the cow for it. We all honor this touching maternal instinct wherever we find it, be it in the home of luxury or in the humble cow-shed. But really, madam, when I come to examine the matter in all its bearings, I find that the correctness of your assertion does not assert itself in all cases. A soiled baby, with a neglected nose, cannot be conscientiously regarded as a thing of beauty; and inasmuch as babyhood spans but three short years, no baby is competent to be a joy "forever." It pains me thus to demolish two-thirds of your pretty sentiment in a single sentence; but the position I hold in this chair requires that I shall not permit you to deceive and mislead the public with your plausible figures of speech. I know a female baby, aged eighteen months, in this city, which cannot hold out as a "joy" twenty-four hours on a stretch, let alone "forever." And it possesses some of the most remarkable eccentricities of character and appetite that have ever fallen under my notice. I will set down here a statement of this infant's operations (conceived, planned, and carried out by itself, and without suggestion or assistance from its mother or any one else), during a single day; and what I shall say can be substantiated by the sworn testimony of witnesses.

It commenced by eating one dozen large blue-mass pills, box and all; then it fell down a flight of stairs, and arose with a blue and purple knot on its forehead, after which it proceeded in quest of further refreshment and amusement. It found a glass trinket ornamented with brass-work—smashed up and ate the glass, and then swallowed the brass. Then it drank about twenty drops of laudanum, and more than a dozen tablespoonfuls of strong spirits of camphor. The reason why it took no more laudanum was because there was no more to take. After this it lay down on its back, and shoved five or six inches of a silver-headed whalebone cane down its throat; got it fast there, and it was all its mother could do to pull the cane out again, without pulling out some of the child with it. Then, being hungry for glass again, it broke up several wineglasses, and fell to eating and swallowing the fragments, not minding a cut or two. Then it ate a quantity of butter, pepper, salt, and California matches, actually taking a spoonful of butter, a spoonful of salt, a spoonful of pepper, and three or four lucifer matches at each mouthful. (I will remark here that this thing of beauty likes painted German lucifers, and eats all she can get of them; but she prefers California matches, which I regard as a compliment to our home manufactures of more than ordinary value, coming, as it does, from one who is too young to flatter.) Then she washed her head with soap and water, and afterward ate what soap was left, and drank as much of the suds as she had room for; after which she sallied forth and took the cow familiarly by the tail, and got kicked heels over head. At odd times during the day, when this joy forever happened to have nothing particular on hand, she put in the time by climbing up on places and falling down off them, uniformly damaging herself in the operation. As young as she is, she speaks many words tolerably distinctly; and being plain-spoken in other respects, blunt and to the point, she opens conversation with all strangers, male or female, with the same formula, "How do, Jim?" Not being familiar with the ways of children, it is possible that I have been magnifying into matter of surprise things which may not strike any one who is familiar with infancy as being at all astonishing. However, I cannot believe that such is the case, and so I repeat that my report of this baby's performances is strictly true; and if any one doubts it, I can produce the child. I will further engage that she will devour anything that is given her (reserving to myself only the right to exclude anvils), and fall down from any place to which she may be elevated (merely stipulating that her preference for alighting on her head shall be respected, and, therefore, that the elevation chosen shall be high enough to enable her to accomplish this to her satisfaction). But I find I have wandered from my subject; so, without further argument, I will reiterate my conviction that not *all* babies are things of beauty and joys forever.

"*Arithmeticus.*" Virginia, Nevada.—"*I am an enthusiastic student of mathematics, and it is so vexatious to me to find my progress constantly impeded by these mysterious arithmetical technicalities. Now do tell me what the difference is between geometry and conchology?*"

Here *you* come again with your arithmetical conundrums, when I am suffering death with a cold in the head. If you could have seen the expression of scorn that darkened my countenance a moment ago, and was instantly split from the center in every direction like a fractured looking-glass by my last sneeze, you never would have written that disgraceful question. Conchology is a science which has nothing to do with mathematics; it relates only to shells. At the same time, however, a man who opens oysters for a hotel, or shells a fortified town, or sucks eggs, is not, strictly speaking, a conchologist—a fine stroke of sarcasm that, but it will be lost on such an unintellectual clam as you. Now compare conchology and geometry together, and you will see what the difference is, and your question will be answered. But don't torture me with any more arithmetical horrors until you know I am rid of my cold. I feel the bitterest animosity toward you at this moment—bothering me in this way, when I can do nothing but sneeze and rage and snort pocket-handkerchiefs to atoms. If I had you in range of my nose now I would blow your brains out.

"True Son of the Union."—Very well, I will publish the following extract from one of the dailies, since you seem to consider it necessary to your happiness, and since your trembling soul has found in it evidence of lukewarm loyalty on the part of the Collector—but candidly, now, don't you think you are in rather small business? I do, anyhow, though I do not wish to flatter you:

"*Battle of Bunker Hill.*—San Francisco, June 17, 1865. *Messrs. Editors: Why is it that on this day, the greatest of all in the annals of the rights of man—viz.: the Glorious Anniversary of the Battle of Bunker Hill*—our Great Ensign of Freedom does not appear on the Custom House? *Perhaps our worthy Collector is so busy Senator-making that it might have escaped his notice. You will be pleased to assign an excuse for the above official delinquency, and oblige*

A New England Mechanic"

Why was that published? I think it was simply to gratify a taste for literary pursuits which has suddenly broken out in the system of the artisan from New England; or perhaps he has an idea, somehow or other, in a general way, that it would be a showing of neat and yet not gaudy international politeness for Collectors of ports to hoist their flags in commemoration of British victories, (for the physical triumph was theirs, although we claim all the moral effect of a victory); or perhaps it struck him that "this day, the greatest of all *in the annals of the rights of man,*" (whatever that may mean, for it is a little too deep for me), was a fine, high-sounding expression, and yearned to get it off in print; or perhaps it occurred to him that "the Glorious Anniversary," and "our Great Ensign of Freedom," being new and startling figures of speech, would probably create something of a sensation if properly marshalled under the leadership of stunning capitals, and so he couldn't resist the temptation to trot them out in grand dress parade before the reading public; or perhaps, finally, he really *did* think the Collector's atrocious conduct partook of the character of a devilish "official delinquency," and imperatively called for explanation or "excuse." And still, after all this elaborate analysis, I am considerably "mixed" as to the actual motive for publishing that thing.

But observe how quibbling and fault-finding breed in a land of newspapers. Yesterday I had the good fortune to intercept the following bitter communication on its way to the office of a contemporary, and I am happy in being able to afford to the readers of the *Californian* the first perusal of it:

"Editors of the Flaming Loyalist: *What does it mean? The extraordinary conduct of Mr. John Doe, one of the highest Government officials among us, upon the anniversary of the battle of Bunker Hill—that day so inexpressibly dear to every loyal American heart—is matter of grave suspicion. It was observed (by those who have closely watched Mr. Doe's actions ever since he has been in office, and who have thought his professions of loyalty lacked the genuine ring,) that this man,* who has uniformly got drunk, heretofore, upon all the nation's great historical days, remained thoroughly sober upon the hallowed 17th of June. *Is not this significant? Was this the pardonable forgetfulness of a loyal officer, or rather, was it not the deliberate act of a malignant and a traitorous heart? You will be pleased to assign an excuse for the above official delinquency, and oblige.*

A Sentinel Agriculturist upon the National Watchtower"

Now isn't that enough to disgust any man with being an office-holder? Here is a drudging public servant who has always served his masters patiently and faithfully, and although there was nothing in his instructions requiring him to get drunk on national holidays, yet with an unselfishness, and an enlarged public spirit, and a gushing patriotism that did him infinite credit, he *did* always get as drunk as a loon on these occasions—ay, and even upon any occasion of minor importance when an humble effort on his part could shed additional lustre upon his country's greatness, never did he hesitate a moment to go and fill himself full of gin. Now observe how his splendid services have been appreciated—behold how quickly the remembrance of them hath passed away—mark how the tried servant has been rewarded. This grateful officer—this pure patriot—has been known to get drunk five hundred times in a year for the honor and glory of his country and his country's flag, and no man cried "Well done, thou good and faithful servant" —yet the very first time he ventures to remain sober on a battle anniversary (exhausted by the wear and tear of previous efforts, no doubt,) this spying "Agriculturist," who has deserted his onion-patch to perch himself upon the National Watch-Tower at the risk of breaking his meddlesome neck, discovers the damning fact that he is firm on his legs, and sings out: "He don't keep up his lick!—he's DISLOYAL!"

Oh, stuff! a public officer has a hard enough time of it, at best, without being constantly hauled over the coals for inconsequential and insignificant trifles. If you *must* find fault, go and ferret out something worth while to find fault with—if John Doe or the Collector neglect the actual business they are required by the Government to transact, impeach them. But pray allow them a little poetical license in the choice of occasions for getting drunk and hoisting the National flag. If the oriental artisan and the sentinel agriculturalist held the offices of these men, would they ever *attend to anything else* but the flag-flying and gin-soaking outward forms of patriotism and official industry?

June, 1865—*Californian.*

Emperor Norton dines regally at one of the magnificent free-lunch counters of the day, as Bummer and Lazarus look hungrily on. Norton was a merchant, who went mad after going bankrupt. He proclaimed himself "Norton I, Emperor of North America and Protector of Mexico." San Francisco indulged him in his madness. He roamed the town freely, inspecting his realm in a lordly way, levied small taxes on businessmen, which they obligingly paid, and issued stately proclamations, which the newspapers solemnly published.

Bummer and Lazarus have been sometimes described as having been Emperor Norton's dogs, but they were not; it is possible that Jump's cartoon may have engendered that notion. Bummer, a black Newfoundland of a sort, with a white stripe, first came to the city's attention one day in 1861 when he slew an epic number of rats that had swarmed out of an excavation outside the Blue Wing Saloon. A dog of great dignity and presence, as well as valor, he patrolled a regular beat down Montgomery Street, where he would present himself at restaurants to be fed. Lazarus was, as Twain wrote, Bummer's "obsequious vassal"—a cur whom Bummer rescued during a fight one day and who thereafter attached himself to Bummer and went everywhere with him.

[In the following three articles Twain perpetrates a hoax, indignantly exposes himself, and then sentences himself to punishment. He would seem to be playing on the reputation his "Petrified Man" and "Bloody Massacre" stories brought him as a shameless manufacturer of hoaxes. Though most bibliographers include these articles as by Twain, I should mention that in a 1964 scholarly article Lawrence A. Melder asserted his belief that these were written not by Twain but by other staff members of the *Golden Era*, enjoying an extended in-house joke.]

SMITH BROWN JONES

A NEW CONTRIBUTOR

We take pleasure in announcing to our readers that we have secured the services of the eminent Smith B. Jones, Esq., whose arrival by the last steamer has already been announced, and who will henceforth contribute weekly to our columns.

Mr. Jones needs no introduction from us. His brilliant effusions have charmed the *literati* of both Europe and America, and are familiar to all. Although the literary services of Mr. Jones have been procured by us only at a large pecuniary outlay—as will be seen by the subjoined correspondence—yet we heartily congratulate ourselves as well as our readers on the acquisition of our new contributor.

On Tuesday last, we addressed Mr. Jones the following note:

Editorial Rooms *Golden Era*,
San Francisco, June 27th, 1865.

Smith Brown Jones, Esq., Consequental Hotel. Dear Sir:—Seeing your name in the list of arrivals by the steamship *Sacramento*, we take the liberty of addressing you at this early moment, to secure, if possible, the productions of your pen for the columns of the *Era*.

Pardon us for the business tenor of this note, and for any seeming intrusion upon your privacy. We are aware that the immense literary labors to which you have been subjected for years past have somewhat impaired your health, and that you have come to our golden shores to seek, in quiet and retirement, that rest so much needed; but our standing as the first literary paper of the Pacific coast—if not of the world—demands of us that we should not allow the opportunity to pass unheeded.

What we ask is but a mere dash of your pen. Our readers will be grateful for a weekly contribution—half a column or more in length—to suit your own convenience of course—and for which we will be glad to pay you at the rate of two hundred and fifty dollars per week.

We hope other engagements will not preclude your acceptance of our offer. Should our terms not meet your approval, please bind yourself to no periodical until we have had an interview.

Very Respectfully,
Editors *Golden Era.*

In reply, we received the following somewhat incomprehensible production, which, however, we place before our readers, conscious that what flows from the pen of the gifted Jones—however erratic—must be esteemed as beyond price.

Consequental Hotel,
San Francisco, June 28th, 1865.

Editors *Golden Era*—Gentlemen: In reply to your kind and flattering note, allow me to say at once that I accept your offer of the Senatorship. I do it advisedly, and without fear of contradiction.

Hon. John C——s says, "close at once with them!" John is a friend of mine—came out on the steamer—and, as I before remarked, advised me to appoint you next Senator—no—I mean you remarked me to advise you to appoint him in succession to Senator to be me. I'm afraid that is not quite clear. The fact is, I'm laboring under a slight indisposition, arising from change of water, I presume, although I've taken but very little. It's funny about that water. I felt the change before we got in sight of the Heads. C——s affects me in the same way, too. I mean, he affects the water in the same way. No, that's not it, either. What I mean to say is, the water affects him. I know it does. Said he, with tears in his eyes, "Jones, I love you. You are the apple of my eye—may we always be friends! Jones, vote for me!"

I assured him I would—that I always had from infancy. Shook my hand affectionately and asked me to go below. Immediately descended to his state room, in second cabin, and took a glass of lemonade at my expense. Talked of old times—of our adventures on the voyage—last day board ship—grew convivial, and took a glass of lemonade for which I paid. Said he was our only sober Senator, and sent for some lemonade—kindly allowed me to pay for it. Went on deck. John said, "There Jones! Can you see the Heads?"

Felt annoyed—thought John was too familiar—was indignant—rebuked him. "Lemonade doesn't affect me in that way, of course I can see ahead!"

Think that went home. John smiled sarcastic—said, "Don't mean can you see ahead,—but can you see the Heads?"

Told him "couldn't see anything else unless I stood on tip-toe, or went on upper deck"—which Cap'n didn't allow to second-class passengers.

Saw at once lemonade affected my friend—laughed immoderately—said I had made a joke. Abjured me above all things to vote for him. Called my attention to Lime Point. Said he was concerned in the swindle—or at least he thought 'twas him. Said United States wanted to buy Lime Point—owners anxious to sell—in fact very anxious to sell—big price—big thing—pulled wool over U.S.—U.S. agreed to buy. Then he and Broderick—but especially he—thought so at least—stepped in—advised U.S. not to buy—stood by U.S. like a brother. U.S. backed out—didn't buy—saved millions—didn't make a cent out of himself—didn't, 'pon his word.

Asked me if I saw Meiggs' wharf on right—Meiggs his friend, but unfortunate. Said that was Alcatraz on my left. Immediately turned to gentleman on my left—Mr. Alcatraz—was happy to meet him—sorry friend John hadn't introduced him before. Think gentleman on left had a pain in stomach. Said intoxicated beast made him sick. Looked for intoxicated beast—didn't see him—saw John—John looked silly—asked me if I was sick, and if I didn't want to go ashore—said he'd introduce Gov. Low to me—Gov. was friend of his—anxious to see him—I could vote for him, but he was tricky. Thought we'd better take a hack and he could dumfoozle Gov. every time.

Called hack. Hack said twenty dollars. Told him I'd see him first! John said to hush—said he'd make contract with hack—was great on contracts. Then we made contract. Hack said where did he want to go. Told him yes, we would, and how did he know it? Man said we would take him, ten dollars and the Russ House to us for three trunks—best carriage in State—both white—had preference for fast carriages that were white—always drove 'em.

Told man ten horses too much, would he give us fifteen. Man with carriage impertinent. Think man intoxicated. Said he was no member of Congress, and had no poor relations. Know man was intoxicated. Tried to be funny—said I was drunk. John asked him to sing—carriage and I was to come in heavy on the chorus. Man failed to come to time. Said he couldn't sing except on flute. All of him laughed—thought he was funny carriage—fact was, all six of him too drunk.

John said 'twas time to go home—but would have one more game—ten cent ante and his deal. Low's chance wasn't worth a copper—he'd taken his straight. Also said he was sick—wished he hadn't come, and asked policeman if he was on it and to beware of bowl—intoxication was best policy, and he'd been a missionary once himself. Policeman very attentive. John wanted policeman to sing. Had great difficulty in getting policeman in carriage. John felt bad—wanted to know where Gov. Low was—said policeman was dearest friend—gave policeman his spectacles. Began to think John was 'toxicated. Said never min' ole boy—may be happy yet. Wanted to know if Russ Hotel dead-headed me—didn't cost him cent—asked policeman to dine with him. Said if I paid, I'd better go to Consequental Hotel—chock up house—and pay greenbacks. Said he was glad the war was over and would call policeman Gen. McDowell and was glad to see him.

Gen. McDowell—I mean policeman—borrowed two and half of me and said I was all right. Think he had been drinking some, but apologised to him. Consequental House arrived—said good-bye to John—John wept bitterly, and I am here, some sickly, but

Truly Yours,
S. B. Jones

July 2, 1865—*Golden Era.*

S. BROWNE JONES

AN ASTOUNDING FRAUD PRACTICED UPON US.—THE EDITOR OF THE "BOHEMIAN" THE GUILTY PARTY.—CRIMINAL PROCEEDINGS INSTITUTED AGAINST HIM.

In our issue of last week we announced to our readers that we had made an engagement with S. Browne Jones Esq., for weekly contributions to the *Era,* and gave the correspondence that passed between the editors of this paper and that gentleman.

We have since discovered that the answer published over the signature of Mr. Jones was written by Mr. Mark Twain, the Editor of the *Bohemian,* who by accident obtained information of the contents of our note to Mr. Jones, and basely took advantage of the knowledge so acquired, to not only impose upon us, but to injure the reputation of several gentlemen of high position. Mr. Mark Twain may think that he has done something very funny. We shall endeavor to teach him, however, that such practical jokes cannot be played upon us with impunity. We intend to follow the matter up.

Immediately upon the discovery of this imposition, we had Mr. Mark Twain placed under arrest. He is now at liberty, on bail. His examination will take place sometime this week. We shall place before our readers, in our next issue, a full report of the proceedings, taken down by one of our corps of phonographic reporters.

The following note from Mr. Jones will be of interest under the circumstances

Consequental Hotel,
San Francisco, July 5th, 1865.

Editors *Golden Era*—Gentlemen: I have the pleasure of acknowledging the receipt of your note of the 27th ultimo, and should have replied long before this, had my health permitted.

When I assure you that this is the first day that I have been able to leave my room since my arrival in California, you will be able to imagine my astonishment upon seeing in your issue of the 2d inst., a most singular communication purporting to have come from me.

Your well-known character as journalists at once forbids the idea that you have taken the liberty of using my name in an improper manner, and I am therefore led to believe that some one has imposed upon you and abused my confidence. I regret this from the fact that it not only places both you and myself in a ridiculous light, but also tends to bring odium upon a gentleman, whom I have every reason to esteem—a gentleman whose character in private life is untarnished—one who has passed through the seething corruptions of public life and has come out undefiled—one whom his most bitter party antagonists confess to be without blemish, and who has so nobly and so zealously represented the interests of your glorious Golden State at our Nation's Capital. Add to all these virtues the remembrance of many personal acts of kindness, and you can appreciate my distress upon reading the communication referred to.

I am happy to add, however, that I have traced out the impostor. To certain circumstances that occurred shortly after the receipt of your note, and which have been recalled to my memory, I am indebted for the discovery. But here allow me the use of your columns to correct an injustice done in the moment of excitement at seeing my name so unceremoniously dragged before the public, and which I fear has caused a worthy gentleman of this community serious annoyance. An hour or two after I had received your note, my friend Mr. Conness called at my apartments, as usual, to inquire after my health, and brought with him a Mr. Pixley—a gentleman of no little distinction in your city, I have since ascertained—and introduced him to me as his friend, stating that Mr. Pixley was an aspirant for Senatorial honors and would be glad of my support.

Informed Mr. Pixley that, owing to my recent arrival, I was necessarily ignorant upon the local politics of the State, and hence could not consistently enter into the approaching Senatorial contest. That otherwise, the mere fact of his endorsement by my friend Conness, was sufficient recommendation to me, and that I should have been pleased to render him any aid in my power.

Mr. Pixley, I thought, felt somewhat piqued; at any rate, there was an awkward silence that I at once proceeded to overcome by changing the subject, and my eye happening to fall on your communication, I passed it to Mr. Conness and asked his advice.

At this moment, a servant presented a card and immediately ushered in a gentleman, whom I requested to be seated for a moment. Mr. Conness read your letter aloud and advised me to accept your offer at once, saying that he had been a constant reader of the *Era* since it was established, and that he frequently contributed to its columns. Other topics of conversation followed rapidly, until Mr. Conness and his friend Pixley took their leave.

Now, when I saw the absurd production attributed to me, in your paper, on Sunday last, it immediately occurred to me that Mr. Pixley was the only person besides Mr. Conness and myself, who was aware of the contents of the note you addressed me, and that he must have written the article referred to, and I at once concluded that a petty spirit of revenge for the refusal of my support to his political schemes, prompted him to bring me into public ridicule by means of the imposition practised upon you. I was all the more confirmed in this view of the matter upon calling to mind his irritated manner during the latter portion of our interview. Accordingly I addressed him a note, expressing in terms not to be mistaken my indignation at his conduct, and demanding an explanation or the satisfaction due a gentleman. Mr. Pixley replied immediately through our mutual friend, Mr. Conness, who hastened to my apartments with flushed face, and assured me that I had made some terrible mistake, that Mr. Pixley was a gentleman of high tone, and far above such a dastardly proceeding, and hinting that he thought I had shown undue haste, and called upon me to substantiate my charges against Mr. Pixley.

I immediately called the attention of Mr. Conness to the circumstances above related; thinking, of course, that he would agree with me in attributing the authorship of the obnoxious communication to Mr. Pixley.

He replied: "You seem to forget there was a fourth person present at that interview. I have occasion to mention it, as, the very next day, that individual called and desired me to lend my name to some swindling operation in petroleum stocks, and when I refused, threatened to 'show me up.' It is to him we are indebted for the scandalous letter in the *Era.*"

It was immediately clear to me that I had deeply wronged Mr. Pixley by my hasty and unjust conclusions. The presence of a fourth person at the interview had entirely escaped my memory.

I begged Mr. Conness to make—in my name—the most ample apologies for my conduct, and to offer any reparation to Mr. Pixley. The latter gentleman—to his honor be it said—was so magnanimous as to perceive the error into which I had fallen, and desired—as public mention had been made of his name—that I should make an explanation through your columns.

Now to the real author of this silly communication.

After Mr. Conness and Mr. Pixley had left my apartments, I gave my attention to the individual who had entered as Mr. Conness was about to read your note. This person—whose card I have unfortunately mislaid—gave his name as Swain or Twain—the latter I think—Mr. Marcus Twain—and represented himself to be the editor of the *Bohemian* newspaper, and said that he had called to solicit contributions for which he would pay liberally.

In reply to some questions as to the general character of the *Bohemian,* he said that paper was a religious journal, now in the forty-third year of its existence, and had a circulation throughout the world. I expressed some surprise at this, as I had not even heard the paper mentioned before, although I thought myself well posted in the literary world, but he assured me such was the fact.

He said he had necessarily overheard the contents of your letter, and that he would not be able to pay me so large a sum as was offered by you, as the *Bohemian* endeavored to live up to its principles, and gave away much in charity, and, therefore, had to depend to a great extent upon the charity of its contributors.

Mr. Twain suggested that I take as a topic for my introductory article to the *Bohemian,* "Death, Hell, and the Grave"; stating that owing to the evil days into which we have fallen, many of the readers of the *Bohemian* had backslidden and needed to be frightened back into the walls of righteousness; and that a few words of timely warning from a person of my known ability would help on the good work.

With shame I confess that I was completely deceived by this plausible young man, with his sanctimonious air and conversation, and I told him that I would give his application serious consideration.

I have since ascertained that the *Bohemian* is not a religious paper; and the bold impudence of this Mr. Marcus Twain astounds me. It seems he is in some way connected with that newspaper.

I do not know what course you intend to pursue. Be assured I shall not let this matter rest here. I intend to prosecute this Mr. Marcus Twain, and have already entered a complaint against him in your municipal Court.

In closing this lengthy but unavoidable explanation, I cannot but express my surprise that gentlemen of your well known information and literary attainments should have been for a moment deceived by this glaring imposition, and can only attribute it to the hurry and confusion attendant on the issue of a journal of the size and circulation of the *Era.*

I must also add my regrets at being unable to appear before the good people of your city on the Fourth. The committee on the celebration waited on me and honored me with a request to deliver the Oration at the Metropolitan theatre. I thankfully accepted their kind offer and prepared the Oration, but on Monday last I was so unwell that I gave my manuscript to John H. Dwinelle, Esq., who kindly volunteered to read it for me. I here return my thanks to Mr. Dwinelle; his masterly delivery added much to the beauty of the Oration.

Allow me to say Messrs. editors, that I shall accept your offer with thanks, and shall be happy to be numbered among your contributors.

I see you have fallen into the common error in regard to my name. I spell the Brown with a final e, and never write my Christian name in full, I am,

Very Respectfully,
S. Browne Jones.

July 9, 1865—*Golden Era.*

S. BROWNE JONES

FULL REPORT OF THE PROCEEDINGS UPON THE EXAMINATION OF MARK TWAIN ON THE CHARGE OF FRAUD, IN THE POLICE COURT. THE DEFENDANT FOUND GUILTY AND SENTENCED TO FORTY-EIGHT HOURS IN THE CITY PRISON.

Probably the largest and most respectable audience that was ever seen in San Francisco on a similar occasion, met at the Police Court Room, on Thursday last, to witness the proceedings in the examination of Mr. Mark Twain, one of the editors of the *Bohemian,* upon the charge of unlawfully and maliciously defrauding the editors and proprietors of this paper, by writing, and transmitting to them for publication, a communication purporting to come from the pen of the eminent S. Browne Jones, Esq., by means of which the proprietors of this paper were placed in a false position before the public, and ridicule brought upon S. Browne Jones, Esq., and other distinguished gentlemen of this community.

Mr. Mark Twain, who, upon giving bond, had been released from arrest, appeared with his usual unblushing effrontery, and bold-faced impudence, attended by his counsel U.S. District Attorney Delos Freshwater,—who, it is said, writes nearly all of the editorial matter of the *Bohemian,* as well as the *News Note,* and *Philosophic Mining Press.*

We do not know but that we ought to do the *Bohemian* people the justice to say that they are heartily ashamed of the conduct of Mr. Mark Twain, and have endeavored to induce us to drop the prosecution of this matter. Even Mr. Mark Twain himself has tried —in an indifferent way, it is true—to buy us off. We rejected his offer with scorn. We deemed it due our readers, as well as ourselves, that this matter should be thoroughly investigated and the evil doers be brought to justice.

Below we give a full report of the testimony elicited on the examination, taken down by one of our efficient corps of phonographic reporters.

The Prosecuting Attorney was assisted by Messrs. Hall McCannister, Samuel M. Williamson and John W. Dwindle, who had been retained in the case of Mr. S. Browne Jones, Esq.

Among the spectators, we observed the Hon. Schuyler Colfax and party, who, being personal friends of Mr. S. Browne Jones, Esq., took great interest in the proceedings.

S. Browne Jones, Esq., was the first witness called on the part of the prosecution, and testified as follows:

"Am devoted to literature. Have been in California about two weeks, only. Arrived on the steamship *Sacramento.* A few days after my arrival, I received a note from the Editors of the *Golden Era,* requesting me to write for that paper. The note read as follows—[published in full in our issue of July 2d.—Eds *Era.*] I was unwell at the time; confined to my apartments. While holding the offer under consideration, my friends, Conness and Pixley, called on me. Mentioned the matter to them. While Mr. Conness was reading the note, the defendant, Mark Twain, called. Know the defendant at the bar to be the same person who called. Identify him by his sanctimonious air; also the strawberry mark on his left eyelid. Mark on his nose is not a strawberry mark. Don't know the facts, but should think that resulted from drinking. The simon-pure strawberry marks are usually found under the left arm—some exceptions. Think defendant's true name is not Mark Twain. Have been told that it is one of many *aliases.* Can't say of my own knowledge.

"No one else was present at the time referred to, except Mr. Conness, Mr. Pixley, the defendant, and myself. No one else knew of the contents of the note.

"Defendant said he had overheard the contents of the letter. He wanted me to write for the *Bohemian.* Said he was editor of the paper."

On Cross Examination:—" 'Twas about eleven o'clock in the forenoon when Mr. Mark Twain called. I had never seen him before. I had not been drinking. Seldom drink anything stronger than raw brandy.

"The mark on defendant's left eyelid is a true strawberry mark. Know all about strawberry marks. Wrote a treatise on them once.

When Edward Everett and I wrote for the *New York Ledger,* at $10,000.00 an article, we had frequent use for strawberry marks. Used them in historical characters. I made researches on the subject. Don't know of my own knowledge that defendant is addicted to drinking."

One of the Editors of the *Golden Era* was the next witness called. He testified that as soon as the arrival of Mr. S. Browne Jones, Esq., was announced, he addressed him the note before referred to. "Received a reply next evening. Did not read it until it was in type. Thought 'twas singular that Mr. Jones should write such a letter. The *Era* was just going to press. Didn't notice particularly the person who brought the manuscript to the *Era* office. 'Twas a boy. Think he is employed in the *Bohemian* office. Can't swear to it.

"Am familiar with Mark Twain's handwriting. It's very scrawly—very much like this (referring to manuscript in question). Can't swear that this is Mr. Mark Twain's writing.

"Defendant was at one time employed by the proprietors of the *Era* to compile and condense news items. Never trusted him with anything original, except obituary notices. He had a morbid desire to write such notices. He overdid the matter. Had to drop him. Defendant had three volumes of manuscript obituary notices. His object was, I believe, to have one ready for any emergency. The names of the deceased, as well as the dates, were left blank, ready to be filled in at a moment's notice."

Mr. Conness was then called, as witness for the prosecution.

"Called on my friend S. Browne Jones, Esq., at Consequental Hotel, in this city and county (in reply to a question of Mr. Louderback's).

"Mr. Jones had just received a note from the editors of the *Golden Era.* Saw the note. Read it aloud. While I was reading, defendant came in. Defendant must have heard me read the note. There was no one else present except Mr. Pixley.

"Recognize the defendant as the same person who subsequently called on me and desired me to lend my name to a Petroleum stock operation. He offered me five hundred shares of stock to induce me to become a trustee. He said 'twas a big thing, could make lots of money if I would only go in. I refused to have anything to do with it. Defendant said that was 'played out,' for he knew I 'was on it.' Threatened to 'blow on me,' or something to that effect."

On Cross Examination:—"I might have drank with defendant. Don't remember. Don't make it a rule to drink every hour. Am a Senator. Hope to be re-elected. Low's chances for succeeding McDougall are not good. Low wouldn't do as I told him. Knew he'd slip up. I have nothing to do with the *Alta* newspaper. I appointed Perkins Postmaster. He does about as I direct; if he didn't, he'd lose his head. 'Tis not true that he edits the *Bulletin.*

"I have nothing to do with the *Flag* now. Did at one time. Wrote all the political articles. I paid for the use of the columns. They wanted more; so they oppose me now. The paper has no influence; has not, since I ceased writing for it. Would like to see my friend Pixley, or Sargent, succeed McDougall."

Mr. Pixley was then sworn.

Said he called with Mr. Conness on Mr. S. Browne Jones, Esq. Was anxious to obtain his support. He was before the people as candidate for the U.S. Senate. Hadn't a doubt but that he'd be elected. Mr. Jones thought that he ought not to interfere, as he had come to this coast so recently.

"While Mr. Conness and myself were at Mr. S. Browne Jones' apartments, defendant came in. Mr. Conness was reading a letter from the publishers of some literary paper, asking Mr. S. Browne Jones to write for them. Don't remember the name of the paper. Had my mind on other things. Was thinking of the Senatorship. Think the paper was the *Golden Era;* am not certain. Have written for that paper myself.

"Don't know much about defendant. He offered to come out for me in the *Bohemian* for a consideration. Among other things, I was to pay for his drinks at the Bank Exchange during the campaign. I paid the bill for one month. 'Twas very large. He had not come out for me according to promise, and I refused to pay more. That was about two months ago."

Cross-Examined:—"It is some time since I wrote anything for the *Golden Era.* The last contribution I made to that paper was a pastoral poem in thirty-nine stanzas of eight lines each, entitled *'Pixley and his Mule.'* Would like to read it; 'twould not take long.

Shall be pleased to send the court a copy with compliments of the author.

"At present I write the 'funny' articles in the *News Note* and *Philosophical Mining Press,* and also the communications in the *Bulletin* entitled, 'Personal Reminiscences of the War, by a California Lady.' Edited the *Flag* at one time. Never had a contract to supply dogs to Gridley's Hog Ranch. Am still a candidate for the U.S. Senate. Know I will be elected. Don't care to say how much I paid for the place."

The Prosecution here rested, and Defendant's Counsel called Mr. C. H. W. Inigo to testify to the good character of the defendant.

"Witness knew defendant. Had been associated with him on the *Bohemian* newspaper. Defendant had a good character as far as he knew. Was generous to a fault. Knew the latter fact of his own knowledge. On one occasion he borrowed my best cotton shirt to go to the opera, and had it sent to the laundry before he returned it; he also paid one half the bill.

"He can play draw poker equal to any man. Consider myself some at draw poker, but he can discount me every time. He won those sleeve buttons that he has on from me at draw poker. We are both interested in the Nicholson pavement. The defendant does not write the 'Answers to Correspondents' in the *Bohemian.* I write them myself—that is—the funny ones. Never wrote anything that wasn't funny."

At this stage of the proceedings, the Defendant's Counsel arose and said that after consultation, his client had concluded to withdraw his plea of not guilty, and would throw himself on the mercy of the Court. Whereupon the Court required the Defendant to appear for sentence on Saturday, July 15th.

On Saturday morning, the Court said it had carefuly reviewed the evidence, and taking into consideration all the facts, and it being the first offense charged against the Defendant, and also taking into consideration Defendant's tender years, he had concluded to punish this first offense lightly—more so, perhaps, than it deserved—and admonished the Defendant to beware of a second departure from the paths of honor and rectitude. And then the

Court proceeded to sentence him to forty-eight hours in the City Prison, on bread and water.

The Defendant seemed to have come to a sense of his position, for he shed tears profusely.

We hope this will be a lesson to him that will not have to be repeated. S. Browne Jones

July 16, 1865—*Golden Era.*

[The earthquake which prompted Twain to these dire predictions and Ed Jump to the cartoon reproduced on page 126 was the one which occurred on October 8, 1865. Though the shock was a severe one, the actual damage done was not very consequential. The principal damage, according to a report by Dr. John B. Trask of the California Academy of Sciences, was "the demolition of parts of the parapet walls erected above roofs . . . and fracture of walls in insecure buildings and heavy buildings erected on made lands of the city front."]

EARTHQUAKE ALMANAC

At the instance of several friends who feel a boding anxiety to know beforehand what sort of phenomena we may expect the elements to exhibit during the next month or two, and who have lost all confidence in the various patent medicine almanacs, because of the unaccountable reticence of those works concerning the extraordinary event of the 8th inst., I have compiled the following almanac expressly for this latitude:

Oct. 17.—Weather hazy; atmosphere murky and dense. An expression of profound melancholy will be observable upon most countenances.

Oct. 18.—Slight earthquake. Countenances grow more melancholy.

Oct. 19.—Look out for rain. It will be absurd to look in for it. The general depression of spirits increased.

Oct. 20.—More weather.

Oct. 21.—Same.

Oct. 22.—Light winds, perhaps. If they blow, it will be from the "east'ard, or the nor'ard, or the west'ard, or the suth'ard," or from some general direction approximating more or less to these points of the compass or otherwise. Winds are uncertain—more especially when they blow from whence they cometh and whither they listeth. N. B.—Such is the nature of winds.

Oct. 23.—Mild, balmy earthquakes.

Oct. 24.—Shaky.

Oct. 25.—Occasional shakes, followed by light showers of bricks and plastering. N. B.—Stand from under.

Oct. 26.—Considerable phenomenal atmospheric foolishness. About this time expect more earthquakes, but do not look out for them, on account of the bricks.

Oct. 27.—Universal despondency, indicative of approaching disaster. Abstain from smiling, or indulgence in humorous conversation, or exasperating jokes.

Oct. 28.—Misery, dismal forebodings and despair. Beware of all discourse—a joke uttered at this time would produce a popular outbreak.

Oct. 29.—Beware!

Oct. 30.—Keep dark!

Oct. 31.—Go slow!

Nov. 1.—Terrific earthquake. This is the great earthquake month. More stars fall and more worlds are slathered around carelessly and destroyed in November than in any other month of the twelve.

EARTH QUA
SAN FRANCIS
SALOON
SHAVING

TIMES,
1865.
1865

Nov. 2.—Spasmodic but exhilarating earthquakes, accompanied by occasional showers of rain, and churches and things.

Nov. 3.—Make your will.

Nov. 4.—Sell out.

Nov. 5.—Select your "last words." Those of John Quincy Adams will do, with the addition of a syllable, thus; "This is the last of earthquakes."

Nov. 6.—Prepare to shed this mortal coil.

Nov. 7.—Shed.

Nov. 8.—The sun will rise as usual, perhaps; but if he does he will doubtless be staggered some to find nothing but a large round hole eight thousand miles in diameter in the place where he saw this world serenely spinning the day before.

Oct. 22, 1865—*Golden Era* (as reprinted from the San Francisco *Dramatic Chronicle*).

[*Arrah-na-Pogue,* the hit show of the 1865 season, was written by Twain's friend Charles Webb.]

THE BALLAD INFLICTION

It is bound to come! There is no help for it. I smell it afar off—I see the signs in the air! Every day and every hour of every day I grow more and more nervous, for with every minute of waning time the dreadful infliction comes nearer and nearer in its inexorable march! In another week, maybe, all San Francisco will be singing "Wearing of the Green!" I know it. I have suffered before, and I know the symptoms. This holds off long, but it is partly that the calamity may gather irresistible worrying-power, and partly because it is harder to learn than Chinese. But that is all the worse; for when the people do learn it they will learn it bad—and terrible will be the distress it will bring upon the community. A year ago "Johnny came marching home!" That song was sung by everybody, in every key, in every locality, at all hours of the day and night, and always out of tune. It sent many unoffending persons to the Stockton asylum. There was no stopping the epidemic, and so it had to be permitted to run its course and wear itself out. Short was our respite, and then a still more malignant distemper broke out in the midst of this harried and suffering community. It was "You'll not forget me, mother, mother, mother, mother!" with an ever-accumulating aggravation of expression upon each successive "mother." The fire-boys sat up all night to sing it; and bands of sentimental stevedores and militia soldiers patroled the streets and howled its lugubrious strains. A passion for serenading attacked the youth of the city, and they sang it under verandahs in the back streets until the dogs and cats destroyed their voices in unavailing efforts to lay the devilish spirit that was driving happiness from their hearts. Finally there came a season of repose, and the community slowly recovered from the effects of the musical calamity. The respite was not long. In an unexpected moment they were attacked, front and rear, by a new enemy—"When we were marching through Georgia!" Tongue cannot tell what we suffered while this frightful disaster was upon us. Young misses sang it to the guitar and the piano; young men sang it to the banjo and the fiddle; the un-bloodstained soldier yelled it with enthusiasm as he marched through the imaginary swamps and cotton plantations of the drill-room; the firemen sang it as they trundled their engines home from conflagrations; and the hated serenader tortured it with his dam-ned accordeon. Some of us survived, and some have gone the old road to a haven of rest at Stockton, where the wicked cease from troubling and the popular songs are not allowed. For the space of four weeks the survivors have been happy.

But as I have said before, it is bound to come! *Arrah-na-Pogue* is breeding a song that will bedeck some mountain with new-made graves! In another week we shall be "Wearing of the Green," and in a fortnight some will be wearing of the black in consequence. Three repetitions of this song will produce lunacy, and five will kill—it is that much more virulent than its predecessors. People are finding it hard to learn, but when they get it learned they will find it potent for harm. It is Wheatleigh's song. He sings it in *Arrah-na-Pogue,* with a sprig of shamrock in his hat. Wheatleigh sings it with such aggravated solemnity as to make an audience long for the grave. It is doled out slowly, and every note settles deliberately to its place on one's heart like a solid iceberg—and by the time it is finished the temperature of the theatre has fallen to twenty degrees. Think what a dead-cold winter we shall have here when this Arctic funeral melody becomes popular! Think of it being performed at midnight, in lonely places, upon the spirit-depressing accordeon! Think of being driven to blow your brains out under such circumstances, and then dying to the grave-yard cadences of "Wearing of the Green!" But it is bound to come, and we may as well bow our heads and submit with such degree of Christian resignation as we are able to command.

Nov. 4, 1865—*Californian* (as reprinted from *Territorial Enterprise*).

[The short items which follow are from three "Letters from San Francisco" which Twain, to eke out his meagre funds, dashed off for the *Napa County Reporter* during November, 1865. He did them in the most cursory manner, but I think them worth including to show Twain's touch manifesting itself even in so routine a piece as the reporting of a collision between a buggy and a streetcar or a petty trial of some insignificant fellow named Summerville, who had been accused of insulting schoolgirls "who were strangers to him."]

SINGULAR ACCIDENT

A collision occurred yesterday at the corner of Bush and Montgomery Streets, between a buggy and a street car, which resulted in the almost total destruction of the latter, and the partial annihilation of the former. The car was passing slowly down Montgomery Street, and the assaulting vehicle charged furiously down Bush and struck it fairly amidships. The pole of the buggy passed clear through to the opposite side of the car, and the horses accompanied it part of the distance. One lady sustained a fracture of the thigh, and received other injuries, chiefly about the head. It was also the opinion of the physicians that she was hurt internally. She was sitting on the further side of the car, as was also another lady, whose wrist was severely bruised. The persons who sat on the side entered by the horses, were not hurt. If the car had been set up as a barricade to stop an avalanche, it could hardly have been more completely wrecked.

P.S.—Midnight. The lady above-mentioned as being so badly injured, is thought to be dying. It appears the horses knocked her down and stepped on her.

Nov. 11, 1865—*Napa County Reporter.*

A DANIEL COME TO JUDGMENT

Judge Pratt refuses to divorce Mary C. Wentworth from her husband, Daniel D. Wentworth. I didn't know Mary, but she has my sympathies, anyhow, because she appears to be out of luck. But just on her account, if Daniel has made her unhappy, I wish he could be thrown into a den of wild beasts, like the prophet, his namesake, and give some lion a chance to bite a piece out of him about as big as a dog. It would be a lesson for him; and besides it would be a good thing for the lion.

Nov. 11, 1865—*Napa County Reporter.*

THE "ADDISONIANS"

The "Addisonian Lectures" are in full blast. This is a sort of doctrinal free fight between all kinds and denominations of ministers of the gospel, but I do not know what is the grand result they are striving to arrive at. I do know one thing, though—too many preachers crowd together to hear those lectures. It is to the last degree dangerous to concentrate so much incendiary material under one roof. What produced the great earthquake of the 8th October? What was the earthquake after? It was after the Methodist Conference. And if this thing goes on much longer, another one will come along and shake those Addisonians out of their shirts.

Nov. 11, 1865—*Napa County Reporter.*

AMUSEMENTS

I stopped in at two of the theatres to-night. At the Academy of Music, the play was the *Unequal Match*—the principal characters by the new star, Miss Thorne, Mr. Setchell and Mr. Wall. The latter is an acquisition from New York. I remained until the heroine had got into a good deal of trouble on account of her husband going off with another woman, and then I went off myself, to the Metropolitan, and left her to skirmish out of it the best way she could.—I expect she will come out all right. She will be at the box office after her regular salary Saturday night, no doubt. I will collect it for her myself, though, if her bereavement makes her indifferent to it. If I had a wife and she should go off with another man, I would go and collect that other man's salary and take things easy.

At the Metropolitan they were playing *Arrah-na-Pogue* as usual—forty-fifth night.

At Maguire's Opera House Bandman was playing Hamlet again. He ought to stick to it. He plays no other part half so well, except that of "Narcisse."

Nov. 11, 1865—*Napa County Reporter.*

BENKERT COMETH!

The papers announce that Geo. F. Benkert, an eminent pianist of Philadelphia, is on his way out here to give us some concerts. Now, don't you know that fellow will be mighty popular in California? Certainly he will. That is, if he is the same man who makes the boots. The boys all like those Benkert boots, and they will patronize their manufacturer's concerts liberally. Up in the mining towns they will just take it for granted that it is the boot-making Benkert, unless they are specially notified that it is not, and they will go to the concerts reflecting thus: "Dang this feller, I like his boots, and so I'll give him a hyste with his music."—And I think it will astonish this Benkert some, in the mining camps, to look across the top of his piano, and see the feet of his male patrons, propped on the backs of the benches, and long gleaming rows of brand-new hob-nailed Benkert boots staring him in the face! The boys will naturally hit upon this method of paying him a delicate and appreciative compliment.

Nov. 23, 1865—*Napa County Reporter.*

WEBB'S BENEFIT

The Academy of Music was well filled on Monday night, the occasion being the benefit of C. H. Webb, author of the new burlesque, *Arrah-na-Pogue.* I believe no play written on the Coast has paid the author as much coin as Mr. Webb has made out of this. During the interval between the pieces, Mr. Setchele read a humorous letter from Webb, which was received with hearty laughter, and then followed it up with a speech which was kindly received, until the orator ventured to branch out into a fine flight of eloquence; the audience would not stand that. The venerable expression, "through storm and sunshine," delivered with some little elocutionary flourish, evoked a burst of laughter which swept the house like a tornado. Now isn't it infamous that a professed humorist can never attempt anything fine but people will at once imagine there is a joke about it somewhere, and laugh accordingly. I *did* once see an audience fooled by a humorist, though, or at least badly perplexed. An actress at the Opera House was playing the part of a houseless, friendless, persecuted and heart-broken young girl, and had so wrought upon the audience with her distress, that many were in tears. To heighten the effect, the playwright had put into the mouth of an humble character, the words—"Poor thing, how she sighs!" Mr. Barry delivered these with touching pathos—so far so good—but he could not resist the temptation to add, in an undertone, "Ah me, how she sighs!—if she keeps on increasing her size this way, she'll oversize her grief eventually and die, poor creature!" The sorrowing maiden let her sad face droop gently behind her hand, and Mr. Barry assumed an air of severe and inflexible gravity, and so the audience dared venture nothing further than to look exceedingly uncertain. One irreverent man in the corner did ejaculate "Oh, geewhillikens!" in a subdued tone of dissent, but he received no encouragement from the perplexed audience, and he pushed the matter no further.

Dec. 2, 1865—*Napa County Reporter.*

WRETCHED SUMMERVILLE

John Summerville pleaded guilty to two charges of insulting school girls, yesterday, "who were strangers to him," as the *Bulletin* remarks, whereby it is meant to be intimated, I suppose, that the offense would not have been so aggravating if the girls had been personal friends of John Summerville. This man has been punished several times for his species of meanness, but it does not seem to teach him any better.—Some people never do learn anything. Now a case in point is furnished in that old newspaper anecdote of the boy who could not understand the phrase, "polite attentions.'' The teacher explained it to him elaborately, but it was of no use—it oversized his calibre. Finally, the teacher simplified it and put a plain case to him, thus: ''Suppose I were to take your sister to the circus, and then to the saloon, and give her ice cream, etc., what would you say?'' And the bright boy answered cheerfully, ''I'd say, bully for you!'' John Summerville will keep on refusing to learn anything from his police court lessons until some day his ''polite attentions'' to school girls will bring him a scorching punishment that will not be very bully for *him*.

Dec. 2, 1865—*Napa County Reporter.*

[Here we have Twain's reaction to being billed for income tax for the first time in his life. A Federal tax had been instituted as a temporary war measure in 1862. Twain's tax for 1864 of $31.25 would indicate, it has been calculated, that his income for that year had been about $1,650. The Collector of Internal Revenue in San Francisco—Frank Soulé—was, as Twain suggests, actually a poet of a sort. He was also the author of *The Annals of San Francisco,* the first detailed chronicle of the city's early years. This piece is an item from a series of daily letters from San Francisco which Twain wrote for the *Enterprise* from late November, 1865, to near the end of February, 1866. They totaled about 2,000 words each, and his pay was a hundred dollars a month. Among other aspects, the letters are notable for the series of slashing attacks and satires he conducted on the inefficiency and corruption of the San Francisco police force. It is in these letters to the *Enterprise* that Twain shows himself for the first time a moralist of consequence, not just a humorist.]

GRACEFUL COMPLIMENT

One would hardly expect to receive a neat, voluntary compliment from so grave an institution as the United States Revenue Office, but such has been my good fortune. I have not been so agreeably surprised in many a day. The Revenue officers, in a communication addressed to me, fondle the faltering fiction that I am a man of means, and have got "goods, chattels and effects"—and even "real estate"! Gentlemen, you couldn't have paid such a compliment as that to any man who would appreciate it higher, or be more grateful for it than myself. We will drink together, if you object not.

I am taxed on my income! This is perfectly gorgeous! I never felt so important in my life before. To be treated in this splendid way, just like another William B. Astor! Gentlemen, we *must* drink.

Yes, I am taxed on my income. And the printed page which bears this compliment—all slathered over with fierce-looking written figures—looks as grand as a steamboat's manifest. It reads thus:

S. C. Internal Revenue, First Dist. Cal.
"Collector's Office,

Name	M. Twain
Residence	At Large
List and amount of tax	$31.25
Penalty	3.12
Warrant	2.45
Total amount	$36.82
Date	November 20, 1865.

C. ST GG, Deputy Collector

☞ Please present this at the Collector's office."

Now I consider that really handsome. I have got it framed beautifully, and I take more pride in it than any of my other furniture. I trust it will become an heirloom and serve to show many generations of my posterity that I was a man of consequence in the land—that I was also the recipient of compliments of the most extraordinary nature from high officers of the national government.

On the other side of this complimentary document I find some happy blank verse headed "Warrant," and signed by the poet "Frank Soulé, Collector of Internal Revenue." Some of the flights of fancy in this Ode are really sublime, and show with what facility the poetic fire can render beautiful the most unpromising subject.

For instance: "You are hereby commanded to distrain upon so much of the goods, chattels and effects of the within named person, *if any such can be found, etc.*" However, that is not so much a flight of fancy as a flight of humor. It is a fine flight, though, anyway. But this one is equal to anything in Shakespeare: "But in case sufficient goods, chattels and effects cannot be found, then you are hereby commanded to seize so much of the real estate of said person as may be necessary to satisfy the tax." There's poetry for you! They are going to commence on my real estate. This is very rough. But then the officer is expressly instructed to find it first. That is the saving clause for me. I will get them to take it all out in real estate. And then I will give them all the time they want to find it in.

But I can tell them a way whereby they can ultimately enrich the Government of the United States by a judicious manipulation of this little bill against me—a way in which even the enormous national debt may be eventually paid off! Think of it! Imperishable fame will be the reward of the man who finds a way to pay off the national debt without impoverishing the land; I offer to furnish that method and crown these gentlemen with that fadeless glory. It is so simple and plain that a child may understand it. It is thus: I perceive that by neglecting to pay my income tax within ten days after it was due, I have brought upon myself a "penalty" of three dollars and twelve cents extra tax for that ten days. Don't you see?—let her run! Every ten days, $3.12; every month of 31 days, $10; every year, $120; every century, $12,000; at the end of a hundred thousand years, $1,200,000,000. . . . [*The rest of the text is missing.*]

After Nov. 20, 1865—*Territorial Enterprise.*

[The *Alta* reporter with whom Twain is at odds here is Albert S. Evans, who wrote for that paper under the pseudonym "Fitz Smythe." He also wrote for the *Gold Hill Evening News* under the name "Amigo," reaching much the same audience there as Twain was writing for in his letters to the *Enterprise.* He was as staunch a defender of the San Francisco police force as Twain was an opponent of it, and he and Twain carried on a running feud over this and other topics. The What Cheer House, where the "mysterious robbery" took place, was that rare institution—a cheerful, decent lodging house serving good, moderately priced meals and offering its guests one of the best private libraries in town.]

THE OLD THING

As usual, the *Alta* reporter fastens the mysterious What Cheer robbery on the same horrible person who knocked young Myers in the head with a slung-shot a year ago and robbed his father's pawnbroker shop of some brass jewelry and crippled revolvers, in broad daylight; and he laid that exploit on the horrible wretch who robbed the Mayor's Clerk, who half-murdered detective officer Rose in a lonely spot below Santa Clara; and he proved that this same monster killed the lone woman in a secluded house up a dark alley with a carpenter's chisel, months before; and he demonstrated by inspired argument that the same villain who chiselled the woman tomahawked a couple of defenseless women in the most mysterious manner up another dark alley a few months before that. Now, the perpetrator of these veiled crimes has never been discovered, yet this wicked reporter has taken the whole batch and piled them coolly and relentlessly upon the shoulders of one imaginary scoundrel, with a comfortable, "Here, these are yours," and with an air that says plainly that no denial, and no argument in the case, will be entertained. And every time anything happens that is unlawful and dreadful, and has a spice of mystery about it, this reporter, without waiting to see if maybe somebody else didn't do it, goes off at once and jams it on top of the old pile, as much as to say, "Here—here's some more of your work." Now this isn't right, you know. It is all well enough for Mr. Smythe to divert suspicion from himself—nobody objects to that—but it is not right for him to lay every solitary thing on this mysterious stranger, whoever he is—it is not right, you know. He ought to give the poor devil a show. The idea of accusing 'The Mysterious' of the What Cheer burglary, considering who was the last boarder to bed and the first one up!

Smythe is endeavoring to get on the detective police force. I think it will be wronging the community to give this man such a position as that—now you know that yourself, don't you? He would settle down on some particular fellow, and every time there was a rape committed, or a steamship stolen, or an oyster cellar rifled, or a church burned down, or a family massacred, or a black-and-tan pup stolen, he would march off with portentious mien and snatch that fellow and say, "Here, you are at it again, you know," and snake him off to the Station House.

Nov. 25, 1865—*Californian* (as reprinted from *Territorial Enterprise*).

[San Francisco Society was deadly serious about itself in those days, as one might expect to be the case in this volatile new city, full of strangers whose pasts were uncertain and new millionaires whose social acceptability had to be endlessly discussed each time invitation lists for a cotillon were being made up. Each ball and social gathering was reported in the press in thrilling and meticulous detail. The situation was made to order for Twain's pen.]

THE PIONEERS' BALL

It was estimated that four hundred persons were present at the ball. The gentlemen wore the orthodox costume for such occasions, and the ladies were dressed the best they knew how. N. B.—Most of these ladies were pretty, and some of them absolutely beautiful. Four out of every five ladies present were pretty. The ratio at the

Colfax party was two out of every five. I always keep the run of these things. While upon this department of the subject, I may as well tarry a moment and furnish you with descriptions of some of the most noticeable costumes.

Mrs. W. M. was attired in an elegant *pate de foi gras,* made expressly for her, and was greatly admired.

Miss S. had her hair done up. She was the centre of attraction for the gentlemen, and the envy of all the ladies.

Miss G. W. was tastefully dressed in a *tout ensemble,* and was greeted with deafening applause wherever she went.

Mrs. C. N. was superbly arrayed in white kid gloves. Her modest and engaging manner accorded well with the unpretending simplicity of her costume, and caused her to be regarded with absorbing interest by every one.

The charming Miss M. M. B. appeared in a thrilling waterfall, whose exceeding grace and volume compelled the homage of pioneers and emigrants alike. How beautiful she was!

The queenly Mrs. L. B. was attractively attired in her new and beautiful false teeth, and the *bon jour* effect they naturally produced was heightened by her enchanting and well-sustained smile. The manner of this lady is charmingly pensive and melancholy, and her troops of admirers desired no greater happiness than to get on the scent of her sozodont-sweetened sighs and track her through her sinuous course among the gay and restless multitude.

Miss R. P., with that repugnance to ostentation in dress which is so peculiar to her, was attired in a simple white lace collar, fastened with a neat pearl-button solitaire. The fine contrast between the sparkling vivacity of her natural optic and the steadfast attentiveness of her placid glass eye was the subject of general and enthusiastic remark.

The radiant and sylph-like Mrs. T., late of your state, wore hoops. She showed to good advantage, and created a sensation wherever she appeared. She was the gayest of the gay.

Miss C. L. B. had her fine nose elegantly enameled, and the easy grace with which she blew it from time to time, marked her as a cultivated and accomplished woman of the world; its exquisitely modulated tone excited the admiration of all who had the happiness to hear it.

Being offended with Miss X., and our acquaintance having ceased prematurely, I will take this opportunity of observing to her that it is of no use for her to be slopping off to every ball that takes place, and flourishing around with a brass oyster-knife skewered through her waterfall, and smiling her sickly smile through her decayed teeth, with her dismal pug nose in the air. There is no use in it—she don't fool anybody. Everybody knows that she is old; everybody knows she is repaired (you might almost say built) with artificial bones and hair and muscles and things, from the ground up—put together scrap by scrap—and everybody knows, also, that all one would have to do would be to pull out her key-pin and she would go to pieces like a Chinese puzzle. There, now, my faded flower, take that paragraph home with you and amuse youself with it; and if ever you turn your wart of a nose up at me again I will sit down and write something that will just make you rise up and howl.

Nov. 26, 1865—*Golden Era* (as reprinted from *Territorial Enterprise*).

"MARK TWAIN" OVERPOWERED

The Enterprise, *having recently published one of those "affecting incidents," which are occasionally met with by "local items," when there is a dearth of fires, runaways, etc., "Mark Twain" issues the following as a companion-piece:*

UNCLE LIGE.

I will now relate an affecting incident of my meeting with Uncle Lige, as a companion novelette to the one published by Dan the other day, entitled "Uncle Henry."

A day or two since—before the late stormy weather—I was taking a quiet stroll in the western suburbs of the city. The day was sunny and pleasant. In front of a small but neat "bit house," seated upon a bank—a worn out and discarded faro bank—I saw a man and a little girl. The sight was too much for me, and I burst into tears. Oh, God! I cried, this is too rough! After the violence of my emotion had in a manner spent itself, I ventured to look once more upon that touching picture. The left hand of the girl (how well I recollect which hand it was! by the warts on it)—a fair-haired, sweet-faced child of about eight years of age—rested upon the right shoulder (how perfectly I remember it was his right shoulder, because his left shoulder had been sawed off in a saw mill) of the man by whose side she was seated. She was gazing toward the summit of Lone Mountain, and prating of the gravestones on the top of it and of the sunshine and Diggers resting on its tomb-clad slopes. The head of the man drooped forward till his face almost rested upon his breast, and he seemed intently listening. It was only a pleasing pretense, though, for there was nothing for him to hear save the rattling of the carriages on the gravel road beside him, and he could have straightened himself up and heard that easy enough, poor fellow. As I approached, the child observed me, notwithstanding her extreme youth, and ceasing to talk, smilingly looked at me, strange as it may seem. I stopped, again almost overpowered, but after a struggle I mastered my feelings sufficiently to proceed.

I gave her a smile—or rather, I swapped her one in return for the one I had just received, and she said:

"This is Uncle Lige—poor blind-drunk Uncle Lige."

This burst of confidence from an entire stranger, and one so young withal, caused my subjugated emotions to surge up in my breast once more, but again, with a strong effort, I controlled them. I looked at the wine-bred cauliflower on the poor man's nose and saw how it had all happened.

"Yes," said he, noticing by my eloquent countenance that I *had* seen how it had all happened, notwithstanding nothing had been said yet about anything having happened, "Yes, it happened in Reeseriv' a year ago; since tha(ic)at time been living here with broth—Robert'n lill Addie (*e ick!*)."

"Oh, he's the best uncle, and tells me such stories!" cried the little girl.

"At's aw-ri, you know (ick!)—at's aw ri," said the kind-hearted, gentle old man, spitting on his shirt bosom and slurring it off with his hand.

The child leaned quickly forward and kissed his poor blossomy face. We beheld two great tears start from the man's sightless eyes, but when they saw what sort of country they had got to travel over, they went back again. Kissing the child again and again and once more and then several times, and afterwards repeating it, he said:

"H(o-ook!)—oorah for Melical eagle star-spalgle baller! At's aw ri, you know—(ick!)—at's aw ri"—and he stroked her sunny curls and spit on his shirt bosom again.

This affecting scene was too much for my already over-charged feelings, and I burst into a flood of tears and hurried from the spot.

Such is the touching story of Uncle Lige. It may not be quite as sick as Dan's, but there is every bit as much reasonable material in it for a big calf like either of us to cry over. Cannot you publish the two novelettes in book form and send them forth to destroy such of our fellow citizens as are spared by the cholera?

Dec. 2, 1865—*Californian.*

"CHRISTIAN SPECTATOR"

Rev. O. P. Fitzgerald, of the Minna Street Methodist Church South, is fairly under way, now, with his new *Christian Spectator.* The second number is before me. I believe I can venture to recommend it to the people of Nevada, of both Northern and Southern proclivities. It is not jammed full of incendiary religious matter about hell-fire, and brimstone, and wicked young men knocked endways by a streak of lightning while in the act of going fishing on Sunday. Its contents are not exciting or calculated to make people set up all night to read them. I like the *Spectator* a great deal better than I expected to, and I think you ought to cheerfully spare room for a short review of it. The leading editorial says: "A journal of the character of the *Spectator* is always to a great extent the reflex of the editor's individuality." Then follows a pleasant moral homily entitled "That Nubbin"; then puffs of a religious college and a Presbyterian church; then some poetical reflections on the happy fact "The War is Over"; then a "hyste" of some old slow coach of a preacher "for not getting subscribers for the *Spectator* fast enough"; then a confidential hint to the reader that he turn out and gather subscriptions—and forward the money; then a puff of the Oakland Female Seminary; then a remark that the *Spectator's* terms are cash; then a suggestion that the paper would make a gorgeous Christmas present—the only joke in the whole paper, and even this one is written with a fine show of seriousness; then a complimentary blast for Bishop Pierce; then a column of "Personal Items" concerning distinguished Confederates, chiefly; then something about "Our New Dress"—not one of Ward's shirts for the editor, but the paper's new dress; then a word about "our publishing house at Nashville, Tenn."; then a repetition of the fact that "our terms are cash"; then something concerning "our head" —not the editor's, which is "level," but the paper's; then follow two columns of religious news not of a nature to drive one into a frenzy of excitement. On the outside is one of those entertaining novelettes, so popular among credulous Sabbath-school children, about a lone woman silently praying a desperate and blood-thirsty robber out of his boots—he looking on and fingering his clasp-knife and wiping it on his hand, and she calmly praying, till at last he "blanched beneath her fixed gaze, a panic appeared to seize him, and he closed his knife and went out." Oh, that won't do, you know. That is rather too steep. I guess she must have scalded him a little. There is also a column about a "remarkable police officer," . . . praising him up to the skies, and showing, by facts sufficient to convince me that if he belonged to our force, Mr. Fitzgerald was drawing it rather strong. I read it with avidity, because I wished to know whether it was Chief Burke, or Blitz, or Lees, the parson was trying to curry favor with. But it was only an allegory, after all; the impossible policeman was "Conscience." It was one of these fine moral humbugs, like some advertisements which seduce you down a column of stuff about General Washington and wind up with a recommendation to "try Peterson's aromatic soap."

Subscribe for the vivacious *Christian Spectator;* C. A. Klose is financial agent.

Dec. 11, 1865—*Territorial Enterprise.*

MORE ROMANCE

The pretty waiter girls are always getting people into trouble. But I beg pardon—I should say "ladies," not "girls." I learned this lesson from the days when I went "gypsying," which was a long time ago. I said to one of these self-important hags, "Mary, or Julia, or whatever your name may be, who is that old slab singing at the piano—the girl with the 'bile' on her nose?" Her eyes snapped. "You call her *girl!*—you shall find out yourself—she is a *lady,* if you please!" They are all "ladies," and they take it as an insult when they are called anything else. It was one of these charming ladies who got shot, by an ass of a lover from the wilds of

When Lazarus died, in October, 1863, after having been run over by a fire engine, the whole town turned out and gave the dog a magnificent civic funeral. Two years later

Bummer died—"full of years and honor and disease and fleas," as Twain put in the obituary he wrote.

Arizona, yesterday in the Thunderboldt Saloon, but unhappily not killed. The fellow had enjoyed so long the society of ill-favored squaws who have to be scraped before one can tell the color of their complexions, that he was easily carried away with the well seasoned charms of "French Mary" of the Thunderboldt Saloon, and got so "spooney" in his attentions that he hung around her night after night, and breathed her garlicky sighs with ecstasy. But no man can be honored with a beer girl's society without paying for it. French Mary made this man Vernon buy basket after basket of cheap champagne and got a heavy commission, which is usually their privilege; in the saloon her company always cost him five or ten dollars an hour, and she was doubtless a still more expensive luxury out of it.

It is said that he was always insisting upon her marrying him, and threatening to leave and go back to Arizona if she did not. She could not afford to let the goose go until he was completely plucked, and so she would consent, and set the day, and then the poor devil, in a burst of generosity, would celebrate the happy event with a heavy outlay of cash. This ruse was played until it was worn out, until Vernon's patience was worn out, until Vernon's purse was worn out also. Then there was no use in humbugging the poor numscull any longer, of course; and so French Mary deserted him, to wait on customers who had cash—the unfeeling practice always observed by lager beer ladies under similar circumstances. She told him she would not marry him or have anything more to do with him, and he very properly tried to blow her brains out. But he was awkward, and only wounded her dangerously. He killed himself, though, effectually, and let us hope that it was the wisest thing he could have done, and that he is better off now, poor fellow.

Dec. 11, 1865—*Territorial Enterprise.*

RE-OPENING OF THE PLAZA

The Plaza, or Portsmouth Square, is "done," at last, and by a resolution passed by the Board of Supervisors last night, is to be thrown open to the public henceforth at 7 o'clock A.M. and closed again at 7 o'clock P.M. every day. The same resolution prohibits the visits of dogs to this holy ground, and denies to the public the privilege of rolling on its grass. If I could bring myself to speak vulgarly, I should say that the latter clause is rough—very rough on the people. To be forced to idle in gravel walks when there is soft green grass close at hand, is tantalizing; it is as uncomfortable as to be disabled and thirsty in sight of a fountain; or to look at a feast without permission to participate in it, when you are hungry; and almost as exasperating as to have to smack your chops over the hugging and kissing going on between a couple of sweethearts without any reasonable excuse for inserting your own metaphorical shovel. And yet there is one consolation about it on Nature's eternal equity of "compensation." No matter how degraded and worthless you may become here, you cannot go to grass in the Plaza, at any rate. The Plaza is a different thing from what it used to be; it used to be a text from a desert—it was not large enough for a whole chapter; but now it is traversed here and there by walks of precise width, and which are graded to a degree of rigid accuracy which is constantly suggestive of the spirit level; and the grass plots are as strictly shaped as a dandy's side-whiskers, and their surfaces clipped and smoothed with the same mathematical exactness. In a word, the Plaza looks like the intensely brown and green perspectiveless diagram of stripes and patches which an architect furnishes to his client as a plan for a projected city garden or cemetery. And its glaring greenness in the midst of so much sombreness is startling and yet piercingly pleasant to the eye. It reminds one of old John Dohle's vegetable garden in Virginia, which, after a rain, used to burn like a square of green fire in the midst of the dull, gray desolation around it.

Dec. 13, 1865—*Territorial Enterprise.*

[This story was written in response to a request from the famous humorist Artemus Ward, who had told Mark Twain he would be happy to include something by him in a new book Ward was preparing. By the time it arrived in New York, Ward's book had gone to the printer, so Ward passed it on to the *Saturday Press,* which published it in its November 18, 1865 issue under the title of "Jim Smiley and His Jumping Frog." It was reprinted a month later in the *Californian,* where Twain took advantage of the opportunity to edit it, change the names of its characters, and change its title to the one it now bears. The *Californian* version is the one I include here.

The success of this story astonished Mark Twain and at first he grumbled over the fact that his fame should have derived from "a villainous backwoods squib." But he rushed to its defense when, some time later, a French scholar criticized it in the highbrow *Revue des Deux Mondes* as not being as funny as it was purported to be. That journal had published a translation of the story under the title "La Grenouille Sauteuse du Comte de Calaveras." Mark Twain's response was to translate the translation back into English to show how the French had lost the flavor. His retranslation goes:

> It there was one time here an individual known under the name of Jim Smiley; it was in the winter of '49, possibly well at the spring of '50, I no me recollect not exactly. This which me makes to believe that it was the one or the other, it is that I shall remember that the grand flume is not achieved when he arrives at the camp for the first time, but of all sides he was the man the most fond of to bet which one have seen, betting upon all that which is presented...

And so on. It took Mark Twain five days, he said, to do his retranslation, but he could rest content that he had set the record straight.]

THE CELEBRATED JUMPING FROG OF CALAVERAS COUNTY

Mr. A. Ward—Dear Sir: Well, I called on good-natured, garrulous old Simon Wheeler, and I inquired after your friend Leonidas W. Greeley, as you requested me to do, and I hereunto append the result. If you can get any information out of it you are cordially welcome to it. I have a lurking suspicion that your Leonidas W.

Greeley is a myth—that you never knew such a personage, and that you only conjectured that if I asked old Wheeler about him it would remind him of his infamous *Jim* Greeley, and he would go to work and bore me nearly to death with some infernal reminiscence of him as long and tedious as it should be useless to me. If that was your design, Mr. Ward, it will gratify you to know that it succeeded.

I found Simon Wheeler dozing comfortably by the barroom stove of the old dilapidated tavern in the ancient mining camp at Angel's, and I noticed that he was fat and bald-headed, and had an expression of winning gentleness and simplicity upon his tranquil countenance. He roused up and gave me good-day. I told him a friend of mine had commissioned me to make some inquiries about a cherished companion of his boyhood named Leonidas W. Greeley—Rev. Leonidas W. Greeley—a young minister of the Gospel, who he had heard was at one time a resident of Angel's Camp. I added that if Mr. Wheeler could tell me anything about this Rev. Leonidas W. Greeley, I would feel under many obligations to him.

Simon Wheeler backed me into a corner and blockaded me there with his chair—and then sat me down and reeled off the monotonous narrative which follows this paragraph. He never smiled, he never frowned, he never changed his voice from the gentle-flowing key to which he tuned the initial sentence, he never betrayed the slightest suspicion of enthusiasm—but all through the interminable narrative there ran a vein of impressive earnestness and sincerity, which showed me plainly that so far from his imagining that there was anything ridiculous or funny about his story, he regarded it as a really important matter, and admired its two heroes as men of transcendent genius in *finesse*. To me, the spectacle of a man drifting serenely along through such a queer yarn without ever smiling was exquisitely absurd. As I said before, I asked him to tell me what he knew of Rev. Leonidas W. Greeley, and he replied as follows. I let him go on in his own way, and never interrupted him once:

There was a feller here once by the name of *Jim* Greeley, in the winter of '49—or maybe it was the spring of '50—I don't recollect exactly, some how, though what makes me think it was one or the other is because I remember the big flume wasn't finished when he first come to the camp; but anyway, he was the curiosest man about always betting on anything that turned up you ever see, if he could get anybody to bet on the other side, and if he couldn't he'd change sides—any way that suited the other man would suit *him*—any way just so's he got a bet, *he* was satisfied. But still, he was lucky—uncommon lucky; he most always come out winner. He was always ready and laying for a chance; there couldn't be no solitry thing mentioned but that feller'd offer to bet on it—and take any side you please, as I was just telling you: if there was a horse race, you'd find him flush or you'd find him busted at the end of it; if there was a dog-fight, he'd bet on it; if there was a cat-fight, he'd bet on it; if there was a chicken-fight, he'd bet on it; why if there was two birds sitting on a fence, he would bet you which one would fly first—or if there was a camp-meeting he would be there regular to bet on Parson Walker, which he judged to be the best exhorter about here, and so he was, too, and a good man; if he even see a straddle-bug start to go any wheres, he would bet you how long it would take him to get wherever he was going to, and if you took him up he would foller that straddle-bug to Mexico but what he would find out where he was bound for and how long he was on the road. Lots of the boys here has seen that Greeley and can tell you about him. Why, it never made no difference to *him*—he would bet on *anything*—the dangdest feller. Parson Walker's wife laid very sick, once, for a good while, and it seemed as if they warn't going to save her; but one morning he come in and Greeley asked how she was, and he said she was considerable better—thank the Lord for his inf'nit mercy—and coming on so smart that with the blessing of Providence she'd get well yet—and Greeley, before he thought, says: "Well, I'll resk two-and-a-half that she don't, anyway."

Thish-yer Greeley had a mare—the boys called her the fifteen-minute nag, but that was only in fun, you know, because, of course, she was faster than that—and he used to win money on that horse, for all she was so slow and always had the asthma, or the distemper, or the consumption, or something of that kind. They used to give her two or three hundred yards' start, and then pass her under way; but always at the fag-end of the race she'd get excited and desperate like, and come cavorting and spraddling up, and scattering her legs around limber, sometimes in the air, and sometimes out to one side amongst the fences, and kicking up m-o-r-e dust, and raising m-o-r-e racket with her coughing and sneezing and blowing her nose—and always fetch up at the stand just about a neck ahead, as near as you could cipher it down.

And he had a little small bull pup, that to look at him you'd think he warn't worth a cent, but to set around and look onery, and lay for a chance to steal something. But as soon as money was up on him he was a different dog—his underjaw'd begin to stick out like the for'castle of a steamboat, and his teeth would uncover, and shine savage like the furnaces. And a dog might tackle him, and bully-rag him, and bite him, and throw him over his shoulder two or three times, and Andrew Jackson—which was the name of the pup—Andrew Jackson would never let on but what he was satisfied, and hadn't expected nothing else—and the bets being doubled and doubled on the other side all the time, till the money was all up—and then all of a sudden he would grab that other dog just by the joint of his hind leg and freeze to it—not chaw, you understand, but only just grip and hang on till they throwed up the sponge, if it was a year. Greeley always came out winner on that pup till he harnessed a dog once that didn't have no hind legs, because they'd been sawed off in a circular saw, and when the thing had gone along far enough, and the money was all up, and he come to make a snatch for his pet holt, he saw in a minute how he'd been imposed on, and how the other dog had him in the door, so to speak, and he 'peared surprised, and then he looked sorter discouraged like, and didn't try no more to win the fight, and so he got shucked out bad. He give Greeley a look as much as to say his heart was broke, and it was *his* fault, for putting up a dog that hadn't no hind legs for him to take holt of, which was his main dependence in a fight, and then he limped off a piece, and laid down and died. It was a good pup, was that Andrew Jackson, and would have made a name for hisself if he'd lived, for the stuff was in him, and he had genius—I know it, because he hadn't had no opportunities to speak of, and it don't stand to reason that a dog could make such a fight as he could under them circumstances, if he hadn't no talent. It always makes me feel sorry when I think of that last fight of his'n, and the way it turned out.

Well, thish-yer Greeley had rat-tarriers and chicken cocks, and tomcats, and all them kind of things, till you couldn't rest, and you couldn't fetch nothing for him to bet on but he'd match you. He ketched a frog one day and took him home and said he cal'lated to educate him; and so he never done nothing for three months but set in his back yard and learn that frog to jump. And you bet he *did* learn him, too. He'd give him a little punch behind, and the next minute you'd see that frog whirling in the air like a doughnut—see him turn one summerset, or maybe a couple, if he got a good start, and come down flat-footed and all right, like a cat. He got him up so in the matter of catching flies, and kept him in practice so constant, that he'd nail a fly every time as far as he could see him. Greeley said all a frog wanted was education, and he could do most anything—and I believe him. Why, I've seen him set Dan'l Webster down here on this floor—Dan'l Webster was the name of the frog—and sing out, "Flies! Dan'l, flies," and quicker'n you could wink, he'd spring straight up, and snake a fly off'n the counter there, and flop down on the floor again as solid as a gob of mud, and fall to scratching the side of his head with his hind foot as indifferent as if he hadn't no idea he'd done any more'n any frog might do. You never see a frog so modest and straightfor'ard as he was, for all he was so gifted. And when it come to fair-and-square jumping on a dead level, he could get over more ground at one straddle than any animal of his breed you ever see. Jumping on a dead level was his strong suit, you understand, and when it come to that, Greeley would ante up money on him as long as he had a red. Greeley was monstrous proud of his frog, and well he might be, for fellers that had travelled and been everywheres, all said he laid over any frog that ever *they* see.

Well, Greeley kept the beast in a little lattice box, and he used to fetch him down town sometimes and lay for a bet. One day a feller—a stranger in the camp, he was—come across him with his box, and says:

"What might it be that you've got in the box?"

And Greeley says, sorter indifferent like, "It might be a parrot, or it might be a canary, maybe, but it ain't—it's only just a frog."

And the feller took it, and looked at it careful, and turned it round this way and that, and says, 'H'm—so 'tis. Well, what's *he* good for?"

"Well," Greeley says, easy and careless, "he's good enough for *one* thing I should judge—he can out-jump ary frog in Calaveras county."

The feller took the box again, and took another long, particular look, and give it back to Greeley and says, very deliberate, "Well—I don't see no points about that frog that's any better'n any other frog."

"Maybe you don't," Greeley says. "Maybe you understand frogs, and maybe you don't understand 'em; maybe you've had experience, and maybe you ain't only a amature, as it were. Anyways, I've got *my* opinion, and I'll resk forty dollars that he can outjump ary frog in Calaveras county."

And the feller studied a minute, and then says, kinder sad, like, "Well—I'm only a stranger here, and I ain't got no frog—but if I had a frog I'd bet you."

And then Greeley says, "That's all right—that's all right—if you'll hold my box a minute I'll go and get you a frog;" and so the feller took the box, and put up his forty dollars along with Greeley's, and set down to wait.

So he set there a good while thinking and thinking to hisself, and then he got the frog out and prized his mouth open and took a teaspoon and filled him full of quail-shot—filled him pretty near up to his chin—and set him on the floor. Greeley he went to the swamp and slopped around in the mud for a long time, and finally he ketched a frog and fetched him in and give him to this feller and says:

"Now if you're ready, set him alongside of Dan'l, with his fore-paws just even with Dan'l's, and I'll give the word." Then he says, "one—two—three—jump!" and him and the feller touched up the frogs from behind, and the new frog hopped off, but Dan'l give a heave, and hysted up his shoulders—so—like a Frenchman, but it wa'nt no use—he couldn't budge; he was planted as solid as an anvil, and he couldn't no more stir than if he was anchored out. Greeley was a good deal surprised, and he was disgusted, too, but he didn't have no idea what the matter was, of course.

The feller took the money and started away, and when he was going out at the door he sorter jerked his thumb over his shoulder —this way—at Dan'l, and says again, very deliberate: "Well—I don't see no points about that frog that's any better'n any other frog."

Greeley he stood scratching his head and looking down at Dan'l a long time, and at last he says, "I do wonder what in the nation that frog throw'd off for—I wonder if there ain't something the matter with him—he 'pears to look mighty baggy, somehow," and he ketched Dan'l by the nap of the neck, and lifted him up and says, "Why blame my cats if he don't weigh five pound," and turned him upside down, and he belched out about a double-handful of shot. And then he see how it was, and he was the maddest man—he set the frog down and took out after that feller, but he never ketched him. And—

(Here Simon Wheeler heard his name called from the frontyard, and got up to see what was wanted.) And turning to me as he moved

away, he said: "Just set where you are, stranger, and rest easy—I ain't going to be gone a second."

But by your leave, I did not think that a continuation of the history of the enterprising vagabond Jim Greeley would be likely to afford me much information concerning the Rev. Leonidas W. Greeley, and so I started away.

At the door I met the sociable Wheeler returning, and he buttonholed me and recommenced:

"Well, thish-yer Greeley had a yaller one-eyed cow that didn't have no tail only just a short stump like a bannanner, and—"

"O, curse Greeley and his afflicted cow!" I muttered, good-naturedly, and bidding the old gentleman good-day, I departed.

Yours, truly,
Mark Twain

Dec. 16, 1865—*Californian* (as reprinted from the New York *Saturday Press*).

THIEF-CATCHING

One may easily find room to abuse as many as several members of Chief Burke's civilian army for laziness and uselessness, but the detective department is supplied with men who are sharp, shrewd, always on the alert and always industrious. It is only natural that this should be so. An ordinary policeman is chosen with especial reference to large stature and powerful muscle, and he only gets $125 a month, but the detective is chosen with especial regard to brains, and the position pays better than a lucky faro-bank. A shoemaker can tell by a single glance at a boot whose shop it comes from, by some peculiarity of workmanship; but to a bar-keeper all boots are alike; a printer will take a number of newspaper scraps, that show no dissimilarity to each other, and name the papers they were cut from; to a man who is accustomed to being on the water, the river's surface is a printed book which never fails to divulge the hiding place of the sunken rock, or betray the presence of the treacherous shoal. In ordinary men, this quality of detecting almost imperceptible differences and peculiarities is acquired by long practice, and goes not beyond the limits of their own occupation—but in the detective it is an instinct, and discovers to him the secret signs of all trades, and the faint shades of difference between things which look alike to the careless eye.

Detective Rose can pick up a chicken's tail feather in Montgomery street and tell in a moment what roost it came from at the Mission; and if the theft is recent, he can go out there and take a smell of the premises and tell which block in Sacramento street the Chinaman lives in who committed it, by some exquisite difference in the stink left, and which he knows to be peculiar to one particular block of buildings.

Mr. McCormick, who should be on the detective force regularly, but as yet is there only by brevet, can tell an obscene photograph by the back, as a sport tells an ace from a jack.

Detective Blitz can hunt down a transgressing hack-driver by some peculiarity in the style of his blasphemy.

The forte of Lees and Ellis, is the unearthing of embezzlers and forgers. Each of these men are best in one particular line, but at the same time they are good in all. And now we have Piper, who takes a cake, dropped in the Lick House by a coat-thief, and sits down to read it as another man would a newspaper. It informs him who baked the cake; who bought it; where the purchaser lives; that he is a Mexican; that his name is Salcero; that he is a thief by profession—and then Piper marches away two miles, to the Presidio, and grabs this foreigner, and convicts him with the cake that cannot lie, and makes him shed his boots and finds $200 in greenbacks in them, and makes him shuck himself and finds upon him store of stolen gold. And so Salcero goes to the station-house. The detectives are smart, but I remarked to a friend that some of the other policemen were not. He said the remark was unjust—that those "other policemen were as smart as they could afford to be for $125 a month." It was not a bad idea. Still, I contend that some of them could not afford to be Daniel Websters, maybe, for any amount of money.

Dec. 19, 1865—*Territorial Enterprise.*

[*Outcroppings,* an anthology of California verse which Bret Harte edited, appeared at the end of 1865. The poem that Twain impudently attributes to Fitz Smythe and then solemnly criticizes is a parody of "In Memoriam," an elegy on the death of Lincoln which Smythe—Albert Evans, that is—had published in the *Alta* on April 17, 1865.]

CAUSTIC

Ah, but Fitz Smythe can be severe when it suits his humor. He knocks "Outcroppings" as cold as a wedge in his last "Amigo" letter to the Gold Hill *News,* in a single paragraph—yet it cost you a whole page of the *Enterprise* to express your disapprobation of that volume of poems. He says, "The contents are of course suited to the capacity of children only." This will make those Eastern papers feel mighty bad, because several of them have spoken highly of the book and thought it was written for men and women to read.

But I attach no weight to Smythe's criticisms, because he don't know anything about polite literature; he has had no experience in it further than to write up runaway horse items for the *Alta* and act as Private Secretary to Emperor Norton. And even in the latter capacity he has never composed the Emperor's proclamations; his duties extended no further than to copy them for the Gold Hill *News,* and anybody could do that. As for poetry, he never wrote but two poems in his life. One was entitled, "The Dream of Norton I, Emperor," which was tolerably good, but not as good as the "Chandos Picture," and the other was one which he composed when the news came of the assassination of the President. This latter effort was bad, but I do not really think he knows it, else why should he feel so injured because it was not inserted in "Outcroppings"? But perhaps it is not fair in me thus to pass judgment upon that poem, when possibly I am no more competent to discern poetical merit or demerit than I conceive him to be himself. Therefore, rather than do Fitz Smythe an unintentional injustice, I will quote one verse from the poem which I have called "bad," and leave the people to endorse my criticism or reject it, as shall seem unto them best:

THE MARTYR

Gone! gone! gone!
  Forever and forever!
Gone! gone! gone!
  The tidings ne'er shall sever!
Gone! gone! gone!
  Wherever! Oh, wherever!
Gone! gone! gone!
  Gone to his endeavor!

(RECAPITULATION.)

Gone forever!
To wherever!
Ne'er shall sever!
His endeavor!
From our soul's high recompense!

I consider that the chief fault in this poem is that it is ill-balanced—lop-sided, so to speak. There is too much "gone" in it, and not enough "forever." I will do the author the credit to say, however, that there is in it a manifestation of genius of a high order. It is a dangerous kind of genius, however, as two poets here, gifted exactly similar, have lately demonstrated—they both transgressed laws whereof the penalty is capital punishment. I have to be a little severe, now, because I am a friend to "Outcroppings," and I do not like to see you and Smythe trying to bring the book into disrepute.

Dec. 19, 1865—*Territorial Enterprise.*

[During a quarrel over the affections of a young lady, Tom Maguire—the flamboyant proprietor of the Academy of Music and other noted San Francisco theatres—punched and pummeled an actor named W. J. Macdougall. Macdougall brought suit for $5,000 damages—and Twain commented as follows.]

MACDOUGALL VS. MAGUIRE

Come, now, Macdougall!
Say—
Can lucre pay
For thy dismembered coat—
Thy strangulated throat—
Thy busted bugle?

Speak thou! Poor W. J.!
And say—
I pray—
If gold can soothe your woes,
Or mend your tattered clothes,
Or heal your battered nose,
Oh bunged-up lump of clay!

No!—arise!
Be wise!
Macdougall, d——n your eyes!
Don't legal quips devise
To mend your reputation,
And efface the degradation
Of a blow that's struck in ire!
But 'ware of execration,
Unless you take your station
In a strategic location,
In mood of desperation,
And "lam" like all creation
This infernal Tom Maguire!

Dec. 20, 1865—*Territorial Enterprise.*

EDITORIAL POEM

The following fine Christmas poem appears in the *Alta* of this morning, in the unostentatious garb of an editorial. This manner of "setting it" robs it of half its beauty. I will arrange it as blank verse, and then it will read much more charmingly:

Christmas Comes But Once A Year

The Holidays are approaching. We hear
Of them and see their signs every day.
The children tell you every morn
How long it is until the glad New Year.
The pavements all are covered o'er
With boxes, which have arrived
Per steamer and are being unpacked
In anticipation sweet, of an unusual demand.
The windows of the shops
Montgomery street along,
Do brilliant shine
With articles of ornament and luxury;
The more substantial goods,
Which eleven months now gone
The place have occupied,
Having been put aside for a few revolving weeks.
Silks, satins, laces, articles of gold and silver,
Jewels, porcelains from Sevres,
And from Dresden;
Bohemian and Venetian glass,
Pictures, engravings,
Bronzes of the finest workmanship
And price extravagant, attract
The eye at every step
Along the promenades of fashion.
The hotels
With visitors are crowded, who have come

From the ultimate interior to enjoy
Amusements metropolitan, or to find
A more extensive market, and prices lower
For purchases, than country towns afford.
Abundant early rains a prosperous year
Have promised—and the dry
And sunny weather which prevailed hath
For two weeks past, doth offer
Facilities profound for coming to the city,
And for enjoyment after getting here.
The ocean beach throughout the day,
And theatres, in shades of evening, show
A throng of strangers glad residents as well.
All appearances do indicate
That this blithe time of holiday
In San Francisco will
Be one of liveliness unusual, and brilliancy withal.

[Exit Chief Editor, bowing low—impressive music.]

I cannot admire the overstrung modesty which impels a man to compose a stately anthem like that and run it together in the solid unattractiveness of a leading editorial.

Dec. 22, 1865—*Territorial Enterprise.*

[Here we have the first appearance in Twain's writings of a theme that he would later on put to good use—most notably in *Tom Sawyer* and *Huck Finn:* juvenile delinquency's attractiveness, and how much more rewarding it is to be bad than to be good.]

THE CHRISTMAS FIRESIDE

FOR GOOD LITTLE BOYS AND GIRLS

By Grandfather Twain

THE STORY OF THE BAD LITTLE BOY THAT BORE A CHARMED LIFE

Once there was a bad little boy, whose name was Jim—though, if you will notice, you will find that bad little boys are nearly always called James in your Sunday-school books. It was very strange, but still it was true, that this one was called Jim.

He didn't have any sick mother, either—a sick mother who was pious and had the consumption, and would be glad to lie down in the grave and be at rest, but for the strong love she bore her boy, and the anxiety she felt that the world would be harsh and cold toward him when she was gone. Most bad boys in the Sunday books are named James, and have sick mothers who teach them to say, "Now, I lay me down," etc., and sing them to sleep with sweet plaintive voices, and then kiss them good-night, and kneel down by the bed-side and weep. But it was different with this fellow. He was named Jim, and there wasn't anything the matter with his mother—no consumption, or anything of that kind. She was rather stout than otherwise, and she was not pious; moreover, she was not anxious on Jim's account; she said if he were to break his neck, it wouldn't be much loss; she always spanked Jim to sleep, and she never kissed him good-night; on the contrary, she boxed his ears when she was ready to leave him.

Once, this little bad boy stole the key of the pantry and slipped in there and helped himself to some jam, and filled up the vessel with tar, so that his mother would never know the difference; but all at once a terrible feeling didn't come over him, and something didn't seem to whisper to him, "Is it right to disobey my mother? Isn't it sinful to do this? Where do bad little boys go who gobble up their good kind mother's jam?" and then he didn't kneel down all alone and promise never to be wicked any more, and rise up with a light, happy heart, and go and tell his mother all about it and beg her forgiveness, and be blessed by her with tears of pride and thankfulness in her eyes. No; that is the way with all other bad boys in the books, but it happened otherwise with this Jim, strangely enough. He ate that jam, and said it was bully, in his sinful, vulgar way; and he put in the tar, and said that was bully also, and laughed, and observed that "the old woman would get up and snort" when she found it out; and when she did find it out he denied knowing anything about it, and she whipped him severely, and he did the crying himself. Everything about this boy was curious—everything turned out differently with him from the way it does to the bad Jameses in the books.

Once he climbed up in Farmer Acorn's apple tree to steal apples, and the limb didn't break, and he didn't fall and break his arm, and get torn by the farmer's great dog, and then languish on a sick bed for weeks and repent and become good. Oh, no—he stole as many apples as he wanted, and came down all right, and he was all ready for the dog, too, and knocked him endways with a rock when he came to tear him. It was very strange—nothing like it ever happened in those mild little books with marbled backs, and with pictures in them of men with swallow-tailed coats and bell-crowned hats and pantaloons that are short in the legs, and women with the waists of their dresses under their arms and no hoops on. Nothing like it in any of the Sunday-school books.

Once he stole the teacher's penknife, and when he was afraid it would be found out and he would get whipped, he slipped it into George Wilson's cap—poor Widow Wilson's son, the moral boy, the good little boy of the village, who always obeyed his mother, and never told an untruth, and was fond of his lessons and infatuated with Sunday-school. And when the knife dropped from the cap and poor George hung his head and blushed, as if in conscious guilt, and the grieved teacher charged the theft upon him, and was just in the very act of bringing the switch down upon his trembling shoulders, a white-haired improbable justice of the peace did not suddenly appear in their midst and strike an attitude and say, "Spare this noble boy—there stands the cowering culprit! I was passing the school door at recess, and, unseen myself, I saw the theft committed!" And then Jim didn't get whaled, and the venerable justice didn't read the tearful school a homily, and take George by the hand and say such a boy deserved to be exalted, and then tell him to come and make his home with him, and sweep out the office, and make fires, and run errands, and chop wood, and study law, and help his wife to do household labors, and have all the balance of the time to play, and get forty cents a month, and be happy. No, it would have happened that way in the books, but it didn't happen that way to Jim. No meddling old clam of a justice dropped in to make trouble, and so the model boy George got threshed, and Jim was glad of it. Because, you know, Jim hated moral boys. Jim said he was "down on them milksops." Such was the coarse language of this bad, neglected boy.

But the strangest things that ever happened to Jim was the time he went boating on Sunday and didn't get drowned, and that other time that he got caught out in the storm when he was fishing on Sunday, and didn't get struck by lightning. Why, you might look, and look, and look through the Sunday-school books, from now till next Christmas, and you would never come across anything like this. Oh, no—you would find that all the bad boys who go boating on Sunday invariably get drowned, and all the bad boys who get caught out in storms, when they are fishing on Sunday, infallibly get struck by lightning. Boats with bad boys in them always upset on Sunday, and it always storms when bad boys go fishing on the Sabbath. How this Jim ever escaped is a mystery to me.

This Jim bore a charmed life—that must have been the way of it. Nothing could hurt him. He even gave the elephant in the menagerie a plug of tobacco, and the elephant didn't knock the top of his head off with his trunk. He browsed around the cupboard after essence of peppermint, and didn't make a mistake and drink aqua fortis. He stole his father's gun and went hunting on the Sabbath, and didn't shoot three or four of his fingers off. He struck his little sister on the temple with his fist when he was angry, and she didn't linger in pain through long summer days and die with sweet words of forgiveness upon her lips that redoubled the anguish of his breaking heart. No—she got over it. He ran off and went to sea at last, and didn't come back and find himself sad and alone in the world, his loved ones sleeping in the quiet churchyard, and the vine-embowered home of his boyhood tumbled down and gone to decay. Ah, no—he came home drunk as a piper, and got into the station house the first thing.

And he grew up, and married, and raised a large family, and brained them all with an axe one night, and got wealthy by all manner of cheating and rascality, and now he is the infernalest wickedest scoundrel in his native village, and is universally respected, and belongs to the Legislature.

So you see there never was a bad James in the Sunday-school books that had such a streak of luck as this sinful Jim with the charmed life.

Dec. 23, 1865—*Californian.*

[The garrulous George Marshall would seem to be a forerunner of the nouveau-riche American tourists Twain would satirize in *The Innocents Abroad.*]

ANOTHER ENTERPRISE

A Mr. P. M. Scoofy, of this city, has been raising oysters for two years past, on the Mexican coast, and his first harvest—eight tons—arrived yesterday on the *John L. Stephens.* They arrived in admirable condition—finer and fatter than they were when they started; for oysters enjoy travelling, and thrive on it; and they learn a good deal more on a flying trip than George Marshall did, and nearly as much as some other Washoe European tourists I could mention, but they are dignified and do not gabble about it so much. I would rather have the society of a travelled oyster than that of George Marshall, because I would not hesitate to show my displeasure if that oyster were to suddenly become gay and talkative, and say: "I was in England, you know, by G——; I went up to Liverpool and there I took the cars and went to London, by ———; I been in Pall Mall, and Cheapside, and Whitefriars, and all them places—been in all of 'em: I been in the Tower of London, and seen all them d——d armors and things they used to wear in an early day; I hired a feller for a shil'n', and he took me all around there and showed me the whole hell-fired arrangement, you know, by G——; and I give him a glass of of'n-of, as they call it, and he jus' froze to me. You show one of them fellers the color of a bit, and he'll stay with you all day, by ———. And I went to Rome—that ain't no slouch of a town, you know—and old? ———! you bet your life. There ain't anything like it in this country—*you* can't put up any idea how it is; you can't tell a d——d thing about Rome 'thout you see it, by ———. And I been to Paris—Parree French call it—you never hear them say Par-*riss*—they would laugh if they was to hear any body call it Par-riss, you know. I was there three weeks. I was on the *Pong-Nuff,* and I been to the *Pal-ley Ro-yoll* and the *Tweeleree,* all them d——d places, and the *Boolyver* and the *Boys dee Bullone.* I stood there in the *Boys dee Bullone* and see old Loois Napoleon and his wife come by in his carriage—I was as close to him as from here to that counter there, by G——; I see him take his hat off and bow to them whoopin' French bilks by ———; I stood right there that close—as close as that counter when he went by; I was close enough to a spit in his face if I'd been a mind to, by ———. Hell, a feller might live *here* a million years, and what would he ever see, by G——d. Parree's the place—style, *there,* you know—people got money, *there,* by ———. Let's take a drink, by G——." I wouldn't let a travelled oyster inflict that sort of thing on me, you understand, and refer to the Deity, and to the Savior by his full name, to verify every other important statement. I would rather have the oyster's company than Marshall's when his reminiscences are big within him, but the moment I received the information that "I been to Europe, and all them places, by G——," I would start that oyster on a journey that would astonish it more than all the wonders of "Parree" and "all them d——d places" combined.

I have forgotten what I was going to say about Mr. Scoofy and his Mexican oyster farm, but it don't matter. The main thing is that he will hereafter endeavor to keep the market supplied with his delicious marine fruit, and another great point is that his Mexican oysters are as far superior to the poor little insipid things we are accustomed to here, as is the information furnished by Alexander Van Humboldt concerning foreign lands to that which one may glean from George Marshall in the course of a brief brandy-punch tournament.

Dec. 23, 1865—*Territorial Enterprise.*

["Fourteener" items were stories concerning the depredations of the Fourteenth Regiment, who were stationed at the Presidio, and who were, by all accounts, a riotous and disorderly crew.]

SPIRIT OF THE LOCAL PRESS

San Francisco is a city of startling events. Happy is the man whose destiny it is to gather them up and record them in a daily newspaper! That sense of conferring benefit, profit and innocent pleasure upon one's fellow-creatures which is so cheering, so calmly blissful to the plodding pilgrim here below, is his, every day in the year. When he gets up in the morning he can do as old Franklin did, and say, "This day, and all days, shall be unselfishly devoted to the good of my fellow-creatures—to the amelioration of their condition—to the conferring of happiness upon them—to the storing of their minds with wisdom which shall fit them for their struggle with the hard world, here, and for the enjoyment of a glad eternity hereafter. And thus striving, so shall I be blessed!" And when he goes home at night, he can exult and say: "Through the labors of these hands and this brain, which God hath given me, blessed and wise are my fellow-creatures this day!

"I have told them of the wonder of the swindling of the friend of Bain, the unknown Bain from Petaluma Creek, by the obscure Catharine McCarthy, out of $300—and told it with entertaining verbosity in half a column.

"I have told them that Christmas is coming, and people go strangely about, buying things—I have said it in forty lines.

"I related how a vile burglar entered a house to rob, and actually went away again when he found he was discovered. I told it briefly, in thirty-five lines.

"In forty lines I told how a man swindled a Chinaman out of a couple of shirts, and for fear the matter might seem trivial, I made a pretense of only having mentioned it in order to base upon it a criticism upon a grave defect in our laws.

"I fulminated again, in a covert way, the singular conceit that Christmas is at hand, and said people were going about in the most unaccountable way buying stuff to eat, in the markets—52 lines.

"I glorified a fearful conflagration that came so near burning something, that I shudder even now to think of it. Three thousand dollars worth of goods destroyed by water—a man then went up and put out the fire with a bucket of water. I puffed our fine fire organization—64 lines.

"I printed some other extraordinary occurrences—runaway horse—28 lines; dog fight—30 lines; Chinaman captured by officer Rose for stealing chickens—90 lines; unknown Chinaman dead on Sacramento steamer—5 lines; several "Fourteener" items, concerning people frightened and boots stolen—52 lines; case of soldier stealing a washboard worth fifty cents—three-quarters of a column. Much other wisdom I disseminated, and for these things let my reward come hereafter."

And his reward *will* come hereafter—and I am sorry enough to think it. But such startling things do happen every day in this strange city!—and how dangerously exciting must be the employment of writing them up for the daily papers!

Dec. 23, 1865—*Territorial Enterprise.*

THE BLACK HOLE OF SAN FRANCISCO

If I were Police Judge here, I would hold my court in the city prison and sentence my convicts to imprisonment in the present Police Court room. That would be capital punishment—it would be the Spartan doom of death for all crimes, whether important or insignificant. The Police Court room, with its deadly miasma, killed Judge Shepheard and Dick Robinson, the old reporter, and will kill Judge Rix, and Fitz Smythe also. The papers are just now abusing the police room—a thing which they do in concert every month. This time, however, they are more than usually exercised, because somebody has gone and built a house right before the only window the room had, and so it is midnight there during every hour of the twenty-four, and gas has to be burned while all other people are burning daylight.

That Police Court room is *not* a nice place. It is the infernalest smelling den on earth, perhaps. A deserted slaughter-house, festering in the sun, is bearable, because it only has one smell, albeit it is a lively one; a soap-factory has its disagreeable features, but the soap-factory has but one smell, also; to stand to leeward of a sweating negro is rough, but even a sweating negro has but one smell; the salute of the playful polecat has its little drawbacks, but even the playful polecat has but one smell, and you can bury yourself to the chin in damp sand and get rid of the odor eventually. Once enter the Police Court though—once get yourself saturated with the fearful combination of miraculous stenches that infect its atmosphere, and neither sand nor salvation can ever purify you any more! You will smell like a polecat, like a slaughter-house, like a soap-factory, like a sweating negro, like a graveyard after an earthquake—for all time to come—and you will have a breath like a buzzard. You enter the door of the Police Court, and your nostrils are saluted with an awful stench; you think it emanates from Mr. Hess, the officer in charge of the door; you say to yourself, "Some animal has crawled down this poor man's throat and died"; you step further in, and you smell the same smell, with another, still more villainous, added to it; you remark to yourself, "This is wrong—very wrong; these spectators ought to have been buried

days ago.'' You go a step further and you smell the same two smells, and another more ghastly than both put together; you think it comes from the spectators on the right. You go further and a fourth, still more powerful, is added to your three horrible smells; and you say to yourself, ''These lawyers are too far gone—chloride of lime would be of no benefit here.'' One more step, and you smell the Judge; you reel, and gasp; you stagger to the right and smell the Prosecuting Attorney—worse and worse; you stagger fainting to the left, and your doom is sealed; you enter the fatal blue mist where ten reporters sit and stink from morning until night—and down you go! You are carried out on a shutter, and you cannot stay in the same room with yourself five minutes at a time for weeks.

You cannot imagine what a horrible hole that Police Court is. The cholera itself couldn't stand it there. The room is about 24 x 40 feet in size, I suppose, and is blocked in on all sides by massive brick walls; it has three or four doors, but they are never opened—and if they were they only open into airless courts and closets anyhow; it has but one window, and now that is blocked up, as I was telling you; there is not a solitary air-hole as big as your nostril about the whole place. Very well; down two sides of the room, drunken filthy loafers, thieves, prostitutes, China chicken-stealers, witnesses, and slimy guttersnipes who come to see, and belch and issue deadly smells, are banked and packed, four ranks deep—a solid mass of rotting, steaming corruption. In the centre of the room are Dan Murphy, Zabriskie, the Citizen Sam Platt, Prosecuting Attorney Louderback, and other lawyers, either of whom would do for a censer to swing before the high altar of hell. Then, near the Judge are a crowd of reporters—a kind of cattle that did never smell good in any land. The house is full—so full that you have to actually squirm and shoulder your way from one part of it to another—and not a single crack or crevice in the walls to let in one poor breath of God's pure air! The dead, exhausted, poisoned atmosphere looks absolutely blue and filmy, sometimes—did when they had a little daylight. Now they have only gas-light and the added heat it brings. Another Judge will die shortly if this thing goes on.

Dec. 29, 1865—*Territorial Enterprise.*

In this woodcut, which appeared in *Puck,* Jump is satirizing the San Francisco Board of Supervisors, who are likened to a runaway milk wagon, creating havoc in the streets of San Francisco.

1866

[As a con man, Aleck Badlam, with his carefully fabricated shark scare, can be considered a worthy precursor of the King in *Huck Finn.* Perhaps the real con man is Mark Twain himself, embroidering and selling a good yarn. Research in the surviving San Francisco newspaper files of the day has failed to turn up the shark-scare story as the stock item Twain says it became. At the time of its construction, the new swimming bath on Third Street was described as the largest of its kind in the United States. The "White Man Mighty Onsartain" title and refrain, I presume, refers to a racial jest of the period—one in which it is the white man who, of course, is not to be trusted.]

"WHITE MAN MIGHTY ONSARTAIN"

Nigger never spoke truer word. White man *is* mighty "onsartain." An instance of it is to be found in the ingenious manipulation of a certain recent speculation here by a white man whom I have in my mind's eye at present.

A small swimming bath was constructed out yonder at North Beach, as a sort of novel experiment, and everybody was surprised to see what a rush was made to it and what a thriving speculation it at once became. Many a smart man wished the idea had occurred to him, and then thought no more about it. Others pondered over it and thought the experiment might bear repetition, but then there was an uncomfortable possibility of the reverse proving the case. Mr. Aleck Badlam, late a member of the California Legislature, but latterly acting in the double capacity of nephew and business agent to Mr. Samuel Brannan, belonged to the latter class, but was rather more hopeful, more energetic and more fertile in expedients than the rest. He went to work and got up a joint stock association, composed of men with good bank accounts, and announced in the public prints that this association would immediately commence the construction of a colossal swimming bath, with all manner of admirable conveniences and accommodations, away out in Third Street opposite South Park. Many people went on swimming in the pioneer bath, and many others in the Bay, and both parties said the new speculation would prove a disastrous failure, and that they were sorry for the projectors of it, etc., and then bothered no more about it. In a day or two the local reporters fell heirs to a refreshing sensation and were made happy—a genuine shark was harpooned in the Bay of San Francisco! It was brought to town and was visited by crowds of timid citizens while it lay in state in the market place. Mr. Badlam went at once to the various newspaper offices and told the reporters, and was greeted with the ancient formula: "That's bully—there's pen and ink, write it up for a fellow, can't you?"—(you know if you walk a mile to accommodate one of these thieves with an item, he will always impose upon you, with infernal effrontery, the labor of writing it up for him, if you will stand it). Mr. Badlam wrote up the shark item. A few days elapsed, the sensation was cooling down and beginning to be forgotten, when another shark was harpooned in the Bay and exposed to view in the market. People shuddered again. Mr. Badlam went and told the reporters; the reporters got him to write it up. In the course of three days another shark was harpooned in the Bay and placed on exhibition. People began to show signs of uneasiness. Mr. Badlam told the reporters and wrote it up. The new swimming bath was being rushed forward to completion with all possible dispatch. From this time on, for the next six weeks a shark passed in his checks every twenty-four hours in the Bay of San Francisco. Mr. Badlam discontinued the ceremony of telling the reporters, but he always came at 1 o'clock in the afternoon with several slips of manuscript, laid one down on the reporter's table, said "Shark item," and departed toward the next newspaper office on his regular beat. People began to say "Why, blame these sharks, the Bay's full of them—it ain't hardly as healthy to swim there as it used to was"—and they stopped swimming there. Reporters got to depending on the customary shark item pretty much as a matter of course, and the printers got to making these items "fat" by keeping them "standing" and making such unimportant alterations in them as the variations in the localities of the shark-killing demanded.

The fact of the business was, that Mr. Badlam, that "onsartain white man," had imported the old original shark from the coast of Mexico, and paid some Italian fishermen to take him out in the Bay and harpoon him, and then fetch him ashore and exhibit him in the market place. It was all in the way of business; he wanted to discourage bathing in the Bay and pave the way for the success of his great bath-house scheme at a later day. It is but just to say that he did make bathing in the Bay exceedingly unpopular. He imported all his sharks, and he kept a detachment of shark-killers under regular pay. Sharks come pretty high—sharks are very expensive—and he economized occasionally by having the same old shark harpooned and exhibited over and over again as long as he would hang together; and when he had to bring on a fresh one he would vary the interest in the thing by having the fish captured alive and towed ashore and exposed to public view in all his native ferocity; and once he got a number of young pigs killed and scraped clean, towed a shark out in the Bay, fed the pigs to him, towed him back again and landed him at the head of the Long Bridge when there were about two thousand people promenading on it, got a multitude collected around the spot, killed and cut the shark open, took several chunks of the delicate white young pork out of its stomach, and then hid his face in his handkerchief and said with manifest emotion: "Oh God, this fellow's been eating a child—ah, how sad, how sad!" This culminating stroke of genius crowned Mr. Badlam's patient, long-continued efforts with a splendid success—no man has bathed in the Bay since Mr. B. wrote that item up and travelled his regular newspaper route with it. His labors were over, the bath-house was nearly finished, and he had nothing but easy sailing before him from that time forward. In a few days his monstrous tank was completed and the water turned on, and the very first day he opened business with a hundred and fifty swimmers an hour on an average, and a hundred and fifty more standing around in Menken costume waiting for a chance. There is nothing like trying, you know; and all experience teaches us that the best

SAN FRANCISC

B

H. SWIMMING.

way to ascertain a thing is to find it. But when it comes to believing all the shark items a sagacious strategist favors you with in the papers, it is well to remember that the wise nigger saith "white man mighty onsartain."

Jan. 8, 1866—*Territorial Enterprise.*

THE MINT DEFALCATION

The *Alta* of this morning publishes a correct statement of the embezzlement by young Macy of $39,000 from the mint, and you can copy it; but there are some little matters in the background which always come within a correspondent's province in cases of this kind, but which are usually omitted from the accounts in the local press, and these I will talk about. Mr. Cheeseman is U.S. Sub-Treasurer, and *ex officio* treasurer of the mint. Macy, his brother-in-law, was his paying clerk—his cashier. He is a green, gawky young fellow about twenty-four or -five years old; and by a glance at his gait and the shape of his head and his general appearance, an experienced business man would judge his capacity to be about equal to the earning of, say fifty dollars a month. But he was the Sub-Treasurer's brother-in-law—he was a barnacle, and had to be provided with a place in the Circumlocution Office, whether he knew enough to come in out of the rain or not. So he was made paying clerk, at a salary of $2,500 a year, and placed in a position where twenty millions in gold coin and oceans of greenbacks passed through his hands in the course of a year. Mr. Swain, the Superintendent of the mint, did not fancy this appointment, but it was out of his jurisdiction. Mr. Cheeseman has the appointing of his own clerks, although all their reports must be made finally to the Superintendent, and all their acts come under his supervision.

Naturally there was nothing bad about young Macy, but it is believed—well, I might go so far as to say it was known—that some mining speculators got around him and persuaded him to put mint funds in stocks, promising to "stand behind him." He did so, and they stood behind him until the crash in stocks warned them to stand some where else and then they dropped him—having made what they could out of him, no doubt. He had been speculating on the mint's money six months before he was found out—the workmen occasionally going without their wages in the meantime because of the lack of supplies. Mr. Swain's suspicions were first aroused by seeing him so frequently in company with speculators and hearing so often on the street of his transactions in heavy stocks. But Macy's books came out right every month and nothing could be shown against him. One of his thefts was a bold one. The coiner sent him three "melts" at different times—three batches of gold coin—two of a hundred thousand dollars each and one of a hundred and twenty thousand. Each had the usual "tag," describing the amount contained. Macy removed and tore up the $120,000 "tag," and sent to the coiner a message that he had lost the tag from one of the $100,000 batches—a thing which sometimes occurs. The coiner sent him the necessary substitute, and he altered the date and placed the new tag on the $120,000 "melt"; but he carried off the extra $20,000 first.

At the last quarterly examination the money and the books were all right, but Macy displayed such distress and trepidation during the examination that he excited the suspicions of more than one of the mint officials; he had been shinning around the streets all day long, too, and it was thought that he had been getting a temporary loan to make his accounts straight with. Such a rigid surveillance was commenced then, and so many informal examinations instituted, that Macy finally packed and ran off. This was in December. The facts of this embezzlement have only just come to light and its full extent only just now finally ferreted out and made known to the public, but the Department at Washington has been kept posted upon the subject by telegraph from time to time during the last two or three weeks.

Jan. 8, 1866—*Territorial Enterprise.*

[Items like this one were constantly appearing in all the San Francisco papers. They prepared the way for the Great Diamond Hoax of the next decade—one of the grandest swindles of all time, in which San Francisco's leading financiers were taken for a ride. San Francisco had enjoyed a gold bonanza and then a silver bonanza; precious stones were being counted on to provide the next bonanza.]

PRECIOUS STONES

I have seen some of the beautiful opals they find in Calaveras county near Mokelumne Hill. Some of them are very handsome. A day or two ago I was shown an Idaho diamond. It was very pure and brilliant, and was said to be a genuine diamond, and of the first water. I compared it with a couple of splendid twenty-five hundred dollar Brazilian diamonds in Tucker's window which have been dazzling people's eyes and attracting considerable attention for a few days past, and I could not swear to any difference. That amounts to something although I am not an expert where it comes to estimating the value and fineness of diamonds. And now they are finding superb moss agates and other precious stones on the river bank right up here at Martinez. This reminds me that there is a hill-side down the gulch below Aurora, Esmeralda, which is covered with round, hard, knotty-surfaced little boulders which display the most beautiful agates when broken open. Might not the Esmeralda people find it profitable to send a bushel or two of those things to the Eastern markets? Nobody cared anything about them when I was there three years ago.

Jan. 11, 1866—*Territorial Enterprise.*

NEW YEAR'S DAY

There was a good deal of visiting done here on New Year's Day. The air was balmy and spring-like, and the day was in every way suited to that sort of business. I say business, because it is more like business than pleasure when you call at a house where all are strangers, and the majority of one's New Year's Calls are necessarily of that description. You soon run through the list of your personal friends—and that part of the day's performances affords you genuine satisfaction—and then Smith comes along and puts you through your paces before a hundred people who treat you kindly, but whom you dare not joke with. You can be as easy and comfortable as a mud-turtle astraddle of a sawyer, but you must observe some show of decorum—you must behave yourself. It is irksome to me to behave myself. Therefore, I had rather call on people who know me and will kindly leave me entirely unrestrained, and simply employ themselves in looking out for the spoons.

When I started out visiting, at noon, the atmosphere was laden with a sweet perfume—a grateful incense that told of flowers, and green fields, and breezy forests far away. But this was only soda-water sentiment, for I soon discovered that these were the odors of the barber shop, and came from the heads of small squads of carefully-dressed young men who were out paying their annual calls.

I took wine at one house and some fruit at another, and after that I began to yearn for some breakfast. It took me two hours to get it. A lady had just given me the freedom of her table when a crowd of gentlemen arrived and my sense of propriety compelled me to destroy nothing more than a cup of excellent coffee. At the next house I got no further than coffee again, being similarly interrupted; at the next point of attack there were too many strange young ladies present, and at the next and the next, something always happened to interfere with my arrangements. I do not know, but perhaps it would be better to defer one's New Year's calls until after breakfast. I did finally corral that meal, and in the house of a stranger—a stranger, too, who was so pleasant that I was almost tempted to create a famine in her house.

It used to be customary for people to drink too much in the course of their annual visits, but few offended in this way on this occasion. I saw one well-dressed gentleman sitting on the curb-stone, propping his face between his knees, and clasping his shins with his hands; but he was the only caller I saw so much discouraged during the whole day. He said he had started out most too early, and I suppose he was right. Wisdom teaches us that none but birds should go out early, and that not even birds should do it unless they are out of worms. Some of the ladies dressed "in character" on New Year's. I found Faith, Hope and Charity in one house, dealing out claret punch and kisses to the annual pilgrims. They had two kinds of kisses—those which you bite and "chaw" and swallow, and those which you simply taste, and then lick your chops and feel streaky. The only defect there was in the arrangement was that you were not permitted to take your choice. Two other ladies personated Mary, Queen of Scots, and Queen Elizabeth; I also found a Cleopatra and a Hebe and a Semiramis and a Maria Antoinette; also a Beauty and the Beast. A young lady, formerly of Carson, was the Beauty, and took the character well; and I suppose Beecher was the Beast, but he was not calculated for the part. I think those are very neat compliments for both parties.

When it came to visiting among strangers, at last, I soon grew tired and quit. You enter with your friend and are introduced formally to some formal looking ladies. You bow painfully and wish the party a happy New Year. You then learn that the party desire that a like good fortune may fall to your lot. You are invited to sit down, and you do so. About this time the door-bell rings, and Jones, Brown and Murphy bluster in and bring the familiar fragrance of the barber shop with them. They are acquainted. They inquire cordially after the absent members of the family and the distant relatives of the same, and relate laughable adventures of the morning that haven't got anything funny about them. Then they cast up accounts and determine how many calls

they have made and how many they have got to inflict yet. The ladies respond by exhibiting a balance sheet of their own New Year's Day transactions. Yourself and your friend are then conducted with funeral solemnity into the back parlor, where you sip some wine with imposing ceremony. If your human instincts get the upper hand of you and you explode a joke, an awful sensation creeps over you such as a man experiences when he catches himself whistling at a funeral. It is time for you to go, then.

New Year's was pretty generally enjoyed here, up stairs and down. At one place where I called, a servant girl was needed, for something, and the bell was rung for her several times without effect. Madame went below to see what the matter was, and found Bridget keeping "open house" and entertaining thirteen muscular callers in one batch. Up stairs there had been only eleven calls received, all told. One chambermaid notified her mistress that extra help must be procured for New Year's Day, as she and the cook had made arrangements to keep open house in the kitchen, and they desired that their visitors should not be discómmoded by interruptions emanating from above stairs. I am told that nearly all the Biddies in town kept open house. Some of them set finer tables than their mistresses. The reason was because the latter did not consider anything more than tea and coffee and cakes necessary for their tables (being church members) but the former seized upon wines, brandies and all the hidden luxuries the closets afforded. Some people affect to think servant girls won't take liberties with people's things, but I suppose it is a mistake.

Jan. 14, 1866—*Golden Era* (as reprinted from *Territorial Enterprise*).

WHAT HAVE THE POLICE BEEN DOING?

Ain't they virtuous? Don't they take good care of the city? Is not their constant vigilance and efficiency shown in the fact that roughs and rowdies here are awed into good conduct?—isn't it shown in the fact that ladies even on the back streets are safe from insult in the daytime, when they are under the protection of a regiment of soldiers?—isn't it shown in the fact that although many offenders of importance go unpunished, they infallibly snaffle every Chinese chicken-thief that attempts to drive his trade, and are duly glorified by name in the papers for it?—isn't it shown in the fact that they are always on the look-out and keep out of the way and never get run over by wagons and things? And ain't they spry?—ain't they energetic?—ain't they frisky?—Don't they parade up and down the sidewalk at the rate of a block an hour and make everybody nervous and dizzy with their frightful velocity? Don't they keep their clothes nice—and ain't their hands soft? And don't they work?—don't they work like horses?—don't they, now? Don't they smile sweetly on the women?—and when they are fatigued with their exertions, don't they back up against a lamp-post and go on smiling till they break plumb down? But ain't they nice?—that's it, you know!—ain't they nice? They don't sweat—you never see one of those fellows sweat. And ain't they easy and comfortable and happy—always leaning up against a lamp-post in the sun, and scratching one shin with the other foot and enjoying themselves? Serene?—I reckon not.

I don't know anything the matter with the Department, but may be Dr. Rowell does. Now when Ziele broke that poor wretch's skull the other night for stealing six bits' worth of flour sacks, and had him taken to the Station House by a policeman, and jammed into one of the cells in the most humorous way, do you think there was anything wrong there? I don't. Why should they arrest Ziele and say, "Oh, come, now, you say you found this stranger stealing on your premises, and we know you knocked him on the head with your club—but then you better go in a cell, too, till we see whether there's going to be any other account of the thing—any account that mightn't jibe with yours altogether, you know—you go in for confessed assault and battery, you know.'' Why should they do that? Well, nobody ever said they did.

And why shouldn't they shove that half-senseless wounded man into a cell without getting a doctor to examine and see how badly he was hurt, and consider that next day would be time enough, if he chanced to live that long? And why shouldn't the jailor let him alone when he found him in a dead stupor two hours after—let him alone because he couldn't wake him—couldn't wake a man who was sleeping and with that calm serenity which is peculiar to men whose heads have been caved in with a club—couldn't wake such a subject, but never suspected that there was anything unusual in the circumstance? Why shouldn't the jailor do so? Why certainly—why shouldn't he?—the man was an infernal stranger. He had no vote. Besides, had not a gentleman just said he stole some flour sacks? Ah, and if he stole flour sacks, did he not deliberately put himself outside the pale of humanity and Christian sympathy by that hellish act? I think so. The Department think so. Therefore, when the stranger died at 7 in the morning, after four hours of refreshing slumber in that cell, with his skull actually split in twain from front to rear, like an apple, as was ascertained by post mortem examination, what the very devil do you want to go and find fault with the prison officers for? You are *always* putting in your shovel. Can't you find somebody to pick on besides the police? It takes all my time to defend them from people's attacks.

I know the Police Department is a kind, humane and generous institution. Why, it was no longer ago than yesterday that I was reminded of that time Captain Lees broke his leg. Didn't the free-handed, noble Department shine forth with a dazzling radiance then? Didn't the Chief detail officers Shields, Ward and two others to watch over him and nurse him and look after all his wants with motherly solicitude—four of them, you know—four of the very biggest and ablest-bodied men on the force—when less generous people would have thought two nurses sufficient—had these four acrobats in active hospital service that way in the most liberal manner, at a cost to the city of San Francisco of only the trifling sum of five hundred dollars a month—the same being the salaries of four officers of the regular police force at $125 a month each. But don't you know there are people mean enough to say that Captain Lees ought to have paid his own nurse bills, and that if he had had to do it may be he would have managed to worry along on less than five hundred dollars worth of nursing a month? And don't you know that they say also that interested parties are always badgering the Supervisors with petitions for an increase of the police force, and showing such increase to be a terrible necessity, and yet they have always got to be hunting up and creating new civil offices and berths, and making details for nurse service in order to find something for them to do after they get them appointed? And don't you know that they say that they wish to God the city would hire a detachment of nurses and keep them where they will be handy in case of accident, so that property will not be left unprotected while Policemen are absent on duty in sick rooms. You can't think how it aggravates me to hear such harsh remarks about our virtuous police force. Ah, well, the police will have their reward hereafter—no doubt.

Jan. 21, 1866—*Golden Era*
(as reprinted from *Territorial Enterprise*).

[The boy's style of talk has the ring of Tom Sawyer's voice. Twain was beginning to experiment, in his journalism, with the art of telling stories in the vernacular—an art he developed later to the point of mastery.]

FITZ SMYTHE'S HORSE

Yesterday, as I was coming along through a back alley, I glanced over a fence, and there was Fitz Smythe's horse. I can easily understand, now, why that horse always looks so dejected and indifferent to the things of this world. They feed him on old newspapers. I had often seen Smythe carrying "dead loads" of old exchanges up town, but I never suspected that they were to be put to such a use as this. A boy came up while I stood there, and said: "That hoss belongs to Mr. Fitz Smythe, and the old man—that's my father, you know—the old man's going to kill him."

"Who, Fitz Smythe?"

"No, the hoss—because he et up a litter of pups that the old man wouldn't a taken forty dol—"

"Who, Fitz Smythe?"

"No, the hoss—and he eats fences and everything—took our gate off and carried it home and et up every dam splinter of it; you wait till he gets done with them old *Altas* and *Bulletins* he's a chawin' on now, and you'll see him branch out and tackle a-n-y-thing he can shet his mouth on. Why, he nipped a little boy, Sunday, which was going home from Sunday school; well, the boy got loose, you know, but that old hoss got his bible and some tracts, and them's as good a thing as *he* wants, being so used to papers, you see. You put anything to eat anywheres, and that old hoss'll shin out and get it—and he'll eat anything he can bite, and he don't care a dam. He'd climb a tree, he would, if you was to put anything up there for him—cats, for instance—he likes cats—he's et up every cat there was here in four blocks—he'll take more chances—why, he'll bust in anywheres for one of them fellers; I see him snake a old tom cat out of them there flower-pot over yonder, where she was a sunning of herself, and take her down, and she a hanging on and grabbing for a holt on something, and you could hear her yowl and kick up and tear around after she was inside of him. You see Mr. Fitz Smythe don't give him nothing to eat but them old newspapers and sometimes a basket of shavings, and so you know, he's got to prospect or starve, and a hoss ain't going to starve, it ain't likely, on account of not wanting to be rough on cats and sich things. Not that hoss, anyway, you bet you. Because *he* don't care a dam. You turn him loose once on this town, and don't you know he'd eat up m-o-r-e goods-boxes, and fences, clothing-store things, and animals, and all them kind of valuables? Oh, you bet he would. Because, that's his style, you know, and he don't care a dam. But you ought to see Mr. Fitz Smythe ride him around, prospecting for them items—you ought to see him with his soldier coat on, and his mustashers sticking out strong like a cat-fish's horns, and them long legs of his'n standing out so, like them two prongs they prop up a step-ladder with, and a jolting down street at four mile a week—oh, what a guy!—sets up stiff like a close pin, you know, and thinks he looks like old General Macdowl. But the old man's going to horniss woggle that hoss on account of his gobbling up them pups. Oh, you bet your life the old man's *down* on him. Yes, sir, coming!" and the entertaining boy departed to see what the "old man" was calling him for. But I am glad that I met the boy, and I am glad I saw the horse taking his literary breakfast, because I know now why the animal looks so discouraged when I see Fitz Smythe rambling down Montgomery Street on him—he has altogether too rough a time getting a living to be cheerful and frivolous or anyways frisky.

Jan. 21, 1866—*Golden Era* (as reprinted from *Territorial Enterprise*).

BUSTED, AND GONE ABROAD

The term—"Busted"—applies to most people here. When a noted speculator breaks, you all hear of it; but when Smith and Jones and Brown go under, they make no stir; they are talked about among a small circle of gratified acquaintances, but they industriously keep up appearances, and the world at large go on thinking them as rich as ever. The lists of rich stock operators of two years ago have quietly sunk beneath the wave and financially gone to the devil. Smithers, who owned a hundred and ninety-six feet in one of the big mines, and gave such costly parties, has sent his family to Europe. Blivens, who owned so much in another big mine, and kept such fast horses, has sent his family to Germany, for their health, where they can sport a princely magnificence on fifty dollars a month. Bloggs, who was high-you-a-muck of another great mine, has sent his family home to rusticate a while with his father-in-law. All the nabobs of '63 are pretty much ruined, but they send their families foraging in foreign climes, and hide their poverty under a show of "appearances." If a man's family start anywhere on the steamer now, the public say: "There's the death rattle again—another Croesus has gone in." These are sad, sad, times. We are all "busted," and our families are exiled in foreign lands.

Jan. 28, 1866—*Golden Era* (as reprinted from *Territorial Enterprise*).

THE KEARNY STREET GHOST STORY

Disembodied spirits have been on the rampage now for more than a month past in the house of one Albert Krum, in Kearny Street—so much so that the family find it impossible to keep a servant forty-eight hours. The moment a new and unsuspecting servant-maid gets fairly to bed and her light blown out, one of those dead and damned scalliwags takes her by the hair and just "hazes" her; grabs her by the water-fall and snakes her out of bed and bounces her on the floor two or three times; other disorderly corpses shy old boots at her head, and bootjacks, and brittle chamber furniture—washbowls, pitchers, hair-oil, teethbrushes, hoop-skirts—anything that comes handy those phantoms seize and hurl at Bridget, and pay no more attention to her howling than if it were music. The spirits tramp, tramp, tramp, about the house at dead of night, and when a light is struck the footsteps cease and the promenader is not visible, and just as soon as the light is out that dead man goes waltzing around again. They are a bloody lot. The young lady of the house was lying in bed one night with the gas turned down low, when a figure approached her through the gloom, whose ghastly aspect and solemn carriage chilled her to the heart. What do you suppose she did?—jumped up and seized the intruder?—threw a slipper at him?—"laid" him with a misquotation from Scripture? No—none of these. But with admirable presence of mind she covered up her head and yelled. That is what she did. Few young women would have thought of doing that. The ghost came and stood by the bed and groaned—a deep, agonizing heart-broken groan—and laid a bloody kitten on the pillow by the girl's head. And then it groaned again, and sighed, "Oh, God, and must it be?" and bet another bloody kitten. It groaned a third time in sorrow and tribulation, and went one kitten better. And thus the sorrowing spirit stood there, moaning in its anguish and unloading its mewing cargo, until it had stacked up a whole litter of nine little bloody kittens on the girl's pillow, and then, still moaning, moved away and vanished.

When lights were brought, there were the kittens, with the finger-marks of bloody hands upon their white fur—and the old mother cat, that had come after them, swelled her tail in mortal fear and refused to take hold of them. What do you think of that? what would you think of a ghost that came to your bedside at dead of night and had kittens?

Jan. 28, 1866—*Golden Era* (as reprinted from *Territorial Enterprise*).

THE CHAPMAN FAMILY

The old gentleman and the old lady must be seventy-five years old, now. They used to play with Dan Marble in New Orleans, twenty-five years ago; earlier, they had a theatre built in a "broad horn," and floated down the Ohio and Mississippi clear to the Belize, tying up every night and knocking Richard III endways for the delectation of any number of graybacks that chose to come, from a dozen to a thousand, and selling tickets for money when they could, and taking Salt Lake currency when they couldn't. They have played in Canada and all over California and Washoe—played everywhere in North America, I may say, and lo! I come to tell you that they still "keep up their lick." I have been honored with a letter from the old lady, dated "Helena, Last Chance, Montana Territory, December 16." She says that they are just five miles from the Missouri river. I suppose they will build a raft in the spring and float down the river, astonishing the Indians with Othello, Richard, Jack Sheppard, etc., and the next thing we hear of them they will be in New Orleans again. The old lady further says:

"We have a theatre and company of Denverites, and are doing well. It is so cold that the quicksilver all froze, or I would tell you how many degrees below zero. Provisions high; salt, $1 per lb; butter, $2.50; flour, $30, and it would not do for you to be here, for tobacco is $6 a pound and scarce. . . . So cold that 50 head of cattle and 2 men who were herding them froze to death on the night of the 14th. Great deal of suffering among miners who were out prospecting. This is a lively town; adjoining camps deserted; everybody wintering here. . . . I play the part of Richard III tonight. Next week I appear as Mazeppa. We charge $1.50 for all seats."

The idea of the jolly, motherly old lady stripping to her shirt and riding a fiery untamed Montana jackass up flights of stairs and kicking and cavorting around the stage on him with the quicksilver frozen in the thermometers and the audience taking brandy punches out of their pockets and biting them, same as people eat peanuts in civilized lands! Why, there is no end to the old woman's energy. She'll go through with Mazeppa with flying colors even if she has to do it with icicles a yard long hanging to her jackass's tail.

Jan. 28, 1866—*Golden Era* (as reprinted from *Territorial Enterprise*).

[About this time, according to Edgar M. Branch, a scholar who has made a close study of Twain's early writing, "an enriching quality of primary significance to Mark Twain's greatest fiction began to appear in his journalism. This quality was his sense of the past." As a character, Captain Montgomery reminds Branch of Captain Stormfield, and Mother Utterback is rather like the motherly Mrs. Grangerford in *Huck Finn.*]

CAPTAIN MONTGOMERY

Whenever he commenced helping anybody, Captain Ed Montgomery never relaxed his good offices as long as help was needed.

As soon as he found that no steamboat ever stopped to wood with old Mother Utterback in the bend below Grand Gulf, Mississippi, and that she was poor and needed assistance, he began to stop there every trip and take her little pile of wood and smile grimly, when the engineers protested that it wouldn't burn any more than so many icicles—and stop there again the very next trip. He used to go ashore and talk to the old woman, and it flattered her to the last degree to be on such sociable terms with the high chief officer of a splendid passenger steamer. She would welcome him to her shabby little floorless log cabin with a royal flourish, and make her six gawky "gals" fly around and make him comfortable. He used to bring his lady passengers ashore to be entertained with Mother Utterback's quaint conversation.

I do not know that this incident is worth recording, but still, as it may let in the light of instruction to some darkened mind, I will just set down the circumstances of one of Captain Montgomery's visits to Mother Utterback and her daughters. He brought some fine ladies with him to enjoy the old woman's talk.

"Good morning, Captain Montgomery!" said she with many a bustling bow and flourish; "Good morning, Captain Montgomery; good morning, ladies all; how de do, Captain Montgomery—how de do—how de do? Sakes alive, it 'pears to me it's ben years sense I seed you. Fly around gals, fly around! You Bets, you slut, highst yoself off'n that candle-box and give it to the lady. How *have* you ben, Captain Montgomery?—make yoself at home, ladies all—you 'Liza Jane, stan' out of the way—move yoself! Thar's the jug, help yoself, Captain Montgomery; take that cob out and make yoself free, Captain Montgomery—and ladies all. You Sal, you hussy, git up f'm thar this minit, and take some exercise! for the land's sake, ain't you got no sense at all?—settin' thar on that cold rock and you jes' ben married last night, and your pores all open!"

The ladies wanted to go aboard the boat, they bade the kind, hospitable old woman good by, and went away. But Captain Montgomery staid behind, because he knew how badly the old lady wanted to talk, and he was a good soul and loved to please her.

Ah, that was a good man was Captain Ed Montgomery, and the moment I saw that paragraph about him the other day I remembered how kind it was of him to always stop and buy that old Arkansas woman's green wood and pay her the highest market price for it when he could no more burn it than he could burn an iceberg. It was so soggy, too, and wet, and heavy. I remember how, whenever he blew the whistle to land there, the mate used to sing out hoarsely and in bitterness of spirit, "Larboard watch—turn out! Stand by, men, to take in some ballast!" But you can rest assured I am not sorry old Captain Ed Montgomery is alive and well yet.

Jan. 28, 1866—*Golden Era.*

SABBATH REFLECTIONS

This is the Sabbath to-day. This is the day set apart by a benignant Creator for rest—for repose from the wearying toils of the week, and for calm and serious (Brown's dog has commenced to howl again—I wonder why Brown persists in keeping that dog chained up?) meditation upon those tremendous subjects pertaining to our future existence. How thankful we ought to be (There goes that rooster, now.) for this sweet respite; how fervently we ought to lift up our voice and (Confound that old hen—lays an egg every forty minutes, and then cackles until she lays the next one.) testify our gratitude. How sadly, how soothingly the music of that deep-toned bell floats up from the distant church! How gratefully we murmur (Scat!—that old gray tom-cat is always bully-ragging that other one—got him down now, and digging the hair out of him by the handful.) thanksgiving for these Sabbath blessings. How lovely the day is! ("Buy a broom! buy a broom!") How wild and beautiful the ("*Golden Era* 'n' Sund' *Mercry,* two for a bit apiece!") sun smites upon the tranquil ("*Alta,* Mon' *Call,* an' *Merican Flag!*") city! ("Po-ta-to-o-o-es, ten pounds for two bits—po-ta-to-o-o-es, ten pounds for quart-va-dollar!")

However, never mind these Sunday reflections—there are too many distracting influences abroad. This people have forgotten that San Francisco is not a ranch—or rather, that it ought not properly to be a ranch. It has got all the disagreeable features of a ranch, though. Every citizen keeps from ten to five hundred chickens, and these crow and cackle all day and all night; they stand watches, and the watch on duty makes a racket while the off-watch sleeps. Let a stranger get outside of Montgomery and Kearny from Pacific to Second, and close his eyes, and he can imagine himself on a well-stocked farm, without an effort, for his ears will be assailed by such a vile din of gobbling of turkeys, and crowing of hoarse-voiced roosters, and cackling of hens, and howling of cows, and whinnying of horses, and braying of jackasses, and yowling of cats, that he will be driven to frenzy, and may look to perform prodigies of blasphemy such as he never knew himself capable of before.

Sunday reflections! A man might as well try to reflect in Bedlam as in San Francisco when her millions of livestock are in tune. Being calm, now, I will call down no curse upon these dumb brutes (as they are called by courtesy), but I will go so far as to say I wish they may all die without issue, and that a sudden and violent death may overtake any person who afterwards attempts to reinstate the fowl and brute nuisance.

Jan. 28, 1866—*Territorial Enterprise.*

["Neodamode," a word meaning originally a newly enfranchised Spartan helot, may have appeared once or twice in San Francisco papers but not anywhere near as often as Twain suggests.]

"NEODAMODE"

What a comfort these reporters do take in that graveyard word! They stick it at the head of an item, in all its native impenetrability, and then slash away cheerfully and finish the paragraph. It is too many for me—that word is, for all it is so handy. Sometimes they write up a fine item about the capture of a chicken-thief—and head it "Neodamode"; or an exciting story of an infant with good clothes on and a strawberry on its little left arm, and a coat of arms stitched on its poor little shirt-tail being left in a market basket on some one's doorstep—and head it "Neodamode"; or an entertaining account of a crazy man going through his family and making it exceedingly warm for the same—and head it "Neodamode"; or an item about a large funeral; or a banquet; or a ball; or a wedding; or a prayer-meeting—anything, no matter what—all the same. They head it "Neodamode." It is the handiest heading I ever saw; it appears to fit any subject you please to tack it to. Why here lately they have even got to using it in items concerning the taking out of naturalization papers by foreigners. There is altogether too much Neodamy around to suit me. I would not mind it so much if it were not quite such an ugly word, and if I had a sort of general notion of what in the mischief it means. I would like to hear from one of the Neodamites.

I have got to go now and report a sermon. I trust it will be pleasanter work than writing a letter on Sunday, while the dogs and cats and chickens are glorifying their Maker and raising the mischief.

Jan. 28, 1866—*Territorial Enterprise.*

MISERIES OF WASHOE MEN

Those of you who owe the Russ House for board and expect to save yourselves trouble when you come here by stopping at the Occidental, look out; Mr. Hardenburgh, formerly of the Russ, is in the office of the Occidental now. And you who owe the Cosmopolitan and propose to stop at the Occidental, beware! for Mr. Smith, formerly of the Cosmopolitan, is in the Occidental office now. And you who owe the Occidental and think to shirk calamity by patronizing the Cosmopolitan, go slow! for Mr. Olmstead and Mr. Childs clerk at the latter hotel now, instead of the former. You had better all come down to your work and go and hang out at the Miners' Restaurant. They have gone and changed things around so now that there is no show for me anywhere. I want to keep my friends out of trouble, though, and so I sound the above note of warning. Amiraux was here from Carson the other day, but he would not stay because his feelings were hurt. He said: "I went to the What Cheer, and I found a fellow from the Brooklyn there; and I went to the Occidental, and I found a fellow from the Russ there; and then I went to the Cosmopolitan, and if there was one clerk there from the Occidental there was a thousand. I am not going to stay in this place—you hear *me!* Damn such a town."

Jan. 28, 1866—*Golden Era.*

["Trem" was the pseudonym of one of the writers for the *Californian.*]

MORE OUTCROPPINGS

Ward, the shirt man, has issued a pamphlet of poems—burlesques of some of the poems in "Outcroppings," and purporting to be a second edition of that work, I suppose, as it bears the same title. It is simply an advertising affair, of course. It was written by "Trem." The burlesque of James Linen's "I Feel I'm Growing Auld," is the most outlandish combination of untranslatable Scotch phraseology I ever saw. I think it is a pretty good take-off on the fashion some folks have of humbugging Americans with poetry that defies criticism because its extravagant Scotchiness defies comprehension. We have come to think, in our day and generation, that every piece of Scotch verse which we cannot understand is necessarily pure, sweet poetry, and that all prose which is spelled atrociously is necessarily humorous and intensely funny. Perhaps you can dig some meaning out of—

I Feel I'm Growing Mirk

by Jean Lining

I feel I'm growing mirk, gude wife,
  I feel I'm growing mirk,
Unsicker girns the graith an' doup,
  An' aye, the stound is birk.
I've fash'd mysel' wi' creeshie rax
  O'er jouk an' hallan braw,
An' now I'll stowlins pit my duds
  An' gar sark white as snaw.

I feel I'm growing mirk, gude wife,
  I feel I'm growing mirk,
An' wae an' wae the giglet jinks,
  'Tis wheep-ed wi' my dirk.
My claes are mirk wi' howdie whangs,
  But still my heart is fair,
Though sconnered yowics loup an' blink,
  I'm nae so puir in gear.

I feel I'm growing mirk, gude wife,
  I feel I'm growing mirk,
The howdie bicker skeeps my een—
  Na mair the coof I'll shirk.
I'll get a Ward's Neat Fitting Shirt—
  They'll glint wi' pawky een,
There's sax score Ward's Shirts sold, gude wife,
  Since I called in yestreen.

Feb. 3, 1866—*Territorial Enterprise.*

MORE CEMETERIAL GHASTLINESS

I spoke the other day of some singular proceedings of a firm of undertakers here, and now I come to converse about one or two more of the undertaker tribe. I begin to think this sort of people have no bowels—as the ancients would say—no heart, as we would express it. They appear to think only of business—business first, last, all the time. They trade in the woes of men as coolly as other people trade in candles and mackerel. Their hearts are ironclad, and they seem to have no sympathies in common with their fellow-men.

A prominent firm of undertakers here own largely in Lone Mountain Cemetery and also in the toll-road leading to it. Now if you or I owned that toll-road we would be satisfied with the revenue from a long funeral procession and would "throw in" the corpse—we would let him pass free of toll—we would wink placidly at the gate-keeper and say, "Never mind this gentleman in the hearse—this fellow's a dead-head." But the firm I am speaking of never do that—if a corpse starts to Paradise or perdition by their road he has got to pay his toll or else switch off and take some other route. And it is rare to see the pride this firm take in the popularity and respectability of their cemetery, and the interest and even enthusiasm which they display in their business.

A friend of mine was out at Lone Mountain the other day, and was moving sadly among the tombs thinking of departed comrades and recalling the once pleasant faces now so cold, and the once familiar voices now so still, and the once busy hands now idly crossed beneath the turf, when he came upon Mr. Smith, of the firm.

"Ah, good morning," says Smith, "come out to see us at last, have you?—glad you have! let me show you round—let me show you round. Pretty fine ain't it?—everything in apple pie order, eh? Everybody says so—everybody says mighty few graveyards go ahead of this? We are endorsed by the best people in San Francisco. We get 'em, sir, we get the pick and choice of the departed. Come, let me show you. Here's Major-General Jones—distinguished man, he was—very distinguished man—highsted him up on that mound, there, where he's prominent. And here's MacSpadden—rich?—Oh, my! And we've got Brigadier-General Jollopson here—there he is, over there—keep him trimmed up and spruce as a fresh "plant," all the time. And we've got Swimley, and Stiggers, the bankers, and Johnson and Swipe, the railroad men, and m-o-r-e Admirals and them kind of people—slathers of 'em! And bless you we've got as much as a whole block planted in nothing but hundred-thousand-dollar fellows—and—"

(Here Mr. Smith's face lighted up suddenly with a blaze of enthusiasm, and he rubbed his hands together and ducked his head to get a better view through the shrubbery of the distant toll-road, and then exclaimed):

"Ah! is it another? Yes, I believe it is—yes it *is!* Third arrival to-day! Long procession! 'George this is gay! Well, so-long, Thompson, I must go and *cache* this party!"

And the happy undertaker skipped lightly away to offer the dismal hospitalities of his establishment to the unconscious visitor in the hearse.

Feb. 3, 1866—*Territorial Enterprise.*

[The vogue for spiritualism had begun to subside elsewhere in the United States, but was still going strong in San Francisco. That city was more favored with spiritual manifestations than other localities, according to one adherent, on account of the powerful psychical emanations given off by the gold deposits. Twain was naturally disposed to spoof the spiritualists and their seances; but when he saw them being ridiculed by Methodists and Baptists, who accepted without question the follies and excesses of revival meetings, he rallied to the spiritualists' defense. The phenomenon intrigued him and he investigated it in several articles—in some of which he comes as close to objective reporting as he ever allowed himself.]

AMONG THE SPIRITS

There was an audience of about 400 ladies and gentlemen present, and plenty of newspaper people—neuters. I saw a good-looking, earnest-faced, pale-red-haired, neatly dressed, young woman standing on a little stage behind a small deal table with slender legs and no drawers—the table, understand me; I am writing in a hurry, but I do not desire to confound my description of the table with my description of the lady. The lady was Mrs. Foye.

As I was coming up town with the *Examiner* reporter, in the early part of the evening, he said he had seen a gambler named Gus Graham shot down in a town in Illinois years ago, by a mob, and as probably he was the only person in San Francisco who knew of the circumstance, he thought he would "give the spirits Graham to chaw on awhile." (N. B. This young creature is a Democrat, and speaks with the native strength and inelegance of his tribe.) In the course of the show he wrote his old pal's name on a slip of paper and folded it up tightly and put it in a hat which was passed around, and which already had about five hundred similar documents in it. The pile was dumped on the table and the medium began to take them up one by one and lay them aside, asking "Is this spirit present?—or this?—or this?" About one in fifty would rap, and the person who sent up the name would rise in his place and question the defunct. At last a spirit seized the medium's hand and wrote

"Gus Graham" backwards. Then the medium went skirmishing through the papers for the corresponding name. And that old sport knew his card by the back. When the medium came to it, after picking up fifty others, he rapped! A committee-man unfolded the paper and it was the right one. I sent for it and got it. It was all right. However, I suppose "all them Democrats" are on sociable terms with the devil. The young man got up and asked:

"Did you die in '51?—'52?—'53?—'54?—"

Ghost—"Rap, rap, rap."

"Did you die of cholera?—diarrhea?—dysentery?—dog-bite?—small-pox?—violent death?—"

"Rap, rap, rap."

"Were you hanged?—drowned?—stabbed?—shot?"

"Rap, rap, rap."

"Did you die in Mississippi?—Kentucky?—New York?—Sandwich Islands?—Texas?—Illinois?—"

"Rap, rap, rap."

"In Adams county?—Madison?—Randolph?—"

"Rap, rap, rap."

It was no use trying to catch the departed gambler. He knew his hand and played it like a Major.

I was surprised. I had a very dear friend, who, I had heard, had gone to the spirit land, or perdition, or some of those places, and I desired to know something concerning him. There was something so awful, though, about talking with living, sinful lips to the ghostly dead, that I could hardly bring myself to rise and speak. But at last I got tremblingly up and said with low and reverent voice:

"Is the spirit of John Smith present?"

"Whack! whack! whack!"

God bless me. I believe all the dead and damned John Smiths between hell and San Francisco tackled that poor little table at once! I was considerably set back—stunned, I may say. The audience urged me to go on, however, and I said:

"What did you die of?"

The Smiths answered to every disease and casualty that man can die of.

"Where did you die!"

They answered yes to every locality I could name while my geography held out.

"Are you happy where you are?"

There was a vigorous and unanimous "No!" from the late Smiths.

"Is it warm there?"

An educated Smith seized the medium's hand and wrote:

"It's no name for it."

"Did you leave any Smiths in that place when you came away?"

"Dead loads of them."

I fancied, I heard the shadowy Smiths chuckle at this feeble joke —the rare joke that there could be live loads of Smiths where all are dead.

"How many Smiths are present?"

"Eighteen millions—the procession now reaches from here to the other side of China."

"Then there are many Smiths in the kingdom of the lost?"

"The Prince Apollyon calls all newcomers Smith on general principles; and continues to do so until he is corrected, if he chances to be mistaken."

"What do lost spirits call their dread abode?"

"They call it the Smithsonian Institute."

I got hold of the right Smith at last—the particular Smith I was after—my dear, lost, lamented friend—and learned that he died a violent death. I feared as much. He said his wife talked him to death. Poor wretch!

But without any nonsense, Mrs. Foye's seance was a very astonishing affair to me—and a very entertaining one. The *Examiner* man's "old pard," the gambler, was too many for me. He answered every question exactly right; and his disembodied spirit, invisible to mortal eyes, must have been prowling around that hall last night. That is, unless this pretended spiritualism is only that other black art called clairvoyance, after all. And yet, the clairvoyant can only tell what is in your mind—but once or twice last night the spirits brought facts to the minds of their questioners which the latter had forgotten before. Well, I cannot make anything out of it. I asked the *Examiner* man what he thought of it, and he said, in the Democratic dialect: "Well, I don't know—I don't know—but it's d——d funny." He did not mean that it was laughable—he only meant that it was perplexing. But such is the language of Democracy.

Feb. 4, 1866—*Golden Era* (as reprinted from *Territorial Enterprise*).

MINISTERIAL CHANGE

MINISTERIAL CHANGE.—The Rev. Richard F. Putnam, late Rector of the Episcopal Church at Grass Valley, has assumed the pastorate of the Church of the Advent in this City.—*Call.*

This gentleman, who was long connected with the editorial department of the *Territorial Enterprise,* and was latterly employed on the Sacramento *Union,* was one of the best men I ever knew. He was a man who could not whistle hard tunes—could not whistle easy ones so as to make a person wish him to keep it up long at a time. Some of the printers used to come to listen when he begun, but the more cultured usually went out—but he could swear and make up telegraph news with any man. He was a man who could go down into a beer cellar in the shank of the evening, and curse and swear, and play commercial seven-up with good average luck and without chicanery till dewy morn, and drink beer all the while—all the while. He was a man who was handy with his pen, and would write you a crusher on any subject under the sun, no matter whether he knew anything about it or not—and he would be growling at somebody or other all through; and if everybody went away and left him he would sit there and curse and swear at his lamp till it burned blue; and he cursed that boy that cleaned that lamp till the constitution of the same was permanently impaired. He was a man who would wade through snow up to his neck to serve his friend, and would convey him home when drunk, and peel him and put him to bed if it was a mile and a half. He was a man who was neck and crop and neck and heels for his friends, and blood, hair and the ground tore up to his enemies. Take him how you would, he was an ornament to his species—and there is no man that is more sorry than I am to see him forsake the pleasant fields he was wont to tread and confine himself to a limited beat on the Gospel—to a beat in a town which is small and where he cannot have full swing according to his dimensions, if I may so speak in connection with matters pertaining to the Scriptural line of business.

P.S.—But I find that this Putnam mentioned in the item above, is not the Putnam I have been speaking of. I was talking of C. A. V. Putnam, and I perceive that the above parson is Richard F. Well, I am glad—and it is all the better as it is.

Feb. 6, 1866—*Territorial Enterprise.*

MARK TWAIN A COMMITTEE MAN

I attended the *seance* last night. After the house was crowded with ladies and gentlemen, Mrs. Foye stepped out upon the stage and said it was usual to elect a committee of two gentlemen to sit up there and see that everything was conducted with perfect honesty and fairness. She said she wished the audience to name gentlemen whose integrity, whose conscientiousness—in a word whose high moral character, in every respect, was notorious in the community. The majority of the audience arose with one impulse and called my name. This handsome compliment was as grateful as it was graceful, and I felt the tears spring to my eyes. I trust I shall never do anything to forfeit the generous confidence San Francisco has thus shown in me. This touching compliment is none the less grateful to me when I reflect that it took me two days to get it up. I "put up" that hand myself. I got all my friends to promise to go there and vote for me to be on that committee—and having reported a good deal in Legislatures, I knew how to do it right. I had a two-thirds vote secured—I wanted enough to elect me over the medium's veto, you know. I was elected, and I was glad of it. I thought I would feel a good deal better satisfied if I could have a chance to examine into this mystery myself, without being obliged to take somebody else's word for its fairness, and I did not go on that stand to find fault or make fun of the affair—a thing which would not speak well for my modesty when I reflect that so many men so much older and wiser than I am see nothing in Spiritualism to scoff at, but firmly believe in it as a religion.

Mr. Whiting was chosen as the other committee man, and we sat down at a little table on the stage with the medium, and proceeded to business. We wrote the names of various departed persons. Mr. W. wrote a good many, but I found that I did not know many dead people; however, I put in the names of two or three whom I had known well, and then filled out the list with names of citizens of San Francisco who had been distinguished in life, so that most persons in the audience could tell whether facts stated by such spirits concerning themselves were correct or not. I will remark here that not a solitary spirit summoned by me paid the least attention to the invitation. I never got a word out of any of them. One of Mr. Whiting's spirits came up and stated some things about itself which were correct. Then some five hundred closely folded slips of paper containing names, were dumped in a pile on the table, and the lady began to lay them aside one by one. Finally a rap was heard. I took the folded paper; the spirit, so-called, seized the lady's hand and wrote "J. M. Cooke" backwards and upside down on a sheet of paper. I opened the slip I held, and, as Captain Cuttle would say, "J. M. Cooke" was the "dientical" name in it. A gentleman in the audience said he sent up the name. He asked a question or so, and then the spirit wrote "Would like to communicate with you alone." The privacy of this ghost was respected, and he was permitted to go to thunder again unmolested. "William Nelson" reported himself from the other world, and in answer to questions asked by a former friend of his in the audience, said he was aged 24 when he died; died by violence; died in a battle; was a soldier; had fought both in the infantry and cavalry; fell at Chickamauga; had been a Catholic on earth—was not one now. Then in answer to a pelting volley of questions, the shadowy warrior wrote: "I don't want to answer any more about it." Exit Nelson.

About this time it was suggested that a couple of Germans be added to the committee, and it was done. Mr. Wallenstein, an elderly man, came forward, and also Mr. Ollendorf, a spry young fellow, cocked and primed for a sensation. They wrote some names. Then young Ollendorf said something which sounded like:

"Ist ein geist hierans?" (bursts of laughter from the audience.)

Three raps—signifying that there *was* a geist hierans.

"Vollen sie schriehen?" (more laughter). Three raps.

"Finzig stollen, linsowftterowlickter-hairowfterfrowleineruback-folderol?" (Oh, this is too rough, you know. I can't keep the run of this sort of thing.) Incredible as it may seem, the spirit cheerfully answered yes to that astonishing proposition.

Young Ollendorf sprang to his feet in a state of consuming excitement. He exclaimed:

"Laties and shentlemen! I write de name for a man vot lifs! Speerit rabbing dells me he ties in yahr eighteen hoondert und dwelf, but he yoos as live und helty as—"

The Medium—"Sit down, sir!"

Mr. O.—"But de speerit cheat!—dere is no such speerit—" (All this time applause and laughter by turns from the audience.)

Medium—"Take your seat, sir, and I will explain this matter."

And she explained. And in that explanation she let off a blast which was so terrific that I half expected to see young Ollendorf shoot up through the roof. She said he had come up there with fraud and deceit and cheating in his heart, and a kindred spirit had come from the land of shadows to commune with him! She was terribly bitter. She said in substance, though not in words, that perdition was full of just such fellows as Ollendorf, and they were ready on the slightest pretext to rush in and assume anybody's name, and rap, and write, and lie, and swindle with a perfect looseness whenever they could rope in a living affinity like poor Ollendorf to communicate with! (Great applause and laughter.)

Ollendorf stood his ground with good pluck, and was going to open his batteries again, when a storm of cries arose all over the house. "Get down! Go on! Speak on—we'll hear you! Climb down from that platform! Stay where you are—Vamose! Stick to your post—say your say!"

The medium rose up and said if Ollendorf remained, she would not. She recognized no one's right to come there and insult her by practicing a deception upon her and attempting to bring ridicule upon so solemn a thing as her religious belief.

The audience then became quiet, and the subjugated Ollendorf retired from the platform.

The other German raised a spirit, questioned it at some length in his own language, and said the answers were correct. The medium claims to be entirely unacquainted with the German language.

A spirit seized the medium's hand and wrote "G. L. Smith" very distinctly. She hunted through the mass of papers, and finally the spirit rapped. She handed me the folded paper she had just picked up. It had "T. J. Smith" in it. (You never can depend on these Smiths; you call for one and the whole tribe will come clattering out of hell to answer you.) Upon further inquiry it was discovered that both these Smiths were present. We chose "T. J." A gentleman in the audience said that was his Smith. So he questioned him, and Smith said he died by violence; he had been a teacher; not a school-teacher, but (after some hesitation) a teacher of religion, and was a sort of a cross between a Universalist and a Unitarian; has got straightened out and changed his opinion since he left here; said he was perfectly happy. Mr. George Purnell, having been added to the committee, proceeded in connection with myself, Mrs. Foye and a number of persons in the audience, to question this talkative and frolicksome old parson. Among spirits, I judge he is the gayest of the gay. He said he had no tangible body; a bullet could pass through him and never make a hole; rain could pass through him as through vapor, and not discommode him in the least (wherefore I suppose he don't know enough to come in when it rains—or don't care enough); says heaven and hell are simply mental conditions—spirits in the former have happy and contented minds; and those in the latter are torn by remorse of conscience; says as far as he is concerned, he is all right—he is happy; would not say whether he was a very good or a very bad man on earth (the shrewd old water-proof nonentity!—I asked the question so that I might average my own chances for his luck in the other world, but he saw my drift); says he has an occupation there—puts in his time teaching and being taught; says there are spheres—grades of perfection—he is making pretty good progress—has been promoted a sphere or so since his matriculation; (I said mentally: "Go slow, old man, go slow—you have got all eternity before you"—and he replied not); he don't know how many spheres there are (but I suppose there must be millions, because if a man goes galloping through them at the rate this old Universalist is doing, he will get through an infinitude of them by the time he has been there as long as old Sesostris and those ancient mummies; and there is no estimating how high he will get in even the infancy of eternity—I am afraid the old man is scouring along rather too fast for the style of his surroundings, and the length of time he has got on his hands); says spirits cannot feel heat or cold (which militates somewhat against all my notions of orthodox damnation—fire and brimstone); says spirits commune with each other by thought—they have no language; says the distinctions of the sex are preserved there—and so forth and so on.

The old parson wrote and talked for an hour, and showed by his quick, shrewd, intelligent replies, that he had not been sitting up nights in the other world for nothing, he had been prying into everything worth knowing, and finding out everything he possibly could—as he said himself, when he did not understand a thing he hunted up a spirit who could explain it; consequently he is pretty thoroughly posted; and for his accommodating conduct and its uniform courtesy to me, I sincerely hope he will continue to progress at his present velocity until he lands on the very roof of the highest sphere of all, and thus achieves perfection.

I have made a report of those proceedings which every person present will say is correct in every particular. But I do not know any more about the queer mystery than I did before. I could not even tell where the knocks were made, though they were not two feet from me. Sometimes they seemed to be on the corner of the table, sometimes under the center of it, and sometimes they seemed to proceed from the medium's knee joints. I could not locate them at all, though; they only had a general seeming of being in any one spot; sometimes they even seemed to be in the air. As to where that remarkable intelligence emanates from which directs those strangely accurate replies, that is beyond my reason. I cannot any more account for that than I could explain those wonderful miracles performed by Hindoo jugglèrs. I cannot tell whether the power is supernatural in either case or not, and I never expect to know as long as I live. It is necessarily impossible to *know*—and it is mighty hard to fully believe what you *don't* know.

But I am going to see it through, now, if I do not go crazy—an eccentricity that seems singularly apt to follow investigations of spiritualism.

Feb. 11, 1866—*Golden Era* (as reprinted from *Territorial Enterprise*).

In 1866 a gentleman named Mercer induced a number of respectable young ladies from the East to sail for the Territory of Washington, which suffered from a dearth of women. Here is Jump's comment on the contrast between what the young ladies expect and what they will get.

THE FASHIONS

I once made up my mind to keep the ladies of the State of Nevada posted upon the fashions, but I found it hard to do. The fashions got so shaky that it was hard to tell what was good orthodox fashion, and what heretical and vulgar. This shakiness still obtains in everything pertaining to a lady's dress except her bonnet and her shoes. Some wear waterfalls, some wear nets, some wear cataracts of curls, and a few go bald, among the old maids; so no man can swear to any particular "fashion" in the matter of hair.

The same uncertainty seems to prevail regarding hoops. Little "highflyer" schoolgirls of bad associations, and a good many women of full growth, wear no hoops at all. And we suspect these, as quickly and as naturally as we suspect a woman who keeps a poodle. Some who I know to be ladies, wear the ordinary moderate-sized hoops, and some who I also know to be ladies, wear the new hoop of the "spread-eagle" pattern—and some wear the latter who are not elegant and virtuous ladies—but that is a thing that may be said of any fashion whatever, of course. The new hoops with a spreading base look only tolerably well. They are not bell-shaped—the "spread" is much more abrupt than that. It is tent-shaped; I do not mean an army tent, but a circus tent—which comes down steep and small half way and then shoots suddenly out horizontally and spreads abroad. To critically examine these hoops—to get the best effect—one should stand on the corner of Montgomery and look up a steep street like Clay or Washington. As the ladies loop their dresses up till they lie in folds and festoons on the spreading hoop, the effect presented by a furtive glance up a steep street is very charming. It reminds me of how I used to peep under circus tents when I was a boy and see a lot of mysterious legs tripping about with no visible bodies attached to them. And what handsome vari-colored, gold-clasped garters they wear now-a-days! But for the new spreading hoops, I might have gone on thinking ladies still tied up their stockings with common strings and ribbons as they used to do when I was a boy and they presumed upon my youth to indulge in little freedoms in the way of arranging their apparel which they do not dare to venture upon in my presence now.

But as I intimated before, one new fashion seems to be marked and universally accepted. It is in the matter of shoes. The ladies all wear thick-soled shoes which lace up in front and reach half way to the knees. The shoe itself is very neat and handsome up to the top of the instep—but I bear a bitter animosity to all the surplus leather between that point and the calf of the leg. The tight lacing of this legging above the ankle-bone draws the leather close to the ankle and gives the heel an undue prominence or projection—makes it stick out behind and assume the shape called the "jay-bird heel" pattern. It does not look well. Then imagine this tall shoe on a woman with a large, round, fat foot, and a huge, stuffy, swollen-looking ankle. She looks like she had on an elbow of stove-pipe. Any foot and ankle that are not the perfection of proportion and graceful contour look surpassingly ugly in these high-water shoes. The pretty and sensible fashion of looping up the dress gives one ample opportunity to critically examine and curse an ugly foot. I wish they would cut down these shoes a little in the matter of leggings.

Feb. 12, 1866—*Territorial Enterprise.*

FUNNY

Chief Burke's Star Chamber Board of Police Commissioners is the funniest institution extant, and the way he conducts it is the funniest theatrical exhibition in San Francisco. Now to see the Chief fly around and snatch up accuser and accused before the Commission when any policeman is charged with misconduct in the public prints, you would imagine that fearful Commission was really going to raise the very devil. But it is all humbug, display, fuss and feathers. The Chief brings his policeman out as sinless as an angel, unless the testimony be heavy enough and strong enough, almost, to hang an ordinary culprit, in which case a penalty of four or five days' suspension is awarded.

Wouldn't you call that Legislature steeped in stupidity which appointed a father to try his own son for crimes against the State? Of course. And knowing that the father must share the disgrace if the son is found guilty, would you ever expect a conviction? Certainly not. And would you expect the father's blind partiality for his own offspring to weigh heavily against evidence given against that son. Assuredly you would. Well, this Police Commission is a milder form of that same principle. Chief Burke makes all these policemen, by appointment—breeds them—and feels something of a parent's solicitude for them; and yet, if any charge is brought against them, *he* is the judge before whom they are tried! Isn't it perfectly absurd? I think so. It takes all three of those Commissioners to convict—the verdict must be unanimous—therefore, since every conviction of one of the Chief's offspring must in the nature of things be a sort of reflection upon himself, you cannot be surprised to know that police officers are very seldom convicted before the Police Commissioners. Though the man's sins were blacker than night, the Chief can always prevent conviction by simply withholding his consent. And this extraordinary power works both ways, too. See how simple and easy a matter it was for the Chief to say to a political obstruction in his path: "You are dismissed, McMillan; I know of nothing to your discredit as an officer, but you are an aspirant to my position and I won't keep a stick to break my own back with." He simply said "Go," and he had to shove! If he had been one of the Chief's pets, he might have committed a thousand rascalities, but the powerful Commission would have shielded and saved him every time. Nay, more—it would have made a tremendous hubbub, and a showy and noisy pretense of trying him—and then brought him out blameless and shown him to be an abused and persecuted innocent and entitled to the public commiseration.

Why, the other day, in one of the Commission trials, where a newspaper editor was summoned as a prosecutor, they detailed a substitute for the real delinquent, and tried *him!* There may be more joke than anything else about that statement, but I heard it told, anyhow. And then it is plausible—it is just characteristic of Star Chamber tactics.

You ought to see how it makes the Chief wince for any one to say a word against a policeman; they are his offspring, and he feels all a father's sensitiveness to remarks affecting their good name. It is natural that he should, and it is wrong to do violence to this purely human trait by making him *swear* that he will impartially try them for their crimes, when the thing is perfectly impossible. He *cannot* be impartial—is it human nature to judge with strict impartiality his own friends, his own dependent, his own offspring?

But what I mean to speak of, if I ever get through with these preliminary remarks, is the fact that the *Flag* yesterday said something severe about the police, and right away the reporter was summoned to stand before that terrible tribunal—the Police Commissioners—and prove his charges. Poor innocent! Why, he never can prove anything. They will come "Iowa justice" on him; he will swear he saw the prisoner do so and so, and the Chief will say, "Captain Baker send up thirty-five policemen to swear that they *didn't* see this thing done." They always manage to have the bulk of testimony on their side, anyhow. If Pontius Pilate was on the police he could crucify the Savior again with perfect impunity—but he would have to let Barabbas and that other policeman alone, who were crucified along with him, formerly.

There is a bill in the hands of a San Francisco legislator which proposes to put the police appointing power in the hands of the Mayor, the District Attorney, and the city and county attorney; and the trial of policemen and power to punish or dismiss them, in the hands of the county and police court prosecuting attorney. This would leave Chief Burke nothing to do but attend to his own legitimate business of keeping the police department up to their work all the time, and is just the kind of bill that ought to pass. It would reduce the Chief from autocrat of San Francisco, with absolute power, to the simple rank of Chief of Police with no power to meddle in outside affairs or do anything but mind his own particular business. He told me, not more than a week ago, that such an arrangement would exactly suit him. Now we shall see if it suits him. Don't you dare to send any log-rolling, wire-pulling squads of policemen to Sacramento, Mr. Burke.

Feb. 15, 1866—*Territorial Enterprise.*

LETTER FROM SACRAMENTO

I arrived in the City of Saloons this morning at 3 o'clock, in company with several other disreputable characters, on board the good steamer *Antelope,* Captain Poole, commander. I know I am departing from usage in calling Sacramento the City of Saloons instead of the City of the Plains, but I have my justification—I have not found any plains, here, yet, but I have been in most of the saloons, and there are a good many of them. You can shut your eyes and march into the first door you come to and call for a drink, and the chances are that you will get it. And in a good many instances, after you have assuaged your thirst, you can lay down a twenty and remark that you "copper the ace," and you will find that facilities for coppering the ace are right there in the back room. In addition to the saloons, there are quite a number of mercantile houses and private dwellings. They have already got one capitol here, and will have another when they get it done. They will have fine dedicatory ceremonies when they get it done, but you will have time to prepare for that—you needn't rush down here right away by express. You can come as slow freight and arrive in time to get a good seat.

The "High Grade" Improvement

The houses in the principal thoroughfares here are set down about eight feet below the street level. This system has its advantages. First—It is unique. Secondly—It secures to the citizen a firm, dry street in high water, whereon to run his errands and do her shopping, and thus does away with the expensive and perilous canoe. Thirdly—It makes the first floors shady, very shady, and this is a great thing in a warm climate. Fourthly—It enables the inquiring stranger to rest his elbows on the second story window-sill and look in and criticize the bedroom arrangements of the citizens. Fifthly—It benefits the plebeian second floor boarders at the expense of the bloated aristocracy of the first—that is to say, it brings the plebeians down to the first floor and degrades the aristocrats to the cellar. Lastly—Some persons call it a priceless blessing because children who fall out of second story windows now, cannot break their necks as they formerly did—but that this can strictly be regarded in the light of a blessing, is, of course, open to grave argument.

But joking aside, the energy and the enterprise the Sacramentans have shown in making this expensive grade improvement and raising their houses up to its level is in every way creditable to them, and is a sufficient refutation of the slander so often leveled at them that they are discouraged by the floods, lack confidence in their ability to make their town a success, and are without energy. A lazy and hopeless population would hardly enter upon such costly experiments as these when there is so much high ground in the State which they could fly to if they chose.

Brief Climate Paragraph

This is the mildest, balmiest, pleasantest climate one can imagine. The evenings are especially delightful—neither too warm nor too cold. I wonder if it is always so?

The Lullaby of the Rain

I got more sleep this morning than I needed. When I got tired, very tired, walking around, and went to bed in room No. 121, Orleans Hotel, about sunrise, I asked the clerk to have me called at a quarter past 9 o'clock. The request was complied with, punctually. As I was about to roll out of bed I heard it raining. I said to myself, I cannot knock around town in this kind of weather, and so I may as well lie here and enjoy the rain. I am like everybody else in that I love to lie abed and listen to the soothing sound of pattering rain-drops, and muse upon old times and old scenes of by-gone days. While I was a happy, careless schoolboy again, (in imagination,) I dropped off to sleep. After a while I woke up. Still raining. I said to myself, it will stop directly—I will dream again—there is time enough. Just as (in memory) I was caught by my mother clandestinely putting up some quince preserves in a rag to take to my little sweetheart at school, I dropped off to sleep again, to the soft music of the pattering rain. I woke up again, after a while. Still raining! I said. This will never do. I shall be so late that I shall get nothing done. I could dream no more; I was getting too impatient for that. I lay there and fidgeted for an hour and a half, listening with nervous anxiety to detect the least evidence of a disposition to "let up" on the part of the rain. But it was of no use. It rained on steadily, just the same. So, finally, I said: I can't stand this; I will go to the window and see if the clouds are breaking, at any rate. I looked up, and the sun was blazing overhead. I looked down—and then I "gritted my teeth" and said: "Oh, d——n a d——d landlord that would keep a d——d fountain in his back yard!"

After mature and unimpassioned deliberation, I am still of the opinion that that profanity was justifiable under the circumstances.

I Try to Out "Sass" the Landlord—and Fail

I got down stairs at ten minutes past 12, and went up to the landlord, who is a large, fine-looking man, with a chest on him which must have made him a most powerful man before it slid down, and said, "Is breakfast ready?"

"Is breakfast *ready?*" said he.

"Yes—is breakfast READY?"

"Not quite," he says, with the utmost urbanity, "not quite; you have arisen too early, my son, by a matter of eighteen hours as near as I can come at it."

Humph! I said to myself, these people go slow up here; it is a wonder to me that they ever get up at all.

"Ah, well," said I, "it don't matter—it don't matter. But, ah—perhaps you design to have lunch this week, some time?"

"Yes," he says, "I have designed all along to have lunch this week, and by a most happy coincidence you have arrived on the very day. Walk into the dining room."

As I walked forward I cast a glance of chagrin over my shoulder and observed, "Old Smarty from Mud Springs, I apprehend."

And he murmured, "Young Lunar Caustic from San Francisco, no doubt."

Well, let it pass. If I didn't make anything off that old man in the way of "sass," I cleaned out his lunch table, anyhow. I calculated to get ahead of him some way. And yet I don't know but the old scallawag came out pretty fair, after all. Because I only staid in his hotel twenty-four hours and ate one meal, and he charged me five dollars for it. If I were not just ready to start back to the bay, now, I believe I would go and tackle him once more. If I only had a fair chance, that old man is not any smarter than I am. (I will risk something that it makes him squirm every time I call him "that old man," in this letter. People who voted for General Washington don't like to be reminded that they are old.) But I like the old man, and I like his hotel too, barring the d—— barring the fountain I should say.

Mr. John Paul's Baggage

As I was saying, I took lunch, and then hurried out to attend to business—that is to say, I hurried out to look after Mr. John Paul's baggage. Mr. John Paul is the San Francisco correspondent of the Sacramento *Union,* and "goes fixed." I was down at the wharf when the *Antelope* was about to leave San Francisco, and Captain Poole came to me and said Mr. Paul was going up with him, and he knew by the way he talked that he was going to travel with a good deal of baggage, and it would be quite a favor if I would go along and help look after a portion of it. The Captain then requested Mr. Asa Nudd, and Lieutenant Elhs, and Mr. Bill Stephenson, treasurer of Maguire's Opera House, to keep an eye on portions of Mr. Paul's baggage, also. They cheerfully assented. And by and by Mr. Paul made his appearance, and brought his baggage with him, on a couple of drays. And it consisted of nothing in the world but a toy carpet-sack like a woman's reticule, and had a pair of socks and a tooth-brush in it. We saw in a moment that all that talk of Mr. Paul's had been merely for effect, and that there was really no use in all of us going to Sacramento to look after his baggage; but inasmuch as we had already shipped for the voyage, we concluded to go on. We liked Mr. Paul, and it was a pleasure to us to humor his harmless vanity about his little baggage. Therefore when he said to the chief mate, "Will you please to send some men to get that baggage aboard?" we proceeded to superintend the transportation with becoming ceremony. It was as gratifying to us as it was to Mr. Paul himself, when the second mate afterward reported that the boat was "down by the head" so that she wouldn't steer, and the Captain said, "It's that baggage, I suppose—move it aft." We had a very pleasant trip of it to Sacramento, and said nothing to disabuse the passengers' minds when we found that Paul had disseminated the impression that he had three or four tons of baggage aboard. After we landed at Sacramento there was the infernalest rumbling and thundering of trunks on the main deck for two hours that can be imagined. Finally a passenger who could not sleep for the jarring and the noise, hailed Mr. Bill Stephenson and said he wondered what all the racket was about. Mr. Stephenson said, "It'll be over pretty soon, now—they've been getting that there John Paul's baggage ashore."

I have made this letter so long that I shall have to chop it in two at this point, and send you the remainder of it to-morrow.

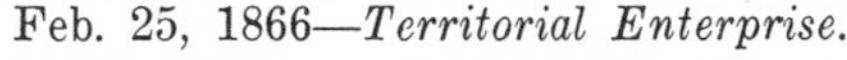
Feb. 25, 1866—*Territorial Enterprise.*

A SAN FRANCISCO MILLIONAIRE

They tell a story of M., a story which shows that once in his life, at any rate, he grew lavish and reckless, and squandered his money with a desperate prodigality.

He had loaned one S. (I cannot recollect his real name,) a thousand dollars or so, at about five per cent a month, and the man invested it in coal, expecting to make a profitable speculation out of it. But the price of coal took a downward track, and went falling, falling, falling, till it was not worth more than half the sum S. had borrowed of M. M. took the place of S.'s shadow, and haunted him day and night. At last the ruined speculator could stand it no longer, and he sought the privacy of his own chamber and blew out his brains. He left M. a heavy loser, and M. abandoned himself to frightful dissipation for a single hour. He was worried by his loss and bothered by the accusation that he was the prime cause of poor S.'s death. He took several friends into a cellar and treated them to a glass of lager apiece. They talked a while, and then got up to leave. The barkeeper reminded them that the beer was not paid for yet. The guests moved up to the counter—each with his hand in his pocket, but M. advanced with a wild light in his eye and waved them impressively aside. He said: "No, I pays for all dis myself! Vot I cares for anydings now? My friend is dead, shentlemen—my friend vot I lofed. Poor S., he's plode his brains out, and didn't pay me. Vot I care for anydings now? I lif, now, after dis, shentlemen—I lif gay und spends my money—I safes no money to loan to people vot go and kill himself before he pay. No, I pays for dis peer myself—I vill be gay und regulus—dam de expensus!"

But that one fearful orgie was his first and his last. The reflections of a cooler moment showed him that the "expensus" were worthy of graver consideration.

Feb. 25, 1866—*Golden Era.*

[Twain's appraisal of the temperament of San Francisco's theatre critics seems quite apt. A decade before, Ferdinand C. Ewer had written in the *Pioneer,* "When we pronounce a favorable verdict, we are able to back it up with a fortune and snap our fingers at the world." Forrest, however, paid no heed to Twain's warning. He *did* go to San Francisco, opening on May 11, 1866, and enjoyed a tremendous success, playing Lear, Macbeth, Othello, and other roles in his repertory. Even before his arrival, demand for seats was so great that the first ticket was auctioned off at $500, and 58 other tickets were sold for $437. As for the critics, they unanimously hailed him as the greatest tragedian of the age.]

ON CALIFORNIA CRITICS

Edwin Forrest is coming here. Very well—good bye, Mr. Forrest. Our critics will make you sing a lively tune. They will soon let you know that your great reputation cannot protect you on this coast. You have passed muster in New York, but they will show you up here. They will make it very warm for you. They will make you understand that a man who has served a lifetime as dramatic critic on a New York paper may still be incompetent, but that a California critic knows it all, notwithstanding he may have been in the shoemaking business most of his life, or a plow-artist on a ranch. You will be the sickest man in America before you get through with this trip. They will set up Frank Mayo for your model as soon as you get here, and they will say you don't play up to him, whether you do or not. And then they will decide that you are a "bilk." That is the grand climax of all criticism. They will say it here, first, and the country papers will endorse it afterwards. It will then be considered proven. You might as well as quit, then.

You see, they always go into ecstasies with an actor the first night he plays, and they call him the most gifted in America the next morning. Then they think they have not acted with metropolitan coolness and self possession, and they slew around on the other tack and abuse him like a pickpocket to get even. This was Bandman's experience, Menken's, Heron's, Vestali's, Boniface's, and many others I could name. It will be yours also. You had better stay where you are. You will regret it if you come here. How would you feel if they told you your playing might answer in places of small consequence but wouldn't do in San Francisco? They will tell you that, as sure as you live. And then say, in the most crushing way:

"Mr. Forrest has evidently mistaken the character of this people. We will charitably suppose that this is the case, at any rate. We make no inquiry as to what kind of people he has been in the habit of playing before, but we simply inform him that he is now in the midst of a refined and cultivated community, and one which will not tolerate such indelicate allusions as were made use of in the play of 'Othello' last night. If he would not play to empty benches, this must not be repeated." They always come the "refined and cultivated" dodge on a new actor—look out for it, Mr. Forrest, and do not let it floor you. The boys know enough that it is one of the most effective shots that can be fired at a stranger. Come on, Forrest—I will write your dramatic obituary, gratis.

Feb. 25, 1866—*Golden Era.*

PRESENCE OF MIND

INCIDENTS OF THE DOWN TRIP OF THE "AJAX."

The Ajax, *according to all accounts, had a rough passage out on her recent trip to the Sandwich Islands, and very many of the passengers for the first time in their lives began to think of their sins. "Mark Twain"—the veracious correspondent of the* Territorial Enterprise, *and a distinguished friend of our Police—relates the following incidents of the storm:*

The storm tore all light rigging to shreds and splinters, upset all furniture that could be upset, and spilled passengers around and knocked them hither and thither with a perfect looseness. For

forty-eight hours no table could be set, and everybody had to eat as best they might under the circumstances. Most of the party went hungry, though, and attended to their praying. But there was one set of "seven-up" players who nailed a card-table to the floor and stuck to their game through thick and thin. Captain Fretz, of the Bank of California, a man of great coolness and presence of mind, was of this party. One night the storm suddenly culminated in a climax of unparalleled fury; the vessel went down on her beam ends, and everything let go with a crash; passengers, tables, cards, bottles—everything—came clattering to the floor in a chaos of disorder and confusion. In a moment fifty sore distressed and pleading voices ejaculated, "Oh, Heaven help us in our extremity!" and one voice rang out clear and sharp above the plaintive chorus and said, "Remember, boys, I played the tray for low!" It was one of the gentlemen I have mentioned who spoke. And the remark showed good presence of mind and an eye to business.

Lewis Leland, of the Occidental, was a passenger. There were some savage grizzly bears chained in cages on deck. One night in the midst of a hurricane, which was accompanied by rain and thunder and lightning, Mr. Leland came up, on his way to bed. Just as he stepped into the pitchy darkness of the deck and reeled to the still more pitchy motion of the vessel (bad) the captain sung out hoarsely through his speaking trumpet, "Bear a hand aft, there!" The words were sadly marred and jumbled by the roaring wind. Mr. Leland thought the captain said, "The bears are after you there!" and he "let go all holts" and went down into his boots. He murmured, "I knew how it was going to be—I just knew it from the start—I said all along that those bears would get loose some time, and now I'll be the first man that they'll snatch. Captain!—Captain!—can't hear me—storm roars so. Oh, God, what a fate! I have avoided wild beasts all my life, and now to be eaten by a grizzly bear in the middle of the ocean, a thousand miles from land! Captain! Oh, Captain!—bless my soul, there's one of them!—I've got to cut and run!" And he did cut and run, and smashed through the door of the first stateroom he came to. A gentleman and his wife were in it. The gentleman exclaimed, "Who's that?" The refugee gasped out, "Oh, great Scotland, those bears are loose, and just raising merry hell all over the ship!" and then sank down exhausted. The gentleman sprang out of bed and locked the door, and prepared for a siege. After a while, no assault being made, a reconnoissance was made from the window and a vivid flash of lightning revealed a clear deck. Mr. Leland then made a dart for his own stateroom, gained it, locked himself in, and felt that his body's salvation was accomplished, and by little less than a miracle. Now I have told this story as I heard it from a passenger, who said he would vouch for every part of it except the language, which is stronger than Mr. Leland ever indulged in. The next day the subject of this memoir, though still very feeble and nervous, had the hardihood to make a joke upon his adventure. He said that when he found himself in so tight a place (as he thought) he didn't bear it with much fortitude, and when he found himself safe at last in his stateroom, he regarded it as the bearest escape he had ever had in his life. He then went to bed and did not get up again for nine days. This unquestionably bad joke cast a gloom over the whole ship's company, and no effort was sufficient to restore their wonted cheerfulness until the vessel reached her port and other scenes erased it from their memories.

March 3, 1866—*Californian.*

THE NEW WILDCAT RELIGION

Another spiritual investigator—G. C. DeMerritt—passed his examination today, after a faithful attendance on the seances of the Friends of Progress, and was shipped, a raving maniac, to the insane asylum at Stockton—an institution which is getting to be quite a College of Progress.

People grow exasperated over these frequently occurring announcements of madness occasioned by fighting the tiger of spiritualism, and I think it is not fair. They abuse the spiritualists unsparingly, but I can remember when Methodist camp meetings and Campbellite revivals used to stock the asylums with religious lunatics, and yet the public kept their temper and said never a word. We don't cut up when madmen are bred by the old legitimate regular stock religions, but we can't allow wildcat religions to indulge in such disastrous experiments. I do not really own in the old regular stock, but I lean strongly toward it, and I naturally feel some little prejudice against all wildcat religions—still, I protest that it is not fair to excuse the one and abuse the other for the self-same rascality. I do not love the wildcat, but at the same time I do not like to see the wildcat imposed on merely because it is friendless. I know a great many spiritualists—good and worthy persons who sincerely and devotedly love their wildcat religion (but not regarding it as wildcat themselves, though, of course,)—and I know them to be persons in every way worthy of respect. They are men of business habits and good sense.

Now when I see such men as these, quietly but boldly come forward and consent to be pointed at as supporters of wildcat religion, I almost feel as if it were presumptuous in some of us to assert without qualification that spiritualism *is* wildcat. And when I see these same persons cherishing, and taking to their honest bosoms and fondling this wildcat, with genuine affection and confidence, I feel like saying, "Well, if this is a wildcat religion, it pans out wonderfully like the old regular, after all." No—it goes against the grain; but still, loyalty to my Presbyterian bringing up compels me to stick to the Presbyterian decision that spiritualism is neither more nor less than a wildcat.

I do not take any credit to my better-balanced head because I never went crazy on Presbyterianism. We go too slow for that. You never see us ranting and shouting and tearing up the ground. You never heard of a Presbyterian going crazy on religion. Notice us, and you will see how we do. We get up of a Sunday morning and put on the best harness we have got and trip cheerfully down town; we subside into solemnity and enter the church; we stand up and duck our heads and bear down on a hymn book propped on the pew in front when the minister prays; we stand up again while our hired choir are singing, and look in the hymn book and check off the verses to see that they don't shirk any of the stanzas; we sit silent and grave while the minister is preaching, and count the waterfalls and bonnets furtively, and catch flies; we grab our hats and bonnets when the benediction is begun; when it is finished, we shove, so to speak. No frenzy—no fanaticism—no skirmishing; everything perfectly serene. You never see any of us Presbyterians getting in a sweat about religion and trying to massacre the neighbors. Let us all be content with the tried and safe old regular religions, and take no chances on wildcat.

March 4, 1866—*Golden Era.*

MORE SPIRITUAL INVESTIGATIONS

I shall have this matter of spiritualism "down to a spot," yet, if I do not go crazy in the meantime. I stumbled upon a private fireside seance a night or two ago, where two old gentlemen and a middle-aged gentleman and his wife were communicating (as they firmly believed) with the ghosts of the departed. They have met for this purpose every week for years. They do not "investigate"—they have long since become strong believers, and further investigations are not needed by them. I knew some of these parties well enough to know that whatever deviltry was exhibited would be honest, at least, and that if there were any humbugging done they themselves would be as badly humbugged as any spectator. We kept the investigations going for three hours, and it was rare fun.

They set a little table in the middle of the floor, and set up a dial on it which bore the letters of the alphabet instead of the figures of a clock-face. An index like the minute hand of a clock was so arranged that the tipping of the table would cause it to move around the dial and point to any desired letter, and thus spell words. The lady and two gentlemen sat at the table and rested their hands gently upon it, no other portion of their persons touching it. And the spirits, and some other mysterious agency, came and tilted the table back and forth, sometimes lifting two of its legs three or four inches from the floor and causing the minute hand to travel entirely around the dial. These persons did not move the table themselves; because when no one's hands rested upon it but the lady's it tilted just the same, and although she could have borne down her side of the table, by an effort, it was impossible for her to *lift up* her side with her hands simply resting on top of it. And then the hands of these persons lay perfectly impassable—not rose or fell, and not a tendon grew tense or relaxed as the table tilted—whereas, when they removed their hands and I tilted the table with mine, it required such exertion that muscles and tendons rose and fell and stretched and relaxed with every movement. I do not know who tilted that table, but it was not the medium at any rate. It tired my arms to death merely to spell out four long words on the dial, but the lady and the ghosts spelled out long conversations without the least fatigue.

The first ghost that announced his presence spelled this on the dial: "My name is Thomas Tilson; I was a preacher. I have been dead many years. I know this man Mark Twain well!"

I involuntarily exclaimed: "The very devil you do?" That old dead parson took me by surprise when he spelled my name, and I felt the cold chills creep over me. Then the ghost and I continued the conversation:

"Did you know me on earth?"

"No. But I read what you write, every day, almost. I like your writings."

"Thank you. But *how* do you read it?—do they take the *Territorial Enterprise* in h—— or rather, heaven, I beg your pardon?"

"No. I read it through my affinity."

"Who is your affinity?"

"Mac Crellish of the *Alta!*"

This excited some laughter, of course—and I will remark here that both ghosts and mediums indulge in jokes, conundrums, doggerel rhymes, and laughter—when the ghost says a good thing he wags the minute hand gaily to and fro to signify laughter.

"Did Mac Crellish ever know you?"

"No. He didn't know me, and doesn't suspect that he is my affinity—but he is, nevertheless. I impress him and influence him every day. If he starts to do what I think he ought not to do, I change his mind."

This ghost then proceeded to go into certain revelations in this connection which need not be printed.

William Thompson's ghost came up. Said he knew me; loved me like a brother; never knew me on earth, though. Said he had been a school teacher in Mott Street, New York; was an assistant teacher when he was only fifteen years old, and appeared to take a good deal of pride in the fact. Said he was with me constantly.

"Well," I said, "you get into some mighty bad company sometimes, Bill, if you travel with me." He said it couldn't hurt him.

One of the irrepressible Smiths took the stand, now. He told his name, and said, "I am here!"

"Staunch and true!" said I.

"Colors blue! and liberty forever!" quoth the poetical Smith.

The medium said, "Mr. Smith, Mr. Twain here has been abusing the Smith family—can't you give him a brush?"

And Smith spelled out, "If I only had a brush!" and wagged the minute hand in a furious burst of laughter. Smith thought that was a gorgeous joke. And it might be so regarded in perdition, where Smith lives, but will not excite much admiration here.

Then Smith asked, "Why don't you have some whiskey here?" He was informed that the decanter had just been emptied. Mr. Smith said: "I'll go and fetch some." In about a minute he came back and said: "Don't get impatient—just sit where you are and wait till you see me coming with that whiskey!" and then shook a boisterous laugh on the dial and cleared out. And I suppose this old Smarty from h—— is going around in the other world yet, bragging about this cheap joke.

A Mr. Wentworth, a very intelligent person for a dead man, came and spelled out a "lecture" of two foolscap pages, on the subject of "Space," but I haven't got space to print it here. It was very beautifully written; the style was smooth, and flowing, the language was well chosen, and the metaphors and similes were apt and very poetical. The only fault I could find about the late Mr. Wentworth's lecture on "Space" was, that there was nothing in it about space. The essayist seemed to be only trying to reconcile people to the loss of friends, by showing that the lost friends were unquestionably in luck in being lost, and therefore should not be grieved for—and the essayist did the thing gracefully and well but devil a word did he say about "Space."

Very well; the *Bulletin* may abuse spiritualism as much as it pleases, but whenever I can get a chance to take a dead and damned Smith by the hand and pass a joke or swap a lie with him, I am going to do it. I am not afraid of such pleasant corpses as these ever running me crazy. I find them better company than a good many live people.

March 11, 1866—*Golden Era.*

REFLECTIONS ON THE SABBATH

The day of rest comes but once a week, and sorry I am that it does not come oftener. Man is so constituted that he can stand more rest than this. I often think regretfully that it would have been so easy to have two Sundays in a week, and yet it was not so ordained. The omnipotent Creator could have made the world in three days just as easily as he made it in six, and this would have doubled the Sundays. Still it is not our place to criticize the wisdom of the Creator. When we feel a depraved inclination to question the judgment of Providence in stacking up double eagles in the coffers of Michael Reese and leaving better men to dig for a livelihood, we ought to stop and consider that we are not expected to help order things, and so drop the subject. If all-powerful Providence grew weary after six days' labor, such worms as we are might reasonably expect to break down in three, and so require two Sundays—but as I said before, it ill becomes us to hunt up flaws in matters which are so far out of our jurisdiction. I hold that no man can meddle with the exclusive affairs of Providence and offer suggestions for their improvement, without making himself in a manner conspicuous. Let us take things as we find them—though, I am free to confess, it goes against the grain to do it, sometimes.

What put me into this religious train of mind, was attending church at Dr. Wadsworth's this morning. I had not been to church before for many months, because I never could get a pew, and therefore had to sit in the gallery among the sinners. I stopped that because my proper place was down among the elect, inasmuch as I was brought up a Presbyterian, and consider myself a brevet member of Dr. Wadsworth's church. I always was a brevet. I was sprinkled in infancy, and look upon that as conferring the rank of Brevet Presbyterian. It affords none of the emoluments of the Regular Church—simply confers honorable rank upon the recipient and the right to be punished as a Presbyterian hereafter; that is, the substantial Presbyterian punishment of fire and brimstone instead of this heterodox hell of remorse of conscience of these blamed wildcat religions. The heaven and hell of the wildcat religions are vague and ill defined but there is nothing mixed about the Presbyterian heaven and hell. The Presbyterian hell is all misery; the heaven all happiness—nothing to do. But when a man dies on a wildcat basis, he will never rightly know hereafter which department he is in—but he will think he is in hell anyhow, no matter which place he goes to; because in the good place they progress, pro-gress, pro-gress—study, study, study, all the time—and if this isn't hell I don't know what is; and in the bad place he will be worried by remorse of conscience. Their bad place is preferable, though, because eternity is long, and before a man got half through it he would forget what it was he had been so sorry about. Naturally he would then become cheerful again; but the party who went to heaven would go on progressing and progressing, and studying and studying until he would finally get discouraged and wish he were in hell, where he wouldn't require such a splendid education.

Dr. Wadsworth never fails to preach an able sermon; but every now and then, with an admirable assumption of not being aware of it, he will get off a first-rate joke and then frown severely at any one who is surprised into smiling at it. This is not fair. It is like throwing a bone to a dog and then arresting him with a look just as he is going to seize it. Several people there on Sunday suddenly laughed and as suddenly stopped again, when he gravely gave the Sunday school books a blast and spoke of "the good little boys in them who always went to Heaven, and the bad little boys who infallibly got drowned on Sunday," and then swept a savage frown around the house and blighted every smile in the congregation.

March 18, 1866—*Golden Era.*

A COMPLAINT ABOUT CORRESPONDENTS

What do you take us for, on this side of the continent? I am addressing myself personally, and with asperity, to every man, woman, and child east of the Rocky Mountains. How do you suppose our minds are constituted, that you will write us such execrable letters—such poor, bald, uninteresting trash? You complain that, by the time a man has been on the Pacific Coast six months, he seems to lose all concern about matters and things and people in the distant East, and ceases to answer the letters of his friends and even his relatives. It is your own fault. You need a lecture on the subject—a lecture which ought to read about as follows:

GRAND MUNICI
DEMOCRATIC TICKET CHIEF POLIC P J WHITE
COBB
FOR CORONER DR HEWER
FOR CORONER
E Jump

The city elections of 1866 saw the Ins ousted.

There is only one brief, solitary law for letter-writing, and yet you either do not know that law, or else you are so stupid that you never think of it. It is very easy and simple: Write only about things and people your correspondent takes a living interest in.

Cannot you remember that law, hereafter, and abide by it? If you are an old friend of the person you are writing to, you know a number of his acquaintances, and you can rest satisfied that even the most trivial things you can write about them will be read with avidity out here on the edge of sunset.

Yet how *do* you write?—how do the most of you write? Why, you drivel and drivel, and drivel along, in your wooden-headed way, about people one never heard of before, and things which one knows nothing at all about and cares less. There is no sense in that. Let me show up your style with a specimen or so. Here is a paragraph from my Aunt Nancy's last letter—received four years ago, and not answered immediately—not at all, I may say.

"St. Louis, 1862.

"Dear Mark: We spent the evening very pleasantly at home, yesterday. The Rev. Mr. Macklin and wife, from Peoria, were here. He is an humble laborer in the vineyard and takes his coffee strong. He is also subject to neuralgia—neuralgia in the head—and is so unassuming and prayerful. There are few such men. We had soup for dinner likewise. Although I am not fond of it. Oh, Mark, why *don't* you try to lead a better life? Read II. Kings, from chap. 2 to chap. 24 inclusive. It would be so gratifying to me if you would experience a change of heart. Poor Mrs. Gabrick is dead. You did not know her. She had fits, poor soul. On the 14th the entire army took up the line of march from——"

I always stopped there, because I knew what was coming—the war news, in minute and dry detail—for I could never drive it into those numsculls that the overland telegraph enabled me to know here in San Francisco every day all that transpired in the United States the day before, and that the pony express brought me exhaustive details of all matters pertaining to the war, at least two weeks before their letters could possibly reach me. So I naturally skipped their stale war reports, even at the cost of also skipping the inevitable suggestions to read this, that, and the other batch of chapters in the Scriptures, with which they were interlarded at intervals like snares wherewith to trap the unwary sinner.

Now what was the Rev. Macklin to me? Of what consequence was it to me that he was "an humble laborer in the vineyard," and "took his coffee strong"?—and was unassuming, and neuralgic, and prayerful? Such a strange conglomeration of virtues could only excite my admiration—nothing more. It could awake no living interest. That there are few such men and that we had soup for dinner, are simply gratifying—that is all. "Read twenty-two chapters of Second Kings" is a nice shell to fall in the camp of a man who is not studying for the ministry. The intelligence that "poor Mrs. Gabrick" was dead, aroused no enthusiasm—mostly because of the circumstance that I had never heard of her before, I presume. But I was glad she had fits—although a stranger.

Don't you begin to understand, now? Don't you see that there is not a sentence in that letter of any interest in the world to me? I had the war news in advance of it; I could get a much better sermon at church when I needed it; I didn't care anything about poor Gabrick, not knowing the deceased: nor yet the Rev. Macklin, not knowing him either. I said to myself, "Here's not a word about Mary Anne Smith—I wish there was; nor about Georgiana Brown, or Zeb Leavenworth, or Sam Bowen, or Strother Wiley—or about anybody else I care a straw for." And so, as this letter was just of a pattern with all that went before it, it was not answered, and one useless correspondence ceased.

My venerable mother is a tolerably good correspondent—she is above the average, at any rate. She puts on her spectacles and takes her scissors and wades into a pile of newspapers and slashes out column after column—editorials, hotel arrivals, poetry, telegraph news, advertisements, novellettes, old jokes, recipes for making pies, cures for "biles"—anything that comes handy; it don't matter to her; she is entirely impartial; she slashes out a column, and runs her eye down it over her spectacles (she looks over them because she can't see through them, but she prefers them to her more serviceable ones because they have got gold rims to them)—

runs her eye down the column and says "Well, it's from a St. Louis paper, anyway," and jams it into the envelope along with her letter. She writes about everybody I ever knew or ever heard of, but unhappily she forgets that when she tells me that "J. B. is dead; and that W. L. is going to marry T. D.;" and that "B. K. and R. M. and L. P. J. have all gone to New Orleans to live," it is more than likely that years of absence may have so dulled my recollection of once familiar names that their unexplained initials will be as unintelligible as Hebrew unto me. She never writes a name in full, and so I never know who she is talking about. Therefore I have to guess—and this was how it came that I mourned the death of Bill Kribben when I should have rejoiced over the dissolution of Ben Kenfuron. I failed to cipher the initials out correctly.

The most useful and interesting letters we get here from home are from children seven or eight years old. This is petrified truth. Happily they have got nothing to talk about but home, and neighbors, and family—things their betters think unworthy of transmission thousands of miles. They write simply and naturally, and without straining for effect. They tell all they know, and then stop. They seldom deal in abstractions or moral homilies. Consequently their epistles are brief; but, treating as they do of familiar scenes and persons, always entertaining. Now therefore, if you would learn the art of letter-writing, let a little child teach you. I have preserved a letter from a small girl eight years of age—preserved it as a curiosity, because it was the only letter I ever got from the States that had any information in it. It runs thus:

St. Louis, 1865.

"Uncle Mark, if you was here I could tell you about Moses in the Bulrushers again. I know it better, now. Mr. Sowerby has got his leg broke off a horse. He was riding it on Sunday. Margaret, that's the maid, Margaret has took all the spittoons, and slop-buckets, and old jugs out of your room, because she says she don't think you're ever coming back any more, you been gone so long. Sissy McElroy's mother has got another little baby. She has them all the time. It has got little blue eyes, like Mr. Swimley that boards there, and looks just like him. I have got a new doll, but Johnny Anderson pulled one of its legs out. Miss Doosenberry was here to day; I give her your picture, but she said she didn't want it. My cat has got more kittens, O, you can't think—twice as many as Lottie Belden's. And there's one such a sweet little buff one with a short tail, and I named it for you. All of them's got names, now—General Grant, and Halleck, and Moses, and Margaret, and Deuteronomy, and Captain Semmes, and Exodus, and Leviticus, and Horace Greeley—all named but one, and I am saving it because the one that I named for You's been sick all the time since, and I reckon it'll die. [It appears to have been mighty rough on the short-tailed kitten, naming it for me—I wonder how the reserved victim will stand it.] Uncle Mark, I do believe Hattie Caldwell likes you, and I know she thinks you are pretty, because I heard her say nothing couldn't hurt your good looks—nothing at all—she said even if you was to have the small-pox ever so bad you would be just as good-looking as you was before. And my ma says she's ever so smart. [Very.] So no more this time, because General Grant and Moses is fighting. Annie"

This child treads on my toes, in every other sentence, with a perfect looseness, but in the simplicity of her time of life she doesn't know it.

I consider that a model letter—an eminently readable and entertaining letter—and, as I said before, it contains more matter of interest and more real information than any letter I ever received from the East. I had rather hear about the cats at home and their truly remarkable names, than listen to a lot of stuff about people I am not acquainted with, or read "The Evil Effects of the Intoxicating Bowl," illustrated on the back with a picture of a ragged scalliwag pelting away right and left, in the midst of his family circle, with a junk bottle.

March 24, 1866—*Californian* (as reprinted from the *New York Review*).

[In the spring of 1866 Twain sailed to Hawaii, or the Sandwich Islands as they were then known, to do a series of articles for the *Sacramento Union.* The resulting series, which have since been published as *Letters from the Sandwich Islands,* were Twain's first extended body of work. The following two pieces are briefer reports from Hawaii which the *Golden Era* published.]

MARK TWAIN'S STEED OAHU

The landlord of the American said the party had been gone nearly an hour, but that he could give me my choice of several horses that could easily overtake them. I said, never mind—I preferred a safe horse to a fast one—I would like to have an excessively gentle horse—a horse with no spirit whatever—a lame one, if he had such a thing. Inside of five minutes I was mounted, and perfectly satisfied with my outfit. I had no time to label him "This is a horse," and so if the public took him for a sheep I cannot help it. I was satisfied, and that was the main thing. I could see he had as many fine points as any man's horse, and I just hung my hat on one of them, behind the saddle, and swabbed the perspiration from my face and started. I named him after this island, "Oahu," (pronounced O-waw-hoo). The first gate he came to he started in; I had neither whip nor spur, and so I simply argued the case with him. He firmly resisted the argument, but ultimately yielded to insult and abuse. He backed out of that gate and steered for another one on the other side of the street. I triumphed by my former process. Within the next six hundred yards he crossed the street fourteen times and attempted thirteen gates, and in the meantime the tropical sun was beating down and threatening to cave the top of my head in, and I was literally dripping with perspiration and profanity. (I am only human and I was sorely aggravated. I shall behave better next time.) He quit the gate business after that and went along peaceably enough, but absorbed in meditation. I noticed this latter circumstance, and it soon began to fill me with the gravest apprehension. I said to myself, this malignant brute is planning some new outrage, some fresh deviltry or another—no horse ever thought over a subject so profoundly as this one is doing just for nothing. The more this thing preyed upon my mind the more uneasy I became, until at last the suspense became unbearable and I dismounted to see if there was anything wild in his eye—for I had heard that the eye of the noblest of our domestic animals is very expressive. I cannot describe what a load of anxiety was lifted from my mind when I found that he was only asleep. I woke him up and started him into a faster walk, and then the inborn villainy of his nature came out again. He tried to climb over a stone wall, five or six feet high. I saw that I must apply force to this horse, and that I might as well begin first as last. I plucked a stout switch from a tamarind tree, and the moment he saw it, he gave in. He broke into a convulsive sort of a canter, which had three short steps in it and one long one, and reminded me alternately of the clattering shake of the great earthquake, and the sweeping plunging of the *Ajax* in a storm.

May 6, 1866—*Golden Era.*

THE SANDWICH ISLAND LEGISLATURE

This Legislature is like all other Legislatures. A wooden-head gets up and proposes an utterly absurd something or other, and he and half a dozen other wooden-heads discuss it with windy vehemence for an hour, the remainder of the house sitting in silent patience the while, and then a sensible man—a man of weight—a big gun—gets up and shows the foolishness of the matter in five sentences; a vote is taken and the thing is tabled. Now, on one occasion, a Kanaka member, who paddled over here from some barren rock or other out yonder in the ocean—some scalliwag who wears nothing but a pair of socks and a plug hat when he is at home, or possibly is even more scantily arrayed in the popular *malo*—got up and gravely gave notice of a bill to authorize the construction of a suspension bridge from Oahu to Hawaii, a matter of a hundred and fifty miles! He said the natives would prefer it to the inter-island schooners, and they wouldn't suffer from sea-sickness on it. Up came Honorables Ku and Kulaui, and Kowkow, and Kiwahoo and a lot of other clacking geese, and harried and worried this notable internal improvement until some sensible person rose and choked them off by moving the previous question. Do not do an unjust thing now, and imagine Kanaka Legislatures do stupider things than other similar bodies. Rather blush to remember that once, when a Wisconsin Legislature had the affixing of a penalty for the crime of arson under consideration, a member got up and seriously suggested that when a man committed the damning crime of arson, they ought either hang him or make him marry the girl! To my mind the suspension bridge man was a Solomon compared to this idiot.

The mental caliber of the Legislative Assembly is up to the average of such bodies the world over—and I wish it were a compliment to say it, but is hardly so. I have seen a number of Legislatures, and there was a comfortable majority in each of them that knew just about enough to come in when it rained, and that was all. Few men of first class ability can afford to let their affairs go to ruin while they fool away their time in Legislatures for months on a stretch. Few such men care a straw for the small-beer distinctions one is able to achieve in such a place. But your chattering, one-horse village lawyer likes it, and your solemn ass from the cow-counties, who don't know the Constitution from the Lord's Prayer, enjoys it, and these you will always find in the Assembly; the one gabble, gabble, gabbling threadbare platitudes and "give-me-liberty-or-give-me-death" buncombe from morning till night and the other asleep, with his slab soled brogans set up like a couple of grave-stones on the top of his desk.

Among the Commons in this Legislature are a number of Kanakas, with shrewd, intelligent faces, and a "gift of gab" that is appalling. The nobles are able, educated, fine-looking men, who do not talk often, but when they do they generally say something—a remark which will not apply to all their white associates in the same house. If I were not ashamed to digress so often I would like to expatiate a little upon the noticeable fact that the nobility of this land, as a general thing, are distinguishable from the common herd by their large stature and commanding presence, and also set forth the theories in vogue for it, but for the present I will pass the subject by.

June 24, 1866—*Golden Era.*

THE MORAL PHENOMENON

Farallones, August 20, 1866.

Publishers *Californian:*

Gentlemen:—You had better hire me to fill the vacant editorship of the *Californian.* What you want is a good Moral tone to the paper. If I have got a strong suit, that is it. If I am a wild enthusiast on any subject, that is the one. I am peculiarly fitted for such a position. I have been a missionary to the Sandwich Islands, and I have got the hang of all that sort of thing to a fraction. I gave such excellent satisfaction in Hawaii nei that they let me off when my time was up. I was justly considered to be the high chief of that Serious Family down there. I mention here—and I mention it modestly—I mention it with that fatal modesty which has always kept me down—that the missionaries always spoke of me as the Moral Phenomenon when I was down there. They were amazed to behold to what a dizzy altitude human morality may be hoisted up, as exemplified in me. I am honestly proud of the title they have conferred upon me, and shall always wear it in remembrance of my brief but gratifying missionary labors in the Islands.

What you want is Morality. You have run too much poetry; you have slathered—so to speak—(missionary term,)—you have slathered too many frivolous sentimental tales into your paper; too much wicked wit and too much demoralizing humor; too much harmful elevating literature. What the people are suffering for, is Morality. Turn them over to me. Give me room according to my strength. I can fetch them!

Let me hear from you. You could not do better than hire me. I can bring your paper right up. You ought to know, yourself, that when I play my hand in the high moral line, I take a trick every time.

Yours,
"Mark Twain"
Surnamed THE MORAL PHENOMENON

Aug. 25, 1866—*Californian.*

ORIGIN OF ILLUSTRIOUS MEN

You have done fair enough about Franklin and Shakespeare, and several parties not so well known—parties some of us never heard of, in fact—but you have shirked the fellows named below. Why this mean partiality?

John Smith was the son of his father. He formerly resided in New York and other places, but he has moved to San Francisco, now.

Wm. Smith was the son of his mother. This party's grandmother is deceased. She was a brick.

John Brown was the son of old Brown. The body of the latter lies mould'ring in the grave.

Edward Brown was the son of old Brown by a particular friend.

Henry Jones was a son of a sea-cook.

Wm. Jones was a son of a gun.

John Jones was a Son of Temperance.

In early life Gabriel Jones was actually a shoemaker. He is a shoemaker yet.

Previous to the age of 85, Caleb Jones had never given any evidence of extraordinary ability. He has never given any since.

Patrick Murphy is said to have been of Irish extraction.

James Peterson was the son of a common weaver, who was so miraculously poor that his friends were encouraged to believe that in case the Scriptures were strictly carried out he would "inherit the earth." He never got his property.

John Davis' father was a soap-boiler, and not a very good soap-boiler at that. John never arrived at maturity—died in childbirth, he and his mother.

John Johnson was a blacksmith. He died. It was published in the papers, with a head over it, "Deaths." It was therefore thought he died to gain notoriety. He has got an aunt living somewheres.

Up to the age of 34, Hosea Wilkerson never had any home but Home, Sweet Home, and even when he had that he had to sing it himself. At one time it was believed that he would have been famous if he had become celebrated. He died. He was greatly esteemed for his many virtues. There was not a dry eye in the crowd when they planted him.

Sept. 29, 1866—*Californian.*

[Not long after Twain's return from Hawaii, the Queen of Hawaii arrived in San Francisco, creating considerable excitement in that city. Twain, an enterprising stringer in those days, promptly sent off this dispatch to the *Daily Hawaiian Herald.*]

THE QUEEN'S ARRIVAL

Queen Emma and suite arrived at noon to-day in the P.M.S.S. *Sacramento,* and was received by Mr. Hitchcock, the Hawaiian Consul, and escorted to the Occidental Hotel, where a suite of neatly decorated apartments had been got ready for her. The U.S. revenue cutter *Shubrick* went to sea and received the guest with a royal salute of 21 guns, and then escorted her ship to the city; Fort Point saluted again, and the colors of the other fortifications and on board the U.S. war steamer *Vanderbilt* were dipped as the *Sacramento* passed. The commander of the fleet in these waters has been instructed to tender the *Vanderbilt* to Queen Emma to convoy her to the Islands when she shall have concluded her visit. The City government worried for days together over a public reception programme, and then, when the time arrived to carry it into execution, failed. But a crowd of gaping American kings besieged the Occidental Hotel and peered anxiously into every carriage that arrived and criticised every woman who emerged from it. Not a lady arrived from the steamer but was taken for Queen Emma, and her personal appearance subjected to remarks—some of them flattering and some otherwise. C. W. Brooks and Jerome Leland, and other gentlemen, are out of pocket and a day's time, in making preparations all day yesterday for a state reception—but at midnight no steamer had been telegraphed, and so they sent their sumptuous carriages and spirited four-horse teams back to the stables and went to bed in sorrow and disappointment.

The Queen was expected at the public tables at dinner to-night, (in the simplicity of the American heart,) and every lady was covertly scrutinized as she entered the dining room—but to no purpose—Her Majesty dined in her rooms, with her suite and the Consul.

She will be serenaded to-night, however, and to-morrow a numerous cortege will march in procession before the hotel and give her three cheers and a tiger, and then, no doubt, the public will be on hand to see her if she shows herself.

Oct. 17, 1866—*Daily Hawaiian Herald.*

THE STORY OF A SCRIPTURAL PANORAMIST

This story is going the rounds of the Eastern press wrongly credited to the Alta California. *It was written more than a year ago, at the time the steamer* Capital *was launched, for the* Californian. *"Mark" starts on a steamer to report the launch for us, when he meets a number of prospecting friends, who, having discovered a bar on the lower-deck, invite him down to sample its contents. At the bar a number of interesting "bar stories" are told, when a Mr. Nickerson is reminded of an incident that occurred during his temporary sojourn in Connecticut some months previous, which he proceeds to relate. In the meanwhile the launch takes place, and "Mark" sees nothing of it, but he reports the story.*

There was a fellow traveling in that country (said Mr. Nickerson) with a moral-religious show—a sort of Scriptural panorama—and he hired a wooden-headed old slab to play the piano for him. After the first night of his performance the showman said:

"My friend, you seem to know pretty much all the tunes there are, and you worry along first-rate. But then, didn't you notice that sometimes last night, the piece you happened to be playing was a little rough on the proprieties, so to speak—didn't seem to jibe with the general gait of the picture that was passing at the time, as it were—was a little foreign to the subject, you know—as if you didn't neither follow suit nor trump, you understand?"

"Well, no," the fellow said. He hadn't noticed, but it might be; he had played along, just as it came to hand.

So they put it up so that the simple old dummy was to keep his eyes on the panorama after that, and as soon as a stunning picture rolled out, he was to fit it to a dot with a piece of music that would help the audience to get an idea of the subject, and warm them up like a camp-meeting revival. That sort of thing would corral their sympathies, the showman said.

There was a big audience that night—mostly middle-aged and old people, who belonged to the church and took a strong interest in Bible matters, and the balance were young bucks and heifers—they always come out strong on panoramas, you know, because it gives them a chance to kiss one another's mugs in the dark.

Well, the showman began to swell himself up for this lecture, and the old mud-dobber tackled the piano, and run his fingers up and down once or twice to see that she was all right, and then the fellows behind the curtain commenced to grind out the panorama. The showman balanced his weight on his right foot, propped his hands on his hips, flung his eyes over the scenery, and said:

"Ladies and gentlemen, the painting now before you illustrates the beautiful and touching parable of the Prodigal Son. Observe the happy expression breaking over the features of the poor suffering youth—so worn and weary with his long march; note also the ecstasy beaming from the uplifted countenance of the aged father, and the joy that sparkles in the eyes of the excited group of youths and maidens, and seems ready to burst in a welcoming chorus from their lips. The lesson, my friends, is as solemn and instructive as the story is tender and beautiful."

The mud-dobber was ready, and the second the speech was finished, he struck up:

"O, we'll all get blind drunk,
When Johnny comes marching home!"

Some of the people giggled, and some groaned a little. The showman could not say a word. He looked at the piano man sharp, but he was all lovely and serene—he didn't know there was anything out of gear.

The panorama moved on, and the showman drummed up his grit, and started in afresh:

"Ladies and gentlemen, the fine picture now unfolding itself to your gaze, exhibits one of the most notable events in Bible history—our Savior and his disciples upon the sea of Galilee. How grand, how awe-inspiring are the reflections which the subject invokes! What sublimity of faith is revealed to us in this lesson from the sacred writings! The Savior rebukes the angry waves, and walks securely upon the bosom of the deep!"

All around the house they were whispering, "O, how lovely, how beautiful!" and the orchestra let himself out again:

"O, a life on the ocean wave,
And a home on the rolling deep!"

There was a good deal of honest snickering turned on this time, and considerable groaning, and one or two old deacons got up and went out. The showman gritted his teeth, and cursed the piano man to himself, but the fellow sat there like a knot on a log, and seemed to think he was doing first-rate.

After things got quiet, the showman thought he would make one more stagger at it anyhow, though his confidence was mighty shaky. The supes started the panorama to grinding again, and he says:

"Ladies and gentlemen, this exquisite painting illustrates the raising of Lazarus from the dead by our Savior. Observe the half confused, half inquiring look upon the countenance of the awakening Lazarus. Observe also the attitude and expression of the Savior, who takes him gently by the sleeves of his shroud by one hand, while he points with the other toward the distant city."

Before anybody could get off an opinion in the case, the innocent old ass at the piano struck up:

"Come, rise up, William R-i-l-e-y,
And come along with me!"

All the solemn old floats got up in a huff to go, and everybody else laughed till the windows rattled.

The showman went down and grabbed the orchestra, and shook him up, and said:

"That lets you out, you know, you chowder-headed old clam! Go to the doorkeeper and get your money, and cut stick!"

Nov. 18, 1866—*Californian.*

HOW, FOR INSTANCE?

Coming down from Sacramento on the *Capital* the other night, I found on a center table, a pamphlet advertisement of an Accident Insurance Company. It interested me a good deal with its General Accidents and its Hazardous tables, and Extra Hazardous furniture of the same description, and I would like to know something more about it. It is a new thing to me. I want to invest if I come to like it. I want to ask merely a few questions of the man who carries on this Accident shop, if you think you can spare so much space to a far-distant stranger. I am an Orphan.

He publishes this list as accidents he is willing to insure people against:

General Accidents

Include the Traveling Risk, and also all forms of Dislocations, Broken Bones, Ruptured Tendons, Sprains, Concussions, Crushings, Bruising, Cuts, Stabs, Gunshot Wounds, Poisoned Wounds, Burns and Scalds, Freezing, Bites, Unprovoked Assaults by Burglars, Robbers or Murderers, the action of Lightning or Sunstroke, the Effects of Explosions, Chemicals, Floods and Earthquakes, Suffocation by Drowning or Choking—where such accidental injury totally disables the person insured from following his usual avocation or causes death within three months from the time of the happening of the injury.

I want to address this party as follows:

Now, Smith—I suppose likely your name is Smith—you don't know me and I don't know you, but I am willing to be friendly. I am acquainted with a good many of your family—I know John as well as I know any man—and I think we can come to an understanding about your little game without any hard feelings. For instance:

Do you allow the same money on a dog-bite that you do on an earthquake?

Do you take special risks for specific accidents?—that is to say, could I, by getting a policy for dog-bites alone, get it cheaper than if I took a chance in your whole lottery? And if so, and supposing

I got insured against earthquakes, would you charge any more for San Francisco earthquakes than for those that prevail in places that are better anchored down?

And if I had a policy on earthquakes alone, I couldn't collect on a dog-bite, may be, could I?

If a man had such a policy and an earthquake shook him up and loosened his joints a good deal, but not enough to incapacitate him from engaging in pursuits which did not require him to be tight, wouldn't you pay him some of his pension?

I notice you do not mention Biles. How about biles?

Why do you discriminate between Provoked and Unprovoked Assaults by Burglars? If a burglar entered my house at dead of night, and I, in the excitement natural to such an occasion, should forget myself and say something that provoked him, and he should cripple me, wouldn't I get anything?

But if I provoked him by pure accident, I would have you there I judge?—because you would have to pay for the Accident part of it anyhow, seeing that insuring against accident is just your strong suit, you know.

Now that item about protecting a man against freezing is good. It will procure you all the custom you want in this country. Because, you understand, the people hereabouts have suffered a good deal from just such climatic drawbacks as that. Why, three years ago, if a man—being a small fish in the matter of money went over to Washoe and bought into a good silver mine, they would let that man go on and pay assessments till his purse got down to about thirty-two Fahrenheit, and then the big fish would close in on him and freeze him out. And from that day forth you might consider that man in the light of a bankrupt community. And you would have him down to a spot, too. But if you are ready to insure against that sort of thing, and can stand it, you can give Washoe a fair start. You might send me an agency. Business? Why, Smith, I could get you more business than you could attend to. With such an understanding as that the boys would all take a chance.

You don't appear to make any particular mention of taking risks on Blighted Affections. But if you should conclude to do a little business in that line, you might put me down for six or seven chances. I wouldn't mind expense—you might enter it on the Extra Hazardous. I suppose I would get ahead of you in the long run anyhow, likely. I have been blighted a good deal in my time.

But now as to those "Effects of Lightning." Suppose the lightning were to strike out at one of your men and miss him, and fetch another party—could that other party come on you for damages? Or could the relatives of the party thus suddenly snaked out of the bright world in the bloom of his youth come on you in case he was crowded for time?—as of course he would be, you know, under such circumstances.

You say you have "issued over sixty thousand policies, forty-five of which have proved fatal and been paid for." Now, do you know, Smith, that that looks just a little shaky to me, in a measure? You appear to have it pretty much all your own way, you see. It is all very well for the lucky forty-five that have died "and been paid for," but how about the other fifty-nine thousand nine hundred and fifty-five? You have got their money, haven't you? but somehow the lightning don't seem to strike and they don't get any chance at you. Won't their families get fatigued waiting for their dividends? Don't your customers drop off rather slow, so to speak?

You will ruin yourself publishing such damaging statements as that, Smith. I tell you as a friend. If you had said that the fifty-nine thousand nine hundred and fifty-five died and that forty-five lived, you would have issued about four tons of policies the next week. But people are not going to get insured, when you take so much pains to prove that there is such precious little use in it. Good-bye, Smith.

Yours,
Mark Twain

Aug. 1866—*Territorial Enterprise*
(as reprinted from *New York Weekly Review*).

MARK TWAIN MYSTIFIED

I cannot understand the telegraphic dispatches now a-days, with their odd punctuation—I mean with so many question marks thrust in where no question is asked. The dispatches appear to me to be in the last degree mysterious. I fear we are on the eve of fearful things. Now, read this ominous telegram. I cut it out of this morning's papers, and have been studying it over most of the day, but still I don't consider that I understand it any better than I did at first:

New York, December 6.—The *World's* Brownsville special says: The city of Matamoras was surrounded [?] to Gen. Sedgwick, commanding the United States horses [?] on the Rio Grande, on the evening of the 24th ult. Col. T. G. Perkins, of the 19th U. S. Infantry, being the only artillery regiment [?] now on duty there, was stationed in command of eleven [?] men of the French [?] cavalry, who crossed over and stultified [occupied?] the city that day, but did not return until the previous [?] day, on account of having to remove [remodel?] the pontoon bridge, to let his baggage train cross over, whereby he did not get back again [where?] in time to prevent it, or at least not as much as he might if he had, and certainly not otherwise if he did not or was unable, or even could not and went back on him. So Gen. Wxgrclvtkrvw [?] thinks.

Come, now, this is not right, you know. I have got to lecture Monday night, and my mind ought to be in repose. It is ruinous to me to have my mind torn up in this way on the eve of a lecture. Now, just at the very time that I ought to be serene and undisturbed, comes this dreadful news about Col. T. G. Perkins and his incomprehensible (but I think, wicked) conduct, and Gen. Wxrg (insert remainder of alphabet)'s blood-curding though unintelligible opinion of it. I wish to Heaven I knew what Perkins was trying to do, and what he wanted to do it for, and what he expected to gain by it, and whether he ever accomplished it or not.

I have studied it over patiently and carefully, and it appears that he, with his regiment of American infantry, being the only artillery there, crossed over with his French cavalry and occupied some city or other; and then returned the day before he went over and sent his baggage train across to the other side (of course returning again at some other time not mentioned,) but too late, unfortunately, to prevent it, which this Gen. Wxgr, etc., thinks he might, if he had, or otherwise if he did not or was unable; he therefore—

However, it ain't any use. The telegram is too many for *me.*

Despondently,
Mark Twain

Dec. 9, 1866—*Bulletin.*

[In *Roughing It,* Twain recounted this robbery episode in detail.]

SO-LONG

Editors *Alta:* I leave for the States in the *Opposition* steamer to-morrow, and I ask, as a special favor, that you will allow me to say good-bye to my highway-robber friends of the Gold Hill and Virginia Divide, and convince them that I have got ahead of them. They had their joke in robbing me and returning the money, and I had mine in the satisfaction of knowing that they came near freezing to death while they were waiting two hours for me to come along the night of the robbery. And at this day, so far from bearing them any ill will, I want to thank them kindly for their rascality. I am pecuniarily ahead on the transaction. I got a telegram from New York, last night, which reads as follows:

"New York, December 12th.

"*Mark Twain:* Go to Nudd, Lord & Co., Front Street, collect amount of money equal to what highwaymen took from you.

(Signed.) A.D.N."

I took that telegram and went to that store and called for a thousand dollars, with my customary modesty; but when I found they were going to pay it, my conscience smote me and I reduced the demand to a hundred. It was promptly paid, in coin, and now if the robbers think *they* have got the best end of that joke, they are welcome—they have my free consent to go on thinking so. [It is barely possible that the heft of the joke is on A.D.N., now.]

Good-bye, felons—good-bye. I bear you no malice. And I sincerely pray that when your cheerful career is closing, and you appear finally before a delighted and appreciative audience to be hanged, that you will be prepared to go, and that it will be as a ray of sunshine amid the gathering blackness of your damning recollections, to call to mind that you never got a cent out of me. So-long, brigands.

Dec. 14, 1866—*Alta California.*

Maguire's Academy of Music.

Pine street, near Montgomery.

THE SANDWICH ISLANDS.

MARK TWAIN,

(Honolulu Correspondent of the Sacramento Union,)

WILL DELIVER A

LECTURE ON THE SANDWICH ISLANDS

AT THE ACADEMY OF MUSIC,

ON TUESDAY EVENING....OCT. 2d,

In which passing mention will be made of Harris, Bishop Staley, the American Missionaries, etc., and the absurd Customs and Characteristics of the Natives duly discussed and described. The great VOLCANO OF KILAUEA will also receive proper attention.

A Splendid Orchestra

Is in town, but has not been engaged.

ALSO,

A Den of Ferocious Wild Beasts

Will be on Exhibition in the Next Block.

Magnificent Fireworks

Were in contemplation for this occasion, but the idea has been abandoned.

A Grand Torchlight Procession

May be expected; in fact, the public are privileged to expect whatever they please.

Dress Circle..One Dollar
Family Circle.......................................Fifty Cents

Doors open at 7 o'clock. The Trouble to begin at 8 o'clock.

[This long excerpt from Twain's final lecture before leaving San Francisco is from the *Alta*. Not characteristic Twain in style, it is yet of interest as the conventional rhetoric employed in those times when discussing San Francisco and her destiny.]

"MARK TWAIN'S" FAREWELL

"*My Friends and Fellow-Citizens:* I have been treated with extreme kindness and cordiality by San Francisco, and I wish to return my sincerest thanks and acknowledgments. I have also been treated with marked and unusual generosity, forbearance and good-fellowship, by my ancient comrades, my brethren of the Press—a thing which has peculiarly touched me, because long experience in the service has taught me that we of the Press are slow to praise but quick to censure each other, as a general thing—wherefore, in thanking them I am anxious to convince them, at the same time, that they have not lavished their kind offices upon one who cannot appreciate or is insensible to them.

"I am now about to bid farewell to San Francisco for a season, and to go back to that common home we all tenderly remember in our waking hours and fondly revisit in dreams of the night—a home which is familiar to my recollection, but will be an unknown land to my unaccustomed eyes. I shall share the fate of many another longing exile who wanders back to his early home to find gray hairs where he expected youth, graves where he looked for firesides, grief where he had pictured joy—everywhere change! remorseless change where he had heedlessly dreamed that desolating Time had stood still!—to find his cherished anticipations a mockery, and to drink the lees of disappointment instead of the beaded wine of a hope that is crowned with its fruition!

"And while I linger here upon the threshold of this, my new home, to say to you, my kindest and my truest friends, a warm good-bye and an honest peace and prosperity attend you, I accept the warning that mighty changes will have come over this home also when my returning feet shall walk these streets again.

"I read the signs of the times, and I, that am no prophet, behold the things that are in store for you. Over slumbering California is stealing the dawn of a radiant future! The great China Mail Line is established, the Pacific Railroad is creeping across the continent, the commerce of the world is about to be revolutionized. California is Crown Princess of the new dispensation! She stands in the centre of the grand highway of the nations: she stands midway between the Old World and the New, and both shall pay her tribute. From the far East and from Europe, multitudes of stout hearts and willing hands are preparing to flock hither; to throng her hamlets and villages; to till her fruitful soil; to unveil the riches of her countless mines; to build up an empire on these distant shores that shall shame the bravest dreams of her visionaries. From the opulent lands of the Orient, from India, from China, Japan, the Amoor; from tributary regions that stretch from the Arctic circle to the equator, is about to pour in upon her the princely commerce of a teeming population of four hundred and fifty million souls. Half the world stands ready to lay its contributions at her feet! Has any other State so brilliant a future? Has any other city a future like San Francisco?

"This straggling town shall be a vast metropolis: this sparsely populated land shall become a crowded hive of busy men: your waste places shall blossom like the rose and your deserted hills and valleys shall yield bread and wine for unnumbered thousands: railroads shall be spread hither and thither and carry the invigorating blood of commerce to regions that are languishing now: mills and workshops, yea, and *factories* shall spring up everywhere, and mines that have neither name nor place to-day shall dazzle the world with their affluence. The time is drawing on apace when the clouds shall pass away from your firmament, and a splendid prosperity shall descend like a glory upon the whole land!

"I am bidding the old city and my old friends a kind, but not a sad farewell, for I know that when I see this home again, the changes that will have been wrought upon it will suggest no sentiment of sadness; its estate will be brighter, happier and prouder a hundred fold than it is this day. This is its destiny, and in all sincerity I can say, So mote it be!"

Dec. 5, 1866—*Alta California.*

Ed Jump left San Francisco about the same time as Twain did. Here is how he said goodbye.